David Gentleman

MORE TALES FROM
THE TRAVELLERS

*A further collection of tales
by members of the
Travellers Club, London*

More Tales from the Travellers

selected by

Frank Herrmann

and

Michael Allen

MICHAEL TOMKINSON PUBLISHING

OXFORD

2005

First published in Great Britain 2005
by Michael Tomkinson Publishing
POB 215 Oxford OX2 0NR

© The Travellers Club 2005
for this collected edition

© Each individual author 2005
for his own contribution or contributions

The extract from *The Marsh Arabs* on page 75
is published by courtesy of Curtis Brown
on behalf of the estate of Wilfred Thesiger
© Sir Wilfred Thesiger 1985

The individual contributors have asserted their right
to be identified as the authors respectively of the
individual contributions and the Travellers Club
asserts its own right to be identified as the author
of the collected edition of this work, in accordance
with the Copyright, Designs & Patents Act 1988

A catalogue record for this book is available
from the British Library

ISBN 0 905500 74 1

Printed in Singapore

Contents

*The front endpapers show the Coffee Room (dining-room) and the back end-
papers the Library of the Travellers Club*
Both are from water-colours by DAVID GENTLEMAN RDI *owned by the Club*

Foreword

We were delighted that the first *Travellers' Tales* gave so much pleasure to so many people. The genesis of that book was the centre table of the Coffee Room, where members of the Club dine when they wish to be sociable and recount interesting stories of their experiences. We felt that it would be worth-while to publish some of them for a wider audience.

This second volume has taken much longer than we expected. Our long search for a new publisher finally led us to Michael Tomkinson, as it happens a long-time member of the Club and a publisher of travel books in his own right. He also undertook the editorial work, which such a multi-author volume as this always requires, and we are most grateful for the skilful and painstaking way in which he tackled the task.

Clubs, like other living organisms, change character in the course of time, and the Travellers is no exception. We dare to say that the publication of *Travellers' Tales* in 1999 acted as a mini-catalyst. The Club became better known because of it, and it spawned various imitations from other clubs. A genial and dynamic chairman, Field Marshal Lord Bramall, strengthened the Club enormously with ambitions for the future. A strong revival of interest in the Club's fabulous Library was stimulated by a series of benign but knowledgeable committee members and chairmen and – more important – by a brilliant librarian. It is now much more used and houses frequent and fascinating Library talks.

The Club's membership also increased gently, and particularly with an influx of well-known and distinguished professional travellers and explorers on the one hand, and prominent newsmen on the other. There was a strong incursion from the financial world too, and a most satisfying number of new members from overseas. *More Tales from the Travellers* reflects all these changes to some degree.

Because of its prolonged period of gestation, we received far more material than we could accommodate. The selection process was what the political world calls 'challenging'. We are deeply grateful to our contributors, particularly for their patience, but would also like to thank those members whose work we could not include.

During the interval between our two volumes the Club lost its oldest and, in many ways, its most distinguished member: Sir Wilfred Thesiger had been a member since 1929. Sadly, a number of our other contributors have died since their tales were received.

We hope you will like what we have to offer and look forward, as before, to your comments.

FRANK HERRMANN AND MICHAEL ALLEN

Publisher's Preface

It was an honour to be asked to produce this second collection of tales from the Travellers. To make full disclosure, the request was not wholly unsolicited. There is in I forget which country or culture a saying that to complain is to risk being asked to rectify. So it was that a nudging enquiry about progress on the publication of this edition resulted, after a gentlemanly presentation and acceptance of credentials, in my being given the job.

There is as in the first *Travellers' Tales* no priority or precedence to the order in which pieces appear – the exception being the pride of place given to Patrick Leigh Fermor's memoir on his sixtieth anniversary as a member. Editing our first collection in 1999, Frank Herrmann and Michael Allen chose their sequence 'with one principle in mind: to set each in such a way that it reads well'. That aim has been maintained; and to it has been added a gentle element of continuity. Members and guests enjoy the Club not only for one of the loveliest libraries in London and the magnificent Coffee Room, which serves not coffee but fine meals and wines, but also (often fostered by these last) its excellent conversation. Tales are told around the Coffee Room's centre table and, as in conversation one topic recalls or prompts another, it seemed logical that wherever possible each tale lead loosely to the next. Their ordering in this collection is consequently more what an academic might call thematic.

With Afghan toponymics, Hungarian diacritics and like arcana, a number of acquaintances have, by kindly correcting the many areas of editorial ignorance, exposed them. Sheila Markham, the Club's librarian, provided much-appreciated help, having at her fingertips every volume requested. In Oxford, and with almost telepathic skill, Cathy Brocklehurst conjured near-perfect proofs from a farrago of scripts, notes and scribblings. These were processed professionally and promptly by my long-suffering, father-and-son designers, Roger and Paul Davies.

Most thanks must however go to Frank Herrmann and Michael Allen who conceived, compiled and master-minded *More Tales from the Travellers*.

MICHAEL TOMKINSON

MORE TALES FROM
THE TRAVELLERS

In the Library of the Travellers Club

Sixty years is a long time to belong to any institution, let alone one as venerable and distinguished as The Travellers. Sometimes, looking back, the lapse of time seems far less, and at others (especially if one dabbles in history at all, as I do now and then) it seems to reach very far back, almost out of sight.

My War-time brother-in-arms, Xan Fielding, and I were put up for the Club when we were in our twenties. Arthur E.E. Reade, our sponsor, was rather older, and a member of long standing when the candidature was set in motion in 1942. We were all three at the time SOE captains dressed up as shepherds, deep in ash and lice, huddling cross-legged over the embers and under the stalactites of a cave in German-occupied Crete. Arthur sealed the envelope putting us up. Obviously it would take some time before it could be handed to the next caique or submarine, longer still to reach Pall Mall. To the south of us, on the other side of the Mediterranean, Rommel was hastening on to El-Alamein. Our candidature might take a while.

We asked Arthur what the 'E.E.' stood for in his name on the back of the envelope, and he said 'Essex Edgeworth'. Was this anything to do with Maria Edgeworth, the pre-Jane Austen, Anglo-Irish novelist, we asked, the author of *Castle Rackrent*? We had just about heard of her.

'Yes,' Arthur replied. 'She was a sort of great-great-aunt.' This, we learned, made him a relative of her uncle, the Abbé Edgeworth de Firmont, the Jesuit son of a convert kinsman who had settled in France and, during the Revolution, become chaplain and confessor to Louis XVI. He accompanied the king to the guillotine where he was reputed to have said, just before the blade fell, '*Fils de Saint-Louis, montez au ciel!*' He then hastened down the steps and dashed away through the Jacobin crowd.

We also learned that the Club later on was very much the background of those dilettanti who ventured farther east than Venice and Florence in Regency times; particularly the ones who pushed on to Constantinople where, under the auspices of our fellow-member Sir Charles Barry, the amazing British Embassy – damaged by a bomb only a few months ago –

was soon to be built. It was of course Barry who designed the premises that surround us at this very moment. Many of these travellers would have hobnobbed with our ambassador there, Sir Stratford Canning – the 'Great Elchi' of Kinglake's *Eothen* – who first took up his task at the age of twenty-four and held it all through the Napoleonic Wars, steering Turkey away from hostilities with Russia in order to foil Napoleon's advances in the north-east.

Canning's world was the Levant of the janissaries and the mamelukes, a region wonderfully handled, in those critical times, by Nelson and by Sir William Sidney Smith of Acre, and by Canning himself. The only communication from London throughout Canning's long tour of duty was a very un-urgent and very unimportant enquiry from Wellington's brother Lord Wellesley, about some antiquarian manuscripts he had vaguely heard about, somewhere in the archives of the Grand Seraglio. What an example to us all . . .

Another member, born in the same year as Byron and, like him, a sort of Apollo – as one sees by the portrait painted later in Rome by Ingres – was the architect Charles Robert Cockerell. He was the great-nephew of Pepys, and after exploring Italy and Sicily he had set off from Constantinople into Asia Minor, heading for the Troad and Smyrna, and then crossed the Ægean to continue his researches in the Morea. How little the Napoleonic Wars seemed to hamper archæological research!

In 1811 Cockerell and three scholarly companions discovered – or rather rediscovered – the lonely and wonderful Temple of Apollo Epicurius at Bassæ, built here by Ictinus to celebrate the end of a plague in the same decade that he put the Parthenon together. The temple of Bassæ combined Doric and Ionic columns and, for the first time, launched the Corinthian style into the architecture of the world. (I say 'rediscovered' because halfway through the eighteenth century the French traveller Bochon had barely set eyes on Bassæ when he was murdered by bandits, who thought the brass buttons on his coat were gold.) A generation later the English party, more soberly dressed, gazed at the temple in wonder. There it stood almost complete in its vast and lonely Arcadian glen, one of the wildest and most haunted regions of the Peloponnese. They were struck dumb.

We know the rest of the story: the rescue and the reassembly of the frieze that had run round the cella of the temple; the long *pourparlers* with the Vizir of Tripolitza; the bargaining, the transport of the slabs in a British ship to Zakynthos – Zante, that is – in the newly acquired Ionian Islands; their arrival in England and their final erection in the British Museum, where they were second only to Lord Elgin's Athenian loot.

The Travellers Club was founded three years after Waterloo and very soon up went Cockerell's casts of the never-ending conflict that rages just above our heads.

Arriving back to be demobbed at the end of *our* war, I made a bee-line for Pall Mall. (Xan Fielding and I were members now – Arthur Reade's letter, three years in transit, had worked.) I dashed upstairs, barely touching Talleyrand's ramp, and into the Library, to gaze up at the battling Amazons and Greeks and Lapiths and centaurs that girdle this marvellous room. It was a great moment.

I was back in Greece soon afterwards, a peripatetic deputy-director of the British Institute improvising lectures to patriot warriors all over the country, largely about Dante Gabriel Rossetti and the Pre-Raphaelite Brotherhood – and I'm not sure how gripping the whiskered guerillas found them. Accompanied by Joan, whom I had married, and by Xan Fielding, who was still in the army, we set off in his jeep and drove from Tripoli to Andritsaina into the fierce Arcadian mountains and on to Phigaleia and – at last! – to Bassæ. We trudged the last few miles along goat tracks, reached the austere and silent temple after dark, and dossed down among the pillars. The early sunbeams over Mount Elaios lit up not only the wonderful columns, but also a young fox sitting in the middle of them. He gave us a long pensive look, then trotted off in search of somewhere less crowded.

Back in the Library here, much later, I was led to David Watkin's *Life of C. R. Cockerell* and settled with it in a corner (where the centaurs seemed to be getting the upper hand) and it fell open on the page where Cockerell and his friends were inspecting the ruins: 'One day when they were scrambling about amongst the great fallen columns,' I read, 'a fox that had made its home deep down amongst the stones, disturbed by the unusual noise, got up and ran away'. I nearly jumped out of my skin. 'In

3

the light that streamed into its momentarily emptied lair, they discovered a glint of marble, then the first slab of what turned out to be the fallen bas-relief – then another and another, and yet another, until the whole wonderful cincture was resurrected and linked together.'

Our fox must have been a descendant of theirs, the great-great-great-great-great-great – in fact, the hundred-and-fortieth great-grand-cub of the one that jumped out of its hole on that momentous day a century and a half before. After all, it was only two thousand, three hundred and seventy-odd years since Ictinus and his fifth-century BC team, having finished their task, piled the spirit-levels and hammers and chisels into the panniers of their baggage-train, shut their dividers, coiled their measuring ropes, brushed off the chips and poured a last libation to Apollo and, perhaps, another down their throats – before following our track across the glen; and we were unshakeably convinced that a small fox, ancestor to all the others, must have watched them out of sight.

PATRICK LEIGH FERMOR

The above is the text of a talk given by the author at a Library Dinner in 2004 to celebrate his sixtieth year of membership.

The following excerpt A German Visit to the Travellers in 1826 *is taken from Pückler-Muskau's* Briefe eines Verstorbenen *(Letters of a Man Lately Dead). Prince Hermann von Pückler-Muskau had, with the concurrence of his wife Lucie, come to England in 1826 to seek a marriageable heiress. Although happily married, the couple thought divorce and remarriage the only solution to their financial predicament, caused by extravagance and ill luck. Hermann failed in his mission but, having kept his promise to send Lucie a detailed daily account of his adventures, they decided to publish a carefully edited selection. The four volumes were the literary sensation of the age, and the publisher's payments to the prince the biggest ever known in Europe. The couple lived in comfort for the rest of their lives.*
Pückler-Muskau was a member of the Travellers Club from 1826 until 1829.

A German Visit to the Travellers in 1826

I advise travellers never to take servants out of their fatherland into strange countries, especially if they imagine they shall save by it, – now-a-days always a prime object. . . . One hangs a load round one's neck which is burthensome in various ways.

These wise reflections are excited in me by my old valet, who seems inclined to fall into the English spleen because he finds so many daily difficulties here; – above all, in getting soup for his dinner, the thought of which beloved aliment of his home calls tears into his eyes. He reminds me of the Prussian soldiers, who, amid streams of Champagne, beat the French peasants for not setting Stettin beer before them.

True it is that the English of the middle classes, accustomed to substantial flesh diet, are not acquainted with the Northern broths and soups: what goes under that name in England is an expensive extract of all sorts of peppers and spices from both Indies, like that brewed in a witch's cauldron. The face of my faithful liegeman, at the first spoonful of this compound he put into his mouth, would have been worthy to figure in Peregrine Pickle's antique repast, and turned my anger into loud laughter. . . . In the absence of society, the various Clubs, (to which, contrary to former custom, a stranger can now gain admittance,) are a very agreeable resource. Our ambassador introduced me into two of them, – the United Service Club, into which no foreigners are admitted except ambassadors and military men, – the latter of the rank of staff-officers: and the Travellers' Club, into which every foreigner of education, who has good introductions, is admitted, though every three months he is made to undergo the somewhat humiliating ceremony of requesting a fresh permission, to which he is held with almost uncivil severity.

In Germany, people have as little notion of the elegance and comfort of Clubs, as of the rigorous execution of their laws which prevail here.

All that luxury and convenience, without magnificence, demand, is here to be found in as great perfection as in the best private houses. The stairs and rooms are covered with fresh and handsome carpets, and rugs (sheep-skins with the wool nicely prepared and dyed of bright colours) are laid before the doors to prevent drafts: marble chimney-pieces, handsome looking-glasses (always of one piece, – a necessary part of solid English luxury), a profusion of furniture, etc., render every apartment extremely comfortable. Even scales, by which to ascertain one's weight daily – a strange taste of the English – are not wanting. The numerous servants are never seen but in shoes, and in the neatest livery or plain clothes; and a porter is always at his post to take charge of great-coats and umbrellas. This latter article in England deserves attention, since umbrellas, which are unfortunately so indispensable, are stolen in the most shameless manner, be it where it may, if you do not take particular care of them. This fact is so notorious that I must translate for your amusement a passage from a newspaper, relating to some Society for the encouragement of virtue, which was to award a prize for the most honourable action. "The choice," continues the author, "was become extremely difficult; and it was nearly determined to give the prize to an individual who had paid his tailor's bill punctually for several years; when another was pointed out, who had twice sent home an umbrella left at his house. At this unheard-of act," added the journalist, "the company first fell into mute wonder that so much virtue was still found in Israel; but at length loud and enthusiastic applause left the choice no longer doubtful."

In the elegant and well-furnished library there is also a person always at hand to fetch you the books you want. You find all the journals in a well-arranged reading-room; and in a small room for maps and charts, a choice of the newest and best in their kind. This is so arranged that all the maps, rolled up, hang one over another on the wall, thus occupying but a small space; and each is easily drawn down for use by a little loop in the centre. . . . The table, – I mean the eating, – with most men the first thing, and with me not the last, – is generally prepared by a French cook, as well and as cheaply as it is possible to have it in London. As the Club provides the wines, and sells them again to each member, they are very drinkable and reasonable. But 'gourmands' must ever miss the finest wines, even at the best tables in London. This arises from the strange habit of the English (and these people, too, stick faster to their habits than an oyster to its shell,) of getting their wines from London wine-merchants, instead of importing them from the places where they grow, as we do. Now these wine-merchants adulterate the wine to such a degree, that one who was lately prosecuted for having some thousand bottles of port and claret in his cellars which had not paid duty, proved that all this wine was manufactured by himself in London, and thus escaped the penalty. You may imagine, therefore, what sort of brewage you often get under the high-sounding names of Champagne, Lafitte, etc. The dealers scarcely ever buy the very best which is to be had in the native lands of the several wines, for the obvious reason that they could make little or no profit of it; at best they only use it to enable them to get off other wine of inferior quality…

But let us back to our Clubs.

The peculiarity of English manners may be much better observed here, at the first 'abord', than in the great world, which is everywhere more or less alike; whereas the same individuals, of whom it is in part composed, show themselves here with much less restraint. In the first place, the stranger must admire the refinement of convenience with which Englishmen sit: it must be confessed that a man who is ignorant of the ingenious English chairs, of every form, and adapted to every degree of fatigue, indisposition, or constitutional peculiarity, really loses a large share of earthly enjoyment. It is a positive pleasure even to see an Englishman sit, or rather lie, in one of these couch-like chairs by the fire-side. A contrivance like a reading-desk attached to the arm, and furnished with a candlestick, is so placed before him, that with the slightest touch he can bring it nearer or further, push it to the right or the left, at pleasure. A curious machine, several of which stand around the large fire-place, receives one or both of his feet; and the hat on his head completes this enchanting picture of superlative comfort.

This latter circumstance is the most difficult of imitation to a man brought up in the old school. Though he can never refrain from a provincial sort of shudder when he enters the brilliantly lighted saloon of the Club-house, where dukes, ambassadors and lords, elegantly dressed, are sitting at the card-tables, yet if he wishes to be 'fashionable' he must keep on his hat, advance to a party at whist, nod to one or two of his acquaintances; then carelessly taking up a newspaper, sink down on a sofa, and, not till after some time, 'nonchalamment' throw down his hat (which perhaps has all the while been a horrid annoyance to him). . . .

The practice of half lying instead of sitting; sometimes of lying at full length on the carpet at the feet of ladies; of crossing one leg over the other in such a manner as to hold the foot in the hand; of putting the hands in the arm-holes of the waistcoat, and so on, – are all things which have obtained in the best company and the most exclusive circles: it is therefore very possible that the keeping on the hat may arrive at the same honour. In this case it will doubtless find its way into Paris society, which, after being formerly aped by all Europe, now disdains not to ape the English, – sometimes grotesquely enough, – and, as is usual in such cases, often outdoes its original.

On the other hand, the English take it very ill of foreigners if they reprove a waiter who makes them wait, or brings one thing instead of another, or if they give their commands in a loud or lordly tone of voice; though the English themselves often do this in their own country, and much more in ours, and though the dining-room of the Club is in fact only a more elegant sort of 'restauration', where every man must pay his reckoning after he has dined. It is regarded not only as improper, but as unpleasant and offensive, if any one reads during dinner. It is not the fashion in England; and, as I have had this bad habit in a supreme degree, I have sometimes remarked satirical signs of displeasure on the countenances of a few Islanders of the old school, who shook their heads as they passed me.

None but a nation so entirely commercial as the English can be expected to attain to their perfection of methodizing and arrangement. In no other country are what are here emphatically called 'habits of business' carried so extensively into social and domestic life; the value of time, of order, of despatch, of inflexible *routine* nowhere so well understood. This is the great key to the most striking national characteristics. The quantity of material objects produced and accomplished – *the work done* – in England, exceeds all that man ever effected. The causes and the qualities which have produced these results have as certainly given birth to the dullness, the contracted views, the *routine* habits of thought as well as of action, the inveterate prejudices, the unbounded desire for, and deference to, wealth, which characterize the mass of Englishmen.

HERMANN VON PÜCKLER-MUSKAU

Terribly, Terribly British

I was expelled from my first school. It probably set a pattern. This is how it happened.

In 1950 we had just moved to Malta where my father, who was in the Navy, was taking up a new posting. I was aged seven, and one of my parents' early concerns was to find a school for me. The obvious place was the Dockyard School, but this was full of boys from the rougher parts of Portsmouth and my mother took the view that I was too tender a flower to be exposed to such influences. Fortunately we lived in Sacred Heart Avenue, and right across the street was the Convent of the Sacred Heart which had a well-regarded primary school. True, it was basically for Maltese Catholic girls, whereas I was an English Protestant boy, but anyhow it agreed to take me. Apart from a minor dispute over whether I should have to learn catechism, my first year there went well enough.

The problem arose when we all had to learn a poem. Poetry was rather a forte of mine. In those days I had a naturally retentive memory and had only to hear a poem to remember it. I therefore had quite a repertory but, whereas my classmates' poems were mostly of a pious and uplifting character, I chose something by Kipling which was full of phrases like 'as far as the Devil can spit'. Sister looked a bit pained when she heard this, and after class she took me aside and said: 'Dear Henry, sweet Henry, could you possibly for next week learn a different poem?'

This was no problem: I knew dozens. However, the one I recited the following week was actually the lyric of a popular song which my parents had on a 78rpm record. It began:

'*I'm terribly, terribly British*
And that's what I like about me.
I belong to a type that wears tweeds and a pipe.
I'm the kind of man people call he-.'

This was not quite what Sister wanted to hear, but the trouble only really started when I reached verse five. This went:

'I once knew a bad girl with a good pair of legs.
"You can have what you like," said this girl from the dregs.
I said, "Thanks very much, I'll have bacon and eggs".
'Cos I'm terribly British, you see.'

I was very proud of my poem and puzzled when Sister gave me a note for my parents. They were to see the Reverend Mother. The next term I started at the Dockyard School. It was a rough, tough place, and I picked up a number of bad habits. Some of them I still have.

HENRY BROWNRIGG

A Bookseller Uncovered

We lived in Malta during the late 1950s at Villa Mompalao, a pavilion of a house on a high point of the island at Rabat. The main feature of the interior was an immense Venetian chandelier once coveted by Queen Mary. Her hints on that occasion were politely ignored. My wife and I were glad of that when, many years after her visit, we took the lease.

Malta was at that time headquarters for the Allied Forces, Mediterranean, and the commander of those forces was Admiral Sir Charles Lambe. The admiral's official residence was a baroque palazzo in South Street, Valletta which, like most of the city's transverse streets, was narrow. High balconied houses with wooden jalousies ran down both sides of it. Between the balconies on the upper floors of Admiralty House and those across the way was a space Nijinsky could have leapt with ease.

The Lambes often had unusual and interesting guests to stay whom we were invited to meet. Among them were the painter Derek Hill and, at another time, the bookseller Heywood Hill and his wife, Lady Ann. During their stay the Lambes were obliged to officiate at some NATO event in Naples. They took the opportunity to give most of the Admiralty House staff weekend leave, retaining only two or three to provide the Heywood Hills with bed and board and asking my wife and me to amuse them during the day.

So we took our young boys and the Hills and a huge picnic and had a scorching, salty Saturday in and out of the sea at the Blue Lagoon, a paradisiac swimming place between the islands. At the end of the day the barge put us ashore, we delivered the Hills back to a more or less empty Admiralty House, and took ourselves home to Rabat.

We had not long been back when I had a telephone call from a police inspector in Valletta. I had met him once or twice, a thin, sallow man and no joker. He was on weekend duty, which nobody liked, and sounded grim.

'Mr Grey Hambins? Inspector Saliba. We have arrested a Mr Hay Hill.' He paused. I repeated, stupidly, 'You have arrested Mr Hill?'

'He claims that you can identify him.'

'Of course I can! Why have you arrested him?'

Inspector Saliba took his time. He had caught me out:

'How can you identify a man you cannot see?'

'But what is the charge?'

'Indecent exposure. Do you know this Mr Woodhill?'

There was a tone in Inspector Saliba's voice suggesting that he would think the worse of me were I to admit to such an acquaintance. I said I would come down to the station at once. I drove at some speed. The notion that Heywood, this rather small, mild-mannered proprietor of a fashionable Curzon Street bookshop, should expose himself indecently was ludicrous. That he should do it while I was, as it were, responsible for him was most inconsiderate. I was apprehensive of Admiral Lambe's reaction when he returned to find a guest left in my care had been consigned to a Maltese jail.

At the police station I was shown into a gloomy office. The only windows were high up and grimy. Inspector Saliba was sitting at a table. Heywood Hill, looking dejected, sat on a chair in a corner like a bad boy. Next to him stood a square-shaped policeman. Heywood was properly dressed in shirt and trousers, which was a relief.

'You know this Hay Woodhill?' asked the inspector. He was tapping the table with his pencil.

'Yes, I know him!' I waved reassuringly to Heywood. 'Hullo,' I said, grinning idiotically. The inspector glared at me. Heywood brightened, but not very much.

'Mrs Floridia Grima has laid a complaint against him. Constable Vella confirms that Mr Woodhill was exposing himself naked to the street!'

'I had just had a shower,' cried Heywood. It was clear that he found his situation unfamiliar and upsetting. He was in fact demoralised and had not made a convincing explanation of himself. I urged him to do so. But Inspector Saliba put the case for the prosecution first.

It was alleged that an elderly widow, Mrs Grima, who lived in a room with a balcony opposite Admiralty House, had been shocked and startled to see directly across the narrow street the jalousies burst open and a naked man appear with all his parts. He had stretched his arms high and wide and looked directly at her.

'I did not have my glasses,' interjected Heywood. 'I didn't know she was there!'

He explained that, being coated with salt and sand after our day on the barge, he had gone to his room, stripped off and crossed the corridor to have a good long shower. Refreshed, he had returned to his room, strode to the tall windows and flung open the jalousies to take a deep breath of air.

I suspect that the widow on the balcony opposite had been sitting there for years in hopeful expectation of such a moment.

'*Eheu!*' she had exclaimed on being confronted with this Adonis. A long look, one more '*Eheu!*' and she had screamed for the police. Constable Vella, strolling by the way policemen do, had looked up in time to see Heywood full frontal. In those days Malta was less complaisant about the flesh than it has since become. '*Modestja Nisraniya Jekk-Joggebok*' proclaimed placards in the street: 'Decency in Dress Please!' A woman wearing a summer dress with shoulder straps rather than sleeves would be hustled off by a policeman and her shoulders quickly covered by some decorous page from the *Times of Malta*. She would be warned. But an offence such as Heywood had committed was a serious matter.

I looked long and sorrowfully at Inspector Saliba. I explained that we had all returned from a day in the sea and the sun; that Mr Hill had been shocked to the core by the sight of an old woman on a balcony looking straight in at his bedroom window; that Mr Hill . . .

'Woodhill, he says he is named,' interjected the inspector. He went on tapping the table.

. . . that Mr Woodhill was a guest of the admiral; that he was a gentle-man of the highest references for propriety, sobriety and, indeed, piety; that he, the inspector, could see for himself that this was no boisterous bravo, no lewd exhibitionist . . .

'Lewd?' asked the inspector. 'Like rude,' I explained.

'*Mella!*' said the inspector. He looked at Heywood and saw that I was right. He was a fair man.

'Sur Woodhill,' he addressed Heywood formally. 'You will please in future cover yourself all over. Is that understood?' Then the corners of his mouth twitched very slightly. 'And be careful of the jalousies; they are there to keep away both the sun and the sight!'

We thanked him so profusely that it seemed for a moment he might regret his leniency. We quickly left and were relieved a little later to reach Admiralty House without any more trouble.

'Is she up there?' asked Heywood. 'I daren't look!'

But there was no one on the balcony opposite.

'She's had her fill,' I said, 'metaphorically speaking.'

Then in the hall we met Lady Ann, elegantly whispy.

'Oh there you are!' she said placidly to Heywood. 'I went to sleep, you know. And then I had a wonderful shower. You look as if you need one!'

GRAHAM BINNS

MI5? MI6!

Once in the Eighties when the Coffee Room was being renovated and the Library serving in lieu, Robert Morley and a fellow-member of the Garrick Club were enjoying the Travellers' hospitality. During a lull in the conversation Morley was heard to exclaim loudly:

'There you are, MI5, every one of them!'

A correction came quickly and equally loudly from a neighbouring table: 'Wrong old boy, MI6!'

ST JOHN ARMITAGE

What the Traveller Wore

My mother was a model and my father was in the rag trade. They both had very extensive wardrobes, so it is not surprising that I am interested in clothes.

My father was a keen rowing man and we used to spend a lot of time, my mother and I, helping him propel his double-sculling skiff along the then largely rural reaches of the upper Thames. It was a really large boat which could sleep three, and it was built of mahogany. The seat on which my mother, who was herself a stylish oarswoman, used to sit while steering had a plaited cane back like the body of a Hispano-Suiza. And there were mahogany table-tops that fitted across the gunwales with holes in them for plates and glasses, and a wicker holster in which my mother prudently kept an umbrella.

All sorts of ludicrous misadventures used to befall us, such as the time we were moored at a delightful, arcadian place called Aston Ferry. My father discovered a wasps' nest and insisted on smearing the bottom of a frying-pan with jam so that he could squash the wasps *en masse*. We soon found ourselves rowing for our lives in mid-stream, as heavily engaged as a convoy in the Sula Sea.

He himself used to wear white flannel trousers with a narrow black stripe, turned up to show his black and pink club socks. And he wore white buckskin shoes and a blazer with five buttons made by a tailor in Maddox Street who, when he put a button on, put it on for ever.

On one occasion my father invited a Scotland Yard detective to accompany us. I was consumed with excitement but, when he appeared in scorching weather and took off his black jacket and waistcoat, he displayed a thick flannel shirt and rather grubby braces. From that time onwards my father always referred to him as 'that fellow who wore braces'.

In 1935 when I was sixteen I failed the obligatory Mathematics in School Certificate, the then equivalent of GCSE. So my father took me away from St Paul's and placed me in a large advertising agency in Lower Regent Street where, in his words, I was to 'learn the business' – at a wage so low as to be almost illusory. By this time I had my first suit, bought at a Harrods sale with the help of my mother, of which I was rather proud. I started work in the checking department, where copies of every periodical in the world in which our clients' advertisements had been placed were checked to make sure that they had appeared, and the right way up, which they sometimes failed to do out in the boondocks. When not lusting after the secretaries or pummelling the other boys who made up the permanent staff of the department, I accumulated from these periodicals knowledge about the most recondite subjects: croquet matches between missionaries in Basutoland, great exhibitions of tram tickets in the Midlands, conventions of undertakers in South Bend, Indiana – the whole world seemed at my feet.

From time to time we used to receive visits from the account executives, elegant men in their late twenties or early thirties. Almost all of them wore double-breasted suits made by Hawes & Curtis, a different one for each day of the week. On Saturdays (almost everyone worked Saturday mornings before the War) they appeared in tweeds before setting off for Sunningdale. One had a Bentley. They all wore clove carnations or cornflowers and smelled either of Trumper's Eucris or Penhaligon's Honey And Flowers. In their presence I felt an oaf and began to be ashamed of my Harrods suit.

Here in the checking department I also studied male fashion in *Style for Men* and *The Tailor and Cutter*. In 1936 I could read that the Duke of York, soon to be King George VI, appeared at the Chelsea Flower Show in a double-breasted coat (a jacket is a 'coat' in Savile Row parlance) with ivory buttons, wide trousers with turn-ups and a blue-striped shirt with matching handkerchief.

Around Christmas 1936, by which time Edward VIII had abdicated and left Britain and George VI been proclaimed but not yet crowned, I was moved from the checking department to the outer office. It was then that my father, alarmed by the lack of progress I seemed to be making, told me that he was going to order a couple of grown-up suits.

'I've been making enquiries,' he said, 'and apparently there's a new firm starting up in Bury Street, St James's. The cutter was at Hawes & Curtis and he's taken the new king with him. I've arranged an introduction for you. And don't forget to order two pairs of trousers. It's well worth it.'

Benson & Clegg's premises were only a thimble's toss from St James's Palace, on the extreme southern frontier of tailors' London, which was mostly north of Piccadilly. They were in that slightly raffish area that one used to associate with Edwardian bachelor chambers; middle-aged tarts with names like French Fifi who had daughters at Roedean; a couple of Turkish baths; some of the most fashionable shirtmakers, and chemists who sold 'Male Energisers' that looked like napkin rings fitted with roller bearings. Its hotel was the Cavendish, where Rosa Lewis's cook compounded pâtés that looked and tasted like shot foxes' brains. Its restaurant was Quaglino's.

I was disappointed with Benson & Clegg's premises – none of the rotting stags' heads or other trophies of the chase, no portraits of illustrious personages or cases containing outmoded articles of court dress, the sort of thing I had learned to expect while window-shopping in and around Savile Row. Just a small room with electric wall candelabra that looked as if they had been bought in Tottenham Court Road, and some painted wrought iron of discussible taste. It was like the entrance to some dull night club. Only a framed letter of commendation from the monarch thanking Benson & Clegg for their services was reassuring; they had to wait until 1944 for the Royal Warrant.

The cutter was Clegg, a short, dour Lancastrian who scared the living daylights out of me. Benson was large, amiable and expensive-looking. He, presumably, was the middleman between King and Clegg. In twenty-five minutes I was in the street again. I had expected to spend the best part of the morning deliberating over styles and materials in a Woosterish kind of way, but during this time Clegg had not only indicated what materials were acceptable to him, he had told me that both suits would be double-breasted. The only question he asked me was which side I dressed as my Harrods trousers were, he said, 'cut too high in the rise'. This means, in vulgar parlance, that the crotch of the trousers is a long way from the crotch of the wearer and can in serious cases give him the uncomfortable sensation that his private parts are dragging along the ground. I thought it should be 'too low in the rise' not 'too high'.

Within a month, and after two fittings, I took delivery of two magnificent suits – one grey chalk-stripe, the other light navy, also striped. The coats were long, with side vents, and the lapels rolled to a single button on a level with the flapless pockets, all the stripes being prolonged to the end of the lapel by a miracle of cutting. The waists were small, the shoulders broad, with what is known in the profession as 'drape' – fullness over the chest and shoulders – an invention of Scholte inspired by a similar fullness in the greatcoats worn by officers in the Foot Guards. There were no waistcoats.

The sleeves of these coats were cut very high under the arms, so that if the wearer raised his arms, the shoulders didn't shoot up behind his head like some spectre, as they can be seen to do any evening on TV. ('Could put my head in yours!' was how Clegg described the armholes of the coat I came to be measured in.) The tops of the sleeves were raised in what are known as 'ropeheads' (a characteristic of Hawes & Curtis coats until long after the War). And there was a big buttonhole for a carnation with a twist of silk behind the lapel to keep the stalk in place. The trousers were 19½" at the bottoms and they had turn-ups. There were none of the awful sensations associated with their being cut 'too high in the rise'. I felt comfortably gripped but not as though I was in a vice. The overall effect was athletic and sexy. The only trouble was that, although my father paid for them (fifteen guineas each, with two pairs of trousers) and for some shirts from Turnbull & Asser and some shoes, he gave me no money to pursue the frivolous sort of life for which they were intended.

The first day I wore one of these suits to the office I decided to give it a trial run in Bond Street during the lunch hour. My presence there provoked wild outbursts of laughter, inexplicable to me until some kindly passer-by pointed out that someone had pinned up the flap in the back of my coat between the two side vents. I took a terrible revenge on the perpetrator of this act, who was also in the front office, by sending him to visit a non-existent department of the V&A, an invention of my own known as the Obscene Practices Room, titillating his imagination by describing the apparatus exhibited in it, where he narrowly escaped being put away.

Nineteen thirty-seven marked the end of the royal family's influence on fashion. From then on, although he continued to get his suits from Benson & Clegg, the king became so correctly dressed – no doubt on the advice of grizzled courtiers – that there was nothing remarkable in his clothes at all, except the excellence of their construction: no matching handkerchiefs, long rolling lapels or any of that jazz.

In 1938 I had a beautiful, hand-woven Harris tweed jacket made for me by a Jewish firm called Ley & Ley. It gave off an exquisite smell of what an expert later told me was pee. That year I asked my father if he would allow me to give up the advertising business and be apprenticed in a Finnish four-masted barque bound for Australia, where it would load grain before sailing back to Europe by way of Cape Horn.

The most memorable item of clothing I took with me on this 30,000-mile voyage was a heavy navy-wool pullover, which I still have, made by a firm called Allen Solly and known as 'pig's whiskers' because the wool used to knit it was so hard you could strike a match on it. The trade-mark was a pig dancing a hornpipe. Some of the Finnish crew wore Levis, the first I had ever seen. I had to wait until 1948 before I managed to get myself a couple of pairs in San Francisco.

When the War broke out I took my suits and the jacket that smelled of pee abroad, which was a grievous mistake. On one occasion, on leave in Alexandria, I was a guest in a very grand house. I was asked by Wavell, who was also having lunch there, why I was wearing my Benson & Clegg suit. The Commander-in-Chief was quite testy about it – he was having a rotten time with Churchill – but when I told him that my uniform was upstairs being repaired by the French maid, he said almost wistfully: 'Wish I had a French maid'.

When I was captured in 1942 both my suits and my tweed jacket failed to be returned to my next-of-kin. In captivity efforts were made by MI9, a clandestine organisation dedicated to helping prisoners escape. They sent us thick grey blankets which we were supposed to turn into suits, but the wearer of a prototype looked so incredibly funny that everyone who saw him fell about. What effect he would have had on a German ticket collector could only be imagined. In prison I consorted with a number of amateur explorers, mostly Indian Army officers who had spent their leaves in High Asia, usually without official permission. All said that they would take me with them after the War and I believed them.

One of the first things I did when I got home was to equip myself as an explorer. I ordered a pair of nailed climbing boots from Carter, a firm that had made them for early Everest expeditions; I had a knickerbocker suit made in twenty-one-ounce checked tweed, and I ordered some 'Almost Unwearoutable Socks', some of which are still unwornout.

I was ready, but nothing happened. By this time I was married and a commercial traveller ranging the length and breadth of Britain. Nevertheless I was determined to make use of my outfit, and whenever I was doomed to spend the weekend away from home I took to secreting it at the bottom of one of the wicker baskets in which my dress samples travelled. So that on Friday evening I used to leave my baskets in Left Luggage and set off for whatever wild country was handy – from Newcastle around Hadrian's Wall, from Glasgow around Ben Ime and Ben Vorlich or wherever. Once I made a foolish, nearly fatal crossing of the Moor of Rannoch in snow.

It was not until 1956, when my parents' business was more or less moribund and I was working in a couture house in Grosvenor Street, that a friend in the Foreign Office suggested that I should accompany him on an expedition to Nuristan, a largely unexplored part of Afghanistan in the Hindu Kush. I was to be an explorer at last. At least I thought I was.

For this treat I took with me the Levis I had got from San Francisco, now becoming a bit fragile; two shirts made from flannel manufactured in 1884 and given me by my father, and a hat made by Habig, the one-time imperial *Hutmacher* in Vienna, wearing which I looked rather like one of Edward VII's friends on a weekend at Tranby Croft. Stupidly I didn't take my Carter boots, on the grounds that they were too heavy, and as a result suffered agonies wearing an Italian pair with pointed toes.

After this, whenever we travelled – Wanda, my wife, had long since got in on the act – we tended to buy what we needed on the way: in India cotton outfits from Hindu shops specialising in hand-woven materials called *khadi* or, from Muslim shops, hieratical-looking lawn shifts worn with peg-top trousers – ideal, if Wanda took the trousers off, for paddling while descending the Ganges.

In Siberia we acquired fearfully smelly sheepskin coats on the shores of Lake Baikal; in Australia, Ozzie shorts with twee socks; in Canada, size thirteen boots, my size in Canada, made by the Gorilla Shoe Company and 'Brutally Strong!' according to the label; in Istanbul, black felt suits with double-breasted waistcoats made by Albanians down by the Golden Horn, and endless copies of Savile Row suits that for me always went wrong. The best buys we made anywhere were the Gore-Tex suits we wore to cycle round Ireland in.

My last suits – altogether I had four tailors after the War, recommencing with Benson & Clegg – were made by the Helman brothers, Harry and Burt. They were archetypal Jewish tailors born in Lodz, both amazingly articulate about their craft, both now unfortunately dead. Practical men who could cut and make a suit from start to finish. Harry always carried a thimble to remind himself of his origins. 'Nice coat,' was his comment on one I was wearing when we met in the street, 'but there's something wrong with it. Who made it?'

Personally, I couldn't see anything wrong with it. 'You did, Harry,' I replied.

'What a boy you are,' he said. 'Well, we'd better go to the shop and put it right.'

After the War the upper classes ceased to have any significant influence on fashion, apart from a brief period at the end of the 1940s when some young men ordered from their tailors long coats and drainpipe trousers, or peg-top trousers with fifteen-inch bottoms, and close-fitting overcoats of Edwardian inspiration, outfits worn with Coke hats with curly brims.

The fashion, minus the hat, was almost immediately appropriated by what became known as Teddy Boys in the East End of London, which for a time was a clearing house for new styles. Which is why, if you order a suit from any traditional West End tailor, you will take delivery of one, give or take an inch or two off the lapel and the trouser bottoms, that will be more or less indistinguishable from the ones I ordered from Benson & Clegg almost sixty years ago and which Prince Charles still orders from his tailor. It is remarkable.

ERIC NEWBY

Sailing up Etna

In the autumn of 2002 I travelled to Trapani and, after a week in that pleasant town, crossed Sicily rapidly by bus and train to Catania, base for the ascent of Mount Etna. W. E. Gladstone had climbed the volcano (before becoming Mr Gladstone, so to speak) and had contributed an appealing description of it to *Murray's Handbook*. It was a goal I had promised myself on many Sicilian trips and now meant to fulfil. I had the impression that it would be a bit of a scramble and probably very hot. But how to start? I asked my hotel porter. 'Take the bus,' he said.

So I walked to the station and searched amongst the waiting buses until I found one with 'Etna' on the front. I climbed aboard and waited. Everyone who passed by made it their duty to ask me where I was going and then tell me I was on the wrong bus. But I held firm and at last my bus started off, slowly ascending away from the sea. Above Etna's girdle of vineyards and orchards, which thrive on the vulcanic soil, there is a belt of forest – beech, pine and holm-oak – whilst above the forest begin the lava fields, petrified floods of the stuff with an occasional toppling building caught in its grasp. We climbed and climbed, the bus's sonorous horn like a challenge to any vehicle descending the hairpins.

At last we reached base camp, a commonplace square offering fast food and a million trinkets from temporary buildings like sheds. In one corner, access was to be had to a higher level, and here a group of men and women was gathered, serious-looking folk with heavy satchels. I joined them. We entered the structure, bought tickets, smelled the atmosphere of skiing shelters. The next stage of the upward journey I don't exactly remember, but I do recall an ascent in something like an elevator. I also recall feeling slightly nervous. I had read the back of my ticket and it advised that the guide 'undertook no guarantee for the safety of people who do not have haking-boots'. I looked down at my deck-shoes. Haking-boots they were not. I looked at my fellow-summiteers, who had been employing the time in taking woollen hats and scarves and gloves out of their bags. There was much hissing and rustling as they pulled on voluminous Gore-Tex jackets. I was wearing a light tweed suit, to which I had added that morning, to be absolutely on the safe side, an alpaca pullover. 'How high is Mount Etna?' I asked an official cautiously.

'Eleven thousand feet.'

'And then some.' An efficient-looking woman endorsed this staggering body-blow. She looked Swiss, but that may have been the Alpine atmosphere in the lift. She surveyed me unfavourably. 'You'd better try and borrow a parka.'

'I better had.'

At last the lift stopped, and they all clumped out in their haking-boots, transformed from Mediterranean tourists into a band of mountaineers. I had not made this transformation and, when we stepped out of the lift into a hut trembling in the wind, I began to pay the price. A parka was found for me, an immense, stiff garment which felt like putting on a sentry-box as they shoved me into it. I couldn't get the zip to work, and trying to do up the buttons was hopeless. But I didn't want to be always complaining, especially when I had shown myself incompetent, so I clutched the weighty garment round me and followed the team out of doors.

At once an icy wind shook me, or rather shook the parka to which I was attached. Mist or cloud was driven across leagues of lava, its slopes and ridges forming as barren a scene as ever I saw. Cold? It was freezing. What had happened to the sunlit summit I had gazed upon so often from bars and terraces at sea-level? This was more like Snowdon. A path of sorts had been flattened through the lava field, which resembled ploughed land suddenly petrified, and out set the leaders of our group into the ragged mist.

I fell in well back but the wind was behind me and the wind had my parka to push, which it did with such extraordinary energy as to force me up on tiptoe to patter along rather faster than I liked. As I overtook the mountaineers, I began to reel and yaw like a yacht running under a reefless mainsail. It was not long before there was nobody ahead of me but the guide, and I was close on his heels when the track took a left-hand turn. Too late I attempted a gybe: my parka wouldn't answer the helm and I shot straight on where the rest turned left. In a moment I was fairly skimming over the cinders towards heaven knows what geysers and vents of the waiting mountain.

I've often had the same feeling, running too quick on bad ground. Your head goes faster than your feet. It's bound to end in a tumble. All you can do is look out for somewhere soft to hit the floor. The terrain ahead looked no softer than the rest of the blessed mountain, so I picked a flattish place and threw myself down, skidding a bit and puncturing everything exposed to the needle-sharp lava.

Up the mountaineers all came, the most active eagerly ahead, one lady turning me over like a fish on a slab to spray purple antiseptic over my cut hands. Another, the woman I had thought Swiss, pushed through the ring of watchers and knelt by me, producing a huge pill and, more extraordinary still, a glass of water. After a moment or two of general sympathy, two burly and impatient men put their hands under my arms, lifted me upright and frog-marched me back to the shelter. The only comment they allowed themselves was to gesture at my feet with understandable mutters of exasperation. No haking-boots. My deck-shoes were cut and scraped by the wretched lava, ruined. I was ashamed. I was exactly one of those foolish people in gym shoes and a T-shirt whom mountain-rescue teams are forever finding dead at the foot of Scottish crags. Without farewells the two bouncers pushed me into the lift and pressed button 'B' for basement. My attempt on the summit was over.

One week later there was a major eruption. I rather took it personally as a message from Mount Etna not to go fooling about on its slopes again.

Philip Glazebrook

When I first stepped off the ferry and walked into Trapani I had the name of a hotel but no one to ask where it was. There were no people about; all the shops were shut. I strolled on until one still-shaded street broke into the hot brilliance of a square. On one side a bar had its sunshades up, and at an outside table sat a neat old man in the hat and suit with which a Sicilian of his generation claims his place in the social order.

I crossed the square to ask about my hotel. I took off my hat deferentially and was about to greet him when I saw the tangle of wires connecting two deaf-aids the size of biscuit tins to a battery lashed to his midriff. I roared out my question into the biscuit tin. After searching my face for further signals he came, as the deaf must, to his own conclusions.

He stayed me with a finger, reached inside a pocket and tossed a coin into my hat.

There's Life after Everest

I have often been asked whether everything isn't an anti-climax after climbing Everest. The answer is a resounding No. If anything, it was a relief to get Everest out of the way so that I could concentrate on what I love most: going into areas which are comparatively unknown and attempting unclimbed peaks. I reached the top of Everest in 1985 and have been doing this kind of exploratory climbing ever since.

Take 1993. Four of us, Graham Little, Jim Lowther, Rob Ferguson and myself, set out for East Greenland. Thirty-six hours after leaving Glasgow Airport we were disgorged from a twin-engined Otter ski-plane onto a glacier just inside the Arctic Circle. We quickly unloaded our gear and food, then the 'plane swung round, headed down the glacier and had soon shrunk to a tiny dot before vanishing over the horizon. A day and a half from Glasgow, and we were standing here, the first men ever, on this magnificent cirque. The nearest other human being was some two hundred miles away. It was exploratory adventure the quick and easy way.

We set up camp, had a couple of hours' sleep and set out for our first climb up a shapely peak on the other side of the glacier. There were no time constraints for we had twenty-four hours of daylight. It was just a matter of keeping going and resting when we felt the need. That day we kept going for twelve hours, picking our way up a series of snow scoops, through rocky buttresses and up wider slopes until we were a few hundred feet from the summit. It was midday and pleasantly warm so we stopped for a rest, soon dozing off in the afternoon sun. Later, as it began to cool, we got going again to reach the summit ridge at about ten o'clock.

The sun was low on the north-west horizon and the temperature now below zero. We were climbing one at a time, belaying each other, until around midnight we reached the top, a little pinnacle of rock. The all-round view was magnificent – huge glaciers flanked by jagged peaks and, to the west, the Greenland ice-cap swelling into a great expanse of snow lit reddish-gold by the orb of the sun now touching the horizon.

We didn't stay long – it was too cold – but started back down to reach our two little tents some eight hours later. We had been on the go for thirty hours and had our first peak in the bag just sixty-six hours after leaving Glasgow. You can burn yourself out all too easily with twenty-four hours of daylight. So, being in an Aladdin's Cave of unclimbed treasures, we forced ourselves to take thirty hours' rest before our next climb.

We pulled down our tents, loaded our pulks (man-hauling sledges), put on our Nordic skis and off we went. You can haul around two hundred pounds with very little effort on smooth snow, and our glacier was like a motorway. We skied up to the head of the glacier – which was dominated by a cluster of spiky peaks – and split up into two pairs, Graham and I going for a spire we named the Ivory Tower after a pair of Ivory gulls roosting on it. These are lovely birds, monogamous for life, that nest on high mountain peaks. They soared above us as we climbed, making a raucous screech to show their disapproval. We enjoyed a great technical rock-climb and were up and down in a mere seventeen hours of continuous climbing.

It was then almost a relief to have two days of bad weather. Being a foursome, we could play bridge, a wonderful expedition game that can wile away many an hour. With the Otter due to pick us up from a deserted airstrip on the coast in just a week's time, we were coming to the end of our trip. We could get in just one more climb.

Graham and I selected the most shapely peak we had seen. We called it the Needle. We skirmished round it one afternoon and picked a line that had the charm of being very direct, going straight for the summit. The bottom was steep and uncompromising, so we decided to run out a couple of rope-lengths that afternoon, leave them in place, descend for a few hours' sleep, then go for it. Graham, fifteen years younger than me, set off up the sheer granite. There were few holds and no protection. To safeguard ourselves we would insert metal wedges and camming devices into cracks, clip on a karabiner or snap-link and pass the climbing rope through them. I was heartily glad that Graham was out in front.

Then it was my turn. Graham had reached the foot of an open groove that stretched up the face until it vanished into an overhang far above. I started climbing – it was just off vertical, but I was able to bridge out with my legs against little holds on either side of the groove. Most important of all, there was a crack in the back of the groove which provided handholds and the means of protection. The climbing was superb – each move needed thought to get the sequence right – but it was also unrelenting and seemingly endless. I had run out a hundred and twenty feet of rope and had used up all too many of my protection devices. I was just below the overhang; above it the crack and groove ran out. There was nothing for it, I had to get out onto a smooth prow to the left. The holds were minuscule and I had made a move I knew I couldn't reverse. I just had to keep going towards what looked like a ramp leading up into a broken chimney (a crack wide enough to insert one's body). There must be a ledge and anchors in there.

I pulled up onto the ramp. The angle eased, but there were practically no holds and no cracks for a running belay. I was now about twenty feet above my last runner (protection device). I had nearly run out of rope, which was beginning to drag badly, pulling me back every time I made a delicate, tentative move, relying almost entirely on the friction of the rough granite.

At last I was able to pull up into the chimney – but it wasn't over. The ledge was a few feet higher, and the back of the chimney filled with loose blocks all ready to come tumbling out. By this time my legs were trembling, my arms aching. I was panting hard, with the rope's drag getting steadily worse. And I was now afraid. One more gargantuan move and I'd made it. I was standing in balance on a tiny ledge, with a good crack to put in a belay just in front of my nose. I let out a shriek of relief, joy and total exhilaration. It was the most beautiful, demanding pitch I had ever led – with the wonderful added spice of a very doubtful outcome.

I brought Graham up to join me and we then abseiled back down to the bottom of the climb. A good meal back in the tent – soup, noodles and tinned fish, a few hours' sleep, porridge breakfast, and we were ready for the big push. We set out in the early hours when the rock face was still in shadow and bitterly cold. Climbing the ropes we had left in place the previous day warmed us up, then we pushed on into the unknown. Rope-length followed rope-length. There was plenty of hard climbing, some of it even harder than the pitch I had led the day before, but none as æsthetically pleasing. Near the top we had a shock, coming across an ice-slope covered in soft snow. We were wearing light-weight, rubber-soled rock-shoes and had no crampons or ice-tools. Graham made a precarious and very frightening lead, relying on the thin layer of soft snow to support him. And at last, seventeen hours after setting out, we reached a summit bathed in mellow evening sunlight.

This had been a very special climb in a very special place, its jagged peaks unclimbed and its glaciers pristine, all untouched, unspoiled. It is heartening to know that there are still places like this; a climb can be every bit as rewarding as an ascent of Everest. Indeed, when you might now-adays have to share the Himalayan base camp with several hundred other climbers, and the summit day with fifty or sixty, I would much rather be in the empty wilds of Greenland on an unclimbed peak. Big is not neces-sarily best.

CHRIS BONINGTON

A Memory of Everest

In mid-May of 1953 we were moving up to live at Camp IV, which became our Advance Base and gave a grandstand view of the Lhotse Face. On my way up I had set up the short-wave radio and aerial at Camp III on the lip of the Western Cwm. John Hunt joined me in our little two-man tent and after receiving the met. bulletin we listened to *Scrapbook for 1929*. It was the year I was born. John was nineteen at the time and the Senior Under Officer at Sandhurst. We were both almost weeping with emotion. Then – with the walls of the Western Cwm and the Lhotse Face acting as one huge satellite dish focusing the airwaves perfectly onto the aerial – we sat and enjoyed Beethoven's *Leonora No. 3*, with Sir John Barbirolli conducting the Halle Orchestra at the Free Trade Hall in Manchester.

GEORGE BAND

Maria Callas' Last Opera Recording

I first met Maria Callas when she recorded the long-awaited remake of *Tosca* in December 1964. EMI had been trying for years to persuade her to repeat for stereo her celebrated interpretation, first recorded in 1953 at La Scala with Tito Gobbi as Scarpia and Giuseppe di Stefano as Cavaradossi, and conducted by Victor de Sabata. Both then and now this wonderful performance has been widely regarded as one of the few undisputed masterpieces of recording, but alas it was in mono: from the late 1950s onward, mono records ceased to be stocked by dealers and so disappeared from the catalogue. Many fine records from the early 1950s were deleted for this reason. We knew to our cost that it was usually impossible to repeat a mono triumph in stereo, but we had to keep trying. Up to 1964 it looked as if Callas would never attempt *Tosca* again. Her dazzling but all too brief career was coming to an early end. In the five years from 1953 to 1957 she had recorded for us no less than eighteen complete operas but after that only three in seven years. After the 1960 remake of *Norma* she had recorded nothing. Despite our constant urging and cajoling, her vocal difficulties and personal preoccupations prevented her.

Then in 1964 events took a turn for the better. First she returned to the stage in Zeffirelli's triumphant production of *Tosca* at Covent Garden, and in July 1964 returned to recording with a wonderfully characterised interpretation of *Carmen*, a part she had never sung on stage. We knew immediately that it would be a huge commercial success and began to plan a powerful campaign for its launch that winter. Callas herself felt sufficiently encouraged to discuss ideas for future recording. For some weeks the discussions were mainly about *Macbeth* – she had never recorded the whole opera – but suddenly in early October she plumped for *Tosca* to be recorded at the beginning of December, just eight weeks ahead.

Our production staff jumped into setting up arrangements that are normally made two years in advance, not two months. Our good fortune was that Tito Gobbi was free for that week, Carlo Bergonzi could give us two days, just enough to record the rôle of Cavaradossi, and we could engage as conductor Georges Prêtre, in whom Callas had developed some confidence during the *Carmen* recording. The orchestra would be the Paris Conservatoire, the venue the Salle Wagram, and the recording team from our French company, Pathé Marconi, all as for *Carmen*.

Since that summer, marketing had been added to my responsibilities and so it was my job to provide journalistic coverage of the sessions, something fairly new in those days. For *Carmen* the arrangements had gone badly wrong, as Madame Callas had ignored completely the lady journalist we had brought over from New York especially to do an interview for *High Fidelity*, the leading record magazine in the USA. Its editor happened to be the husband of our lady journalist. Four months later, recriminatory letters were still flying between New York, Paris and London. So I was particularly careful to check that my choice – Charles Reid, the music critic of the *News Chronicle* – would be acceptable to Callas. Charles was a genial old gentleman, adept at getting a story out of a difficult recording session, and for that reason often employed by us. He said that he had interviewed Callas on various occasions and got on with her well. At the same time I heard from our Paris office that Callas approved my choice.

I was therefore taken aback to receive a telephone call from a lachrymose Charles, on the morning of his first day at the recording, to say that Madame Callas had angrily refused to allow him to attend the sessions. Later I discovered that she had a year or so earlier been very irritated by something he had written, but had remembered who he was only that morning. I went off to consult my boss: it was far too late to identify, check and engage another journalist. The sessions would be finished in less than three days, so at my boss' suggestion I went immediately to Paris.

I made straight for the Salle Wagram, a gloomy old dance-hall near L'Étoile said to have been a haunt of Toulouse-Lautrec. Its wonderful acoustics caused us and Pathé Marconi to use it for all our Paris recordings. Pathé's equipment was set up permanently in a small central room called *la cabine*, where now our recording team was at work, led by the producer Michel Glotz of Pathé. He promptly introduced me to Callas as being 'instead of Charles Reid'. She let out a cry and turned on me with blazing eyes. 'Who sent that man?' she demanded. 'Who sent him?'

'I have no idea, Madame Callas,' I said firmly, and fortunately she dropped the matter and turned back to the urgent task of completing the recording.

The schedule was most intensive: each morning there was an orchestral rehearsal (especially necessary for the Conservatoire players), each afternoon a three-hour recording session and in the evening another three hours of recording. By the time I arrived, all the Cavaradossi scenes were finished so Bergonzi departed, leaving to be done the finale of Act I and, the core of the drama, the confrontation between Tosca and Scarpia in Act II. My task was to be unobtrusive, to listen, to watch and to note everything of interest. Sometimes I sat in the hall itself to watch the principals rehearsing. But mostly I was in the cabine, both when the tape was running and for the playbacks. This was a great advantage which would not have been given to an outsider such as an independent writer; it enabled me to listen to all the candid discussion about which takes were good, which would have to be done again and so on.

I was surprised to find that in spite of Callas' fearsome reputation and the storm of anger that had pitchforked me into the situation, the atmosphere in the cabine was remarkably relaxed and friendly. It was almost like a family party, with jokes, giggles and laughter, but also a sense of affectionate regard and confidence between the artists born of long years of work together. This was the eighth opera that Callas and Gobbi had recorded together and, as perhaps the two greatest singing actors of the last century, they clearly found their collaboration intensely stimulating. Callas in recent years had also felt much confidence in Prêtre and Michel Glotz.

The cosy intimacy of the cabine was constantly fostered by Michel as the best way of keeping her relaxed and happy. She enjoyed the feeling of being a member of a little team intent on an all-absorbing project. Mildly risqué jokes were exchanged. Michel had discovered that references to suppositories never failed to make her laugh, particularly if he pronounced *suppositoires* in the growly voice of an old comédien like Raimu.

Since she had been living in Paris, Callas had become an elegant and fashionable figure, always dressed in the most distinguished haute couture. Michel made a point of admiring each successive ensemble, and managed to insinuate that her glamorous appearance had much to do with her well-known relationship with Aristotle Onassis, the billionaire ship-owner. Without actually saying so, he conveyed the impression that Ari's attachment to her must be entirely because of her physical allure. She purred appreciatively. At the time I found it strange that she was so susceptible to flattery about her appearance, rather than about her artistic achievement, but I did not then know about the unhappiness of her childhood as the ugly duckling of the family.

In this happy mood she immersed herself in the whole process of recording and surprisingly often went out of her way to help solve a problem: the orchestra in particular had difficulty in producing an acceptable ensemble, not having played the score before and not having the sight-reading ability of the London orchestras. In one passage the orchestral fluffs were so difficult to eradicate that without demur she repeated her part ten times so as to help get a perfect take.

The penultimate day of recording was again very long. Towards the end of the evening session Tito Gobbi began to feel the strain on his voice after the successful taping of his big scene at the end of Act I and the beginning of the Tosca/Scarpia scenes of Act II. As his voice was no longer at its best, he decided to call a halt and save himself for the morrow. With half an hour of the session remaining, Michel asked Callas to record *Vissi d'arte*, which as a solo passage could be recorded separately and slipped into its place after the rest of the scene had been completed. At first the tired and apprehensive Callas said this would be madness, after she had been singing already for six hours. Michel argued that to get it in the can would give extra scope to the demanding sessions the next day. I suspected that he also thought that it would help if she did not have it hanging over her for most of the morrow.

She said she would just try a rehearsal, but her voice sounded so well that she went straight ahead. She sang five full takes until she declared herself perhaps satisfied. It was characteristic of her that her intense concentration produced a performance that was exactly true to the dramatic situation and the composer's intention. When I listen to it now, almost forty years later, I still find its bleak despair unbearably poignant. That her voice was a little tired adds an extra edge to the sense of relentless misery which infuses this pathetic prayer.

The burden on Callas and Gobbi, as well as on the conductor and the producer, was to make a recording to compare well with the 1953 classic and, they must have hoped, in some ways to surpass it. I think that in one respect they did surpass it and that is in the dramatic intensity of the scenes between Tosca and Scarpia. In the earlier set, and perhaps even more in the Zeffirelli production, the Act II confrontation – the murder scene – had been the core of the drama. This one act was televised from Covent Garden and is, sadly, almost the only visual record of Maria Callas on stage.

How were they going to rekindle the fire of these famous performances? How could they once again reproduce the relentless drive of the drama as Tosca's deepening despair and hatred of the sadistic Scarpia impel her inexorably to the fatal stabbing? After one Covent Garden performance, Gobbi had remarked that on stage he really did begin to feel that his life was in danger.

The next day – 9 December 1964 – was the last day of recording, as before with orchestral rehearsal in the morning. At the afternoon session first the Act I scene was recorded, in which Scarpia arouses Tosca's jealousy, and then they began to prepare for their Act II scene. It was with keen interest that I looked to see how they were rehearsing. Significantly their rehearsals were solitary and apart, not together at all. Callas was out in the corridor repeating and refining key phrases: '*Quanto?*' contemptuously; '*La più breve*' miserably.

At the same time Gobbi was in a corner of the hall rehearsing to himself his own key words: '*Aspetta!*' throatily. I listened enthralled whilst he tried four or five different inflexions of *Ebbene?* It seemed that their method was constantly to bring in unexpected but subtle changes of inflexion, which would come as a surprise to the other and so provoke fresh and spontaneous reactions. As far as I could see, there was no further discussion together before they went to the microphones to record. Many years later Callas told one of the students in her Juilliard master classes that in playing dramatic rôles one must never give the impression that one knows in advance what the other actor is going to say.

The final session was extraordinarily dramatic. There can be no attempt to describe line by line how the two of them drove each other to greater feats of intensity. Anyone can hear it for himself from the records. For those of us listening in the cabine it was spell-binding. Late in the evening came the death of Scarpia. At the playback of the second take, Gobbi said: 'Michel, even if we do that scene ten times, I know you will choose this take. There is a dramatic atmosphere which I never before heard on disc.

To make a beautiful *Tosca* one can of course sing correctly, and he parodied a very correct *Tosca* with every note beautifully sung and in strict time but dull. 'But this . . . *is a real murder!*' He spoke for all of us.

There had nevertheless been some orchestral slips and Callas would not accept that fragments could be recorded separately and edited in. So even though the session had lasted over three hours, they went back and did it again. And this take was even better: the orchestra played with greater intensity, Scarpia's dying groans were even more realistic and Callas' chest notes for '*È morto! Or gli perdono!*' seemed to tear at our hearts.

At the playback there was little more to be said. That was it. Gobbi was content, and departed. Callas said she must go but lingered in the cabine for half an hour chatting and joking. Michel pulled her leg about her magnificent fur coat: 'What did you have to do to earn that, I wonder?'

She smiled contentedly and made her farewells. Past midnight, almost reluctantly, she left.

That was the last session of the last opera she recorded.

MICHAEL ALLEN

One of Them

Whatever association the Travellers Club may have with the various secret services is almost impossible for a lay member to ascertain, as the rules of the game seem to dictate that no member thus genuinely involved would ever admit to it. Some cynics claim that a few members are in the habit of hinting at some such clandestine activity in the hope of earning the occasional fee from the newspapers in the rôle of 'a former member of SIS'.

Only once did I get a sniff of real espionage. This was when I enquired of a senior ex-diplomat what might be the occupation of another distinguished member of the Club, of whose profession I knew nothing.

'Oh,' said the diplomat, 'he's *one of them*, you know.'

'One of them?' I queried.

'Well, how shall I put it? *His office is south of the river.*'

I pretended I understood.

Working with Waugh

As authors go, Evelyn Waugh was particularly difficult to work with. He had a fierce temper and always felt that he knew best. One of his biographers wrote that he was 'the nastiest tempered man in England' but, as I shall show, it was not as bad as that.

In the mid-1960s, when I was production director at Methuen's, a spate of mergers began to take place in the publishing world and I soon found myself coping also with production for Eyre & Spottiswood and Chapman & Hall. The latter's principal claim to fame was as the original publishers of Charles Dickens, but that was truly a thing of the past. Though Chapman & Hall now published books mainly on science and engineering, they also had a tiny general list – preserved only as a framework for their most important author, Evelyn Waugh.

Waugh's father had been managing director of Chapman & Hall for many years, so publishing was mother's milk to his son. The MD in my day was a close friend of his, Jack MacDougall, whose main reason for being with the firm was to look after Evelyn Waugh.

Although everyone else was kept at arm's length when it came to dealing with him, I began to be allowed some contact with Waugh. It was not easy. He had very definite opinions about book production and design. He could be very fierce on the telephone. But I argued when I did not agree with him, not from arrogance but from a genuine wish to give his books a more sympathetic appearance.

We crossed swords first over the typography of his biography of the Oxford cleric, Ronald Knox, who had appointed Waugh as his literary executor. The biography contained a great deal of matter quoted from Knox's and others' writings. Waugh wanted his own text set in Times New Roman and the quotations in Gill Sans, a typeface with no serifs. I was appalled. The finished book would look very 'spotty'.

I appealed to Jack MacDougall who said: 'You must talk to Waugh yourself'. I telephoned him and got my head bitten off. I expounded on the elegance of Bembo, a type based on an ancient Italian model and much in use at the time.

'Show me,' said Waugh. I took great care over some specimen pages and sent them to him. Waugh 'phoned me – an almost unheard-of event: 'Go ahead with Bembo,' he said.

When the book was about to be published I was told that Waugh wanted a special, one-copy edition on hand-made paper with a change on the title page. Instead of 'Compiled from Original Sources by Evelyn Waugh' it was to read 'A Masterpiece by Evelyn Waugh'. This copy was apparently intended for a lady friend: she was said to have a complete set of his books with 'A Masterpiece' on each title page. The special edition was also to be bound in a particular bronze-grey buckram. This had been unavailable for several years, but fortunately I knew of a binder who had some. After all the problems we had had (the cost of author's corrections Waugh made to his proofs was astronomical), I printed and had bound two copies with 'A Masterpiece' on the title page. Some time after the book was published, I sent Waugh the second copy and asked him to sign it for me. On the endpaper he wrote: 'For the reproductive organs of Eyre & Spottiswood this flagrant example of over-production, from Evelyn Waugh'. On the title page he crossed out 'A Masterpiece' and replaced it with 'Not for public use or sale'.

We next had a long tussle over the new editions of his novels *A Handful of Dust* and *The Loved One*, and later the trilogy *Sword of Honour* (all 794 pages of it). These had originally been set very solidly in Times New Roman, which now looked dated. I suggested a more elegant type-face called Walbaum. At first Waugh refused utterly to countenance a change. So we sent him a specimen page; Jack MacDougall said some soothing words – and we were allowed to go ahead with Walbaum.

All Waugh's books had to be bound in a shiny, dark blue cloth. Apparently it reminded him of publications from the Oxford University Press. We lost that battle. The dark blue cloth remained.

I would not claim that we had become friends but at least I was no longer *persona non grata*. Later he telephoned quite often: to say how pleased he was at the appearance of his son Auberon's first novel *The Foxglove Saga*, and how much he liked the design of the limited edition of *Basil Seal Rides Again*. We parted in peace.

FRANK HERRMANN

Dracula, Prince of Darkness

In my experience of the human condition, there is high-life, low-life and no-life.

Personally I prefer the last. Give me, a gentle amateur philosopher in search of understanding and spiritual enlightenment, a quiet evening at home, any time, with St Augustine of Hippo or Jalal ud-Din Rumi, a gas fire and a mug of warm lemon barley water. As for low-life, that is where I get dragged, unwillingly and against my better judgement, by acquaintances who need to be kept an eye on in their hour of need. And high-life? That of course is what goes with the job in the Diplomatic Service.

In the late 1960s the highest high-life of all was at the British Embassy in Paris under Sir Christopher (later Lord) Soames and his wife Mary, the youngest daughter of Winston Churchill. Soames was later to become vice-president of the European Commission. In Paris he was initially an unfamiliar quantity, who took a little getting used to. An unusual but shrewd ambassadorial appointment by Harold Wilson, Soames was a big fish in Paris, politically as well as corporeally. A Tory toff and former cabinet minister, he had been made ambassador with essentially one purpose: to overcome the French president's veto on UK accession to the European Community.

Once I had grown accustomed to the Soames phenomenon, and established what was expected and what I could contribute, I became personally devoted to both of them. But from the point of view of my no-life, there was one drawback: the Soames's mistook me, the shy and intellectual bachelor, for an extrovert playboy and general *beau sabreur*. There were consolations: such as a tutored introduction to serious claret and a social entrée like Clark Gable's in *Gone with the Wind*. Never since the days of Pauline Borghese and the Duke of Wellington had the Faubourg Saint-Honoré found itself so full of handsome and brave men, décolleté and diamond-draped women and the unmistakable whiff of position and power.

One winter the Soames's decided to give a fancy dress ball. It would be like no other in living memory, for *le tout Paris*. All of us in the Chancery were invited to make up suitable little parties of glitterati. I managed to rope in some of the usual suspects – apparatchiks and aristos, rebels and reptiles – but what was I going to wear? We were all busier than usual revising the embassy's Personality Report and I was blowed if I was going to go cap in hand to some theatrical costumier for a cowboy outfit or Caligula's cod-piece. Naturally I had a grass skirt, brought back from a recent trip to Tahiti, a present from a lady of good family, but the embassy ballroom might be too draughty. With three hours to go I was costume-less and clueless.

Suddenly, however, *le coup de foudre*. Wasn't it the Horror Film Festival in Paris this month? Wasn't *Dracule, Prince des Ténèbres* (with a plausibly dubbed Christopher Lee) the current Top of the Pops among *Les Filmes d'Épouvante*? Did I not possess clip-on plastic vampire teeth (a present from the Werewolf Lady at La Poubelle – but that is another story)? And also, somewhere, a white tie and tails? Quickly I togged myself up. To add Transylvanian glamour I slung the red-and-blue-striped belt of my dressing-gown over one shoulder, and tied it to the pommel of the court sword of my diplomatic uniform. But more was needed. So I pinned to my breast the gilt and glass star once given me by a grateful Prussian baron (a fellow-student at a French business school who had broken his spectacles falling down a cliff whilst admiring the moon early one morning and had had to be rescued and consoled with another *digestif*). Looking in the mirror, however, I thought it all looked somehow unconvincing even with the fangs in position. So I covered my face with talcum powder, brushed my hair straight back and slid a small bottle into my tailcoat pocket. I had difficulty finding a taxi-driver willing to convey me to my destination.

The embassy that evening was lit with candelabra. An orchestra played. There was dancing, a delicious buffet too. Liveried footmen in swallow-tails moved softly among the guests, bearing crystal flutes of Pol Roger on silver salvers. There was a gorilla, a Madame de Pompadour, a Mother Superior, a Marie-Antoinette, an Astérix le Gaulois and his twin, several cardinals, a Roman centurion with hairy legs and knobbly knees, a Lawrence of Arabia, one Napoleon, two Mickey Mice, three Vietnamese emperors, four Mexican peasants with ponchos and sombreros, several Cleopatras. Also, I believe, a Jane Birkin (in the flesh) if not a Brigitte Bardot. And one Dracula.

Time for the line-up. A fanfare of trumpets. Christopher and Mary Soames (conventionally attired as befitted their rank and their rôle as judges) took their place on a small dais in front of the orchestra. Guests competing for the fancy-dress prize were invited to circle the ballroom twice. First time round, as it seemed to me, all eyes were on the others. We circled for the second time. Hanging back a little, I drank unobserved from my small bottle. Finally approaching the dais, I snarled: tomato juice poured down from my fangs over the white piqué waistcoat. Sir Christopher recoiled, his expression a struggle between disgust and fascination. Mary Soames screamed, clutching her husband's arm. The prize was mine.

Not everyone was happy. 'Goddamn sonofabitch,' muttered the disappointed gorilla (a gentleman from the *Wall Street Journal*, I believe). '*C'est dégueulasse, ça*,' said the Banque de France. '*Quel cochon*,' opined the Ministre des Ponts et Chaussées. '*Vraiment la fin*,' concluded a Merchant of Death. '*Légèrement excessif, je trouve*,' whispered the high-up chap from the Élysée, cautious as ever.

But then all my life I have tried to live modestly with the understandable envy of those around me. So I bared my fangs one more time and returned to my little party. '*Mais, Less-lee, t'es devenu parfaitement fou*,' said the countess affectionately. '*Dingue comme tout*,' agreed the Directeur from the Quai d'Orsay. '*Chouette*,' conceded *Le Monde Diplomatique*. But the ash-blonde ballerina from Berlin embraced me warmly, her eyes shining. One was always ready to go to extreme lengths to enter into closer Anglo-German relations.

LESLIE FIELDING

A recently retired ambassador was comparing notes with a colleague in the Smoking Room.

'In my last post I spent nearly three years pressing for a certain minister to be invited to the UK as a guest of HMG. When he finally arrived, just after my retirement, I wasn't even asked to come and meet him.'

'I know, I know,' the other nodded. 'There's no swifter transition in this world than from Excellency to ex-.'

ST JOHN ARMITAGE

Excellencies Express

When I arrived in Saudi Arabia in April 1993 to take up my post as ambassador, my New Zealand colleague had been waiting fourteen months to present his credentials to King Fahd. A further twelve envoys designate formed a queue between him and me. He was flattering enough to suggest that the arrival of as important a representative as that of Her Majesty might unblock the logjam. And so, against my more modest expectations, it proved.

At 1.20 a.m. on the morning of 25 May the telephone on my bedside table exploded into life. It was Royal Protocol: the king would like to see me in Jedda (a mere eight hundred miles distant) later the same morning. How, I enquired, was I supposed to get there? 'No problem,' replied the protocol person. 'Please present yourself at the Royal Pavilion at Riyadh Airport at eleven and there will be a 'plane.'

There was: a Saudi Airlines Boeing 747 upgraded with velvet seat covers and the like. Another five colleagues presented themselves and the six of us flew down to Jedda with the remaining three hundred-odd seats empty. It being the Hajj season, eight other potential excellencies were already in Jedda looking after their pilgrims. (One had only his pilgrimage wear with him and was obliged to dive into the Jedda suq to buy a suit.) Three were absent from the kingdom on leave and missed the cut. One of them was said to have threatened to commit hara-kiri.

In Jedda we were met by a fleet of Mercedes and transported to the king's palace where each of us, in protocol order, reviewed a guard of honour to the accompaniment of somewhat shaky renditions of respective national anthems. We were then shepherded into a series of waiting-rooms (oddly enough for Saudi, no coffee or dates in any of them) before being ushered one by one into the presence of the king. Certain of my colleagues, having been caught short by the abruptness of the summons, did not have their credentials with them and were obliged to present impressive – but empty – envelopes.

By the time my turn finally came the Head of Protocol, who was doing the introducing, had clearly become stuck in a rut of republics because he began introducing me as 'the Ambassador of the Republic . . .' I interrupted him (my MECAS Arabic finally paying dividends!) to say that I was representing a monarch and not a president. The king heard and burst into laughter – which is why, according to watchers of Saudi TV, I was the only envoy he greeted with a smile.

Then back into the Mercedes, back into the jumbo and back to Riyadh, exhausted but accredited.

DAVID GORE-BOOTH

A Gentleman's Occupation

My cousin Charles Harding, who was a member of the Travellers, had a talent for telling stories against himself. He told me that one should never ask what someone's occupation was and that to do so was the height of ill manners, the presumption being that gentlemen did not do anything. To this day I find myself as a result asking people how they pass their time.

In 1975 Charles closed the Trafford Gallery in Mount Street where, since the late 1940s, he had put on exhibitions of contemporary artists. Thereafter he had no employment. But he soon found when travelling abroad that people expected you to 'do' something.

Consequently I was solemnly informed of his need to invent a job. This job – as an international art consultant with clients who always had to remain mysterious because they did not exist – involved an imaginary office. As a prop his housekeeper gave him a cheap, black-leather briefcase with which to do his shopping, so that he could always be on the way to or from the office when he met friends in the street.

The employment suffered set-backs: on one occasion he was asked by Lady A. in front of a large audience what his VAT registration number was. This question completely floored him as he had only the haziest idea what VAT was, let alone any number associated with it. Hours were then spent concocting answers to other tricky questions which he might be asked.

THOMAS WOODCOCK

The Triumph of the Truth

When the Foreign Office told me in 1961 where I had been posted, I had to look it up in the atlas. When I told my friends, they asked me what I'd done wrong. But they were the wrong ones, for it turned out to be a splendid job in a splendid place. The work and the title – Her Britannic Majesty's Political Agent Dubai – were remnants of the old Indian empire and nearing their sell-by date. They disappeared a year or two after I left.

Old hands from the Indian Civil Service always said that the best part of their job was the touring. This was certainly true in Dubai. I had to visit the shaikhs and the tribesmen, settle boundary disputes and blood feuds, inspect clinics and schools, choose sites for the well-diggers, fight the locusts. In those days there were no paved roads, only rough tracks in the desert and the mountains, and no transport but that old work-horse, the Land Rover, with its four-wheel drive and high-gear ratio. You shoved a campbed, a valise and a couple of primus stoves in the back and set off for four or five days, sleeping in the sand or occasionally in a tent if the weather was bad.

You depended a lot on the driver: he had to know the tracks, and the technique of desert-driving. Mine was the magnificent Gambar bin Hasan, a black Baluchi, son of a slave. Because of his huge and powerful build we called him *Pahlawan*, the Wrestler. He was illiterate but had a fund of stories, pure Arabian Nights, which he had heard from his mother.

Some of the desert stretches, particularly the soft shifting dunes, were both boring and uncomfortable. I would jam my feet against the dash-board to reduce the pitching and try to sleep. But Gambar would have none of it: my job was to keep him awake.

'*Yallah, ya gunsul*,' he would say. '*Ihki li gissa*. Come on, consul, tell me a story.' The trouble was that I did not have his repertoire and had to dredge my memory for the tales of Somerset Maugham or convert Scottish folk-songs into narratives. He quite liked them but could always be persuaded to dig out some of his own.

It happened once that we were camped on the sea-shore. I had with me a visiting professor from England, his wife and some of my men who were working in the area with a grader and lorry, improving the tracks. We were a mixed lot, British, Arab, Persian and Pakistani, but everyone spoke Arabic to some extent. We were stuck for three days because there had been heavy rain and beneath us was *sabkha*, salt clay, which turned into a morass when it was wet. It rained most of the day but broke clear in the evening, so that we could light a fire and sit round it talking. Gambar's story-telling was well known and each night the men urged him on. On the second night he produced his masterpiece.

'Once upon a time in the early days of Islam (he said), in a small and remote town, a young man, known to be off his head, went too far. He began to roam the streets shouting in a loud and eerie voice: "*Ana 'l-haqq, I am the Truth*".

'His eccentricities had until then always been tolerated with character-istic kindness, but this was blasphemy and therefore unacceptable. Only God is the Truth. His friends urged him to be silent but he would not. They warned him that if he did not stop, they would have to take him to the sultan. But he paid no heed and carried on shouting in that voice of doom: "*Ana 'l-haqq, I am the Truth*".

'So they led him to the sultan and explained the case. The sultan, a pious man, was horrified. He rebuked, he warned, he begged, he threat-ened, but to no effect. To every plea and every menace the young man returned no reply except those same awesome, shocking words: "*Ana 'l-haqq*".

'At last the sultan gave his terrible verdict: "If you do not stop this foul and sinful blasphemy, now and forever, you must be done away with". The watching crowd fell silent, waiting for the young man's reply. The time was between the dusk and the dark. The sunset prayer was over, the night prayer had not yet come round. The fading light made the suspense un-bearable. But finally the whispered reply emerged: "*Ana 'l-haqq*".

'Enough. The sultan had no further recourse. "Cut off his head", he said. And the public executioner came forward, an official whose services in that peaceful town had not been called upon since the time, many years before, when the people had accepted Islam and submitted themselves to the will of the One God.

'The young man knelt down, calm and unresisting. One blow of the heavy sword severed his neck. The head rolled away and lay face up in the dust. As the watchers watched, the lips moved and from them came the same words: "*Ana 'l-haqq*".'

Here Gambar paused, moved by his own story, but not as moved as we were. It was a full night on the beach and we huddled in to the fire, unsure whether to draw comfort from its last warmth or to see in it a foretaste of hell's eternal flames that awaited all sinners.

'The sultan (said Gambar) was much taken aback but soon recovered his authority. He ordered the head to be cut up into tiny pieces, with special attention paid to the lips. The executioner slashed away with his sword until there was nothing left on the ground but a mince of flesh, sinew and bone. To no avail. From the mash of gobbets there rose the distinct and eldritch words, repeated three times: "*Ana 'l-haqq*".

'In a fury the sultan gave orders that a fire should be lit and the remnants of the head burned. Men rushed to carry out his command. For two hours, three hours, the fire burned, the flesh dissolved, the flames roared, then flickered, then died.

'In the morning the people came out to inspect the cold embers. Over and between the dead logs lay the grey ashes which had, the night before, been a man's head. And from the ashes came a murmur, faint and tremulous but horrendously audible: "*Ana 'l-haqq*".

'The sultan himself was now afraid. But he was after all a ruler and must act. Picking out a crew of the town's strongest oarsmen, he told them to gather the ashes in a pot, row far out to sea and scatter them far and wide on the waves. His orders were obeyed, though all of the crew were fearful and some found it hard to pull. After a few hours they returned, their errand accomplished. By the end of the week calm had settled on the little town.'

The calm in our group round the fire was pretty uneasy. Was this the end of the story or was there more? Gambar sucked in his breath with a harsh rasp – to increase the suspense? to ensure our attention? – and went on. Our dread and our delight were not yet over.

'As far as the citizens of the town were concerned (Gambar said) the affair was finished, their fears had gone. But a few days later one of them, a prosperous merchant, was walking along the sea-shore. He was a solitary man, a widower with a daughter in her early teens. The two of them were looked after by a middle-aged woman, herself a widow, as their housekeeper. The merchant had been changed by the loss of his wife and the unmasculine task of bringing up a young girl. As he paced the beach, melancholy, even morose, he heard an unexpected sound, a murmur almost like a human voice. He stopped and listened: it was coming from the breakers as they rolled up the sand. The murmur broke up into words, those awful words that he had thought he would never hear again: "*Ana 'l-ḥaqq*".

'He bent down on one knee. The words were coming from the foam on the top edge of the waves. Without knowing quite why, he emptied the bottle in which he kept his tobacco and scooped up into it some of the articulate foam. Replacing the cork, he hurried home and put the bottle on the top shelf of the cupboard in which he kept his private papers. He said nothing to his fellow-citizens for fear of disturbing the peace which they had only tentatively regained.

'A week later he was to leave on a long journey, master of a caravan carrying imported piece-goods from India into the interior. He called his daughter to his room and spoke sternly to her: she must behave well while he was away, she must be obedient to the housekeeper, who would be in charge. Above all she must on no account touch the bottle on the top shelf of the cupboard, for it contained a deadly poison. He laid great stress on this warning, realising uneasily that he himself had no inkling what it was that the bottle contained, but unwilling to throw it away for fear of witchery. And off he went with his camels and his hopes of gain.

'Now the housekeeper was not the quiet, gentle soul that she appeared. She was tired of her widow's weeds and still young enough to hope for a second husband. Her rich employer would be an ideal catch but hitherto he had been too wrapped up with his daughter to have any heed for another woman. Here was her chance, while he was away, to slacken the daughter's hold, to make her naughty or peevish or malcontent. So she began a campaign of nagging and petty punishment that drove the girl in time to grave unhappiness and finally to the contemplation of suicide. But how? No guns, no gas ovens in those far-off days. Then the memory of her father's warning came back: the bottle in the cupboard. She climbed up and drank from it.

'She did not die.' We all sighed. 'But after a while her belly began to swell. The housekeeper was of course delighted. Here was the very thing.

When the father returned, he would have no choice but to punish with death or banishment. And when, after several months, he did come back, he was indeed appalled. He cross-examined his daughter: what had she done? With which man had she misbehaved? The girl was firm in her denials: she had done no wrong except to drink from the forbidden bottle.

'The merchant was distraught: on the one hand his daughter had always been truthful before, on the other her story was utterly improbable. He took advice from the town's *imam*, a man trusted for his wisdom and skill in solving problems.

"Well," said the imam, "clearly she is pregnant. You must wait till her time is come. If she gives birth in the normal way, you will know that she has been lying, that she has sinned, and you must do what is right in such cases. But if the baby is born by unnatural means, then she has been telling the truth and only the bottle is to blame."

'Patience was prudence. The girl gave birth to a son through a most unnatural orifice, a sudden split in her right knee. He was given the name Ahmad and the merchant accepted him as his grandchild and was reconciled to his daughter. When, after a few years, he died, he left the pair of them well provided for and they lived a quiet and comfortable life in the house which was part of the legacy. The boy grew up, lively, intelligent and good. When he was sixteen or so, his mother died in her turn. It was no great matter. She had never been entirely happy, for the townspeople had not been admitted to the secret of her pregnancy and remained deeply suspicious. In any case, the boy was now old enough to look after himself.

'But he was regarded in the town as odd. His circumstances ensured that: a young lad with the means of a middle-aged merchant, an only child, now an orphan with no uncles or cousins to guard him or speak for him. The oddity increased when it slowly became clear that he could not only speak for himself but had qualities beyond the ordinary, beyond the natural. In particular it was discovered that he had the power to heal the sick by the laying-on of hands. His fame spread throughout the town and his magical help was more and more in demand.

'Now about this time in another town, on an island a day's journey away, a great misfortune had occurred. The emir's daughter, a beautiful girl on the brink of womanhood and marriage, had fallen inexplicably into a coma. Doctors were summoned from far and wide. Week after week they arrived with their phials and their philtres, and week after week they departed, disappointed and disgraced. The emir was in despair. The daughter was his only child and, his wife being long beyond child-bearing, there was no hope of reinforcement. One of his advisers had heard of the young orphan's reputation and suggested calling him in, as a last resort. A delegation was sent and the young man was brought over by ferry and camel.

'The emir explained the situation and put forward a lonely and frightened man's proposal. If Ahmad could cure his daughter he would be given her hand in marriage and become heir to the emirate. Ahmad, stipulating that his powers were unexplained and unexplored, took on the task with the diffidence becoming a young man.

'He went into the room where the girl lay pale and still on a bed. Her eyes were closed, her lips were as white as her face. He put his right hand on her brow and said, quietly and solemnly: "*Qumi, bismi rabbik*. Rise in the name of thy Lord".

'The girl did not stir. Ahmad said again: "*Qumi, bismi rabbik*".

'Again, she did not stir. A third time Ahmad spoke: "*Qumi bismiyya*. Rise in *my* name".

'The girl's eyes opened, the blood flowed into her lips and cheeks, she looked up and caught her father's eye. In a few moments she was helped to her feet, frail but smiling.

'The emir was beside himself. He turned to Ahmad and embraced him. "Thank you, thank you. A thousand thanks and blessings. My promise will be kept. You shall be my son-in-law and my successor. Have no doubt of that. But now you must tell me: Where did you get these powers? Who are you?"

'And Ahmad replied: "*Ana 'l-haqq*".'

JAMES CRAIG

Educating Princes

Dumbfounding his wives by first asking their opinion, the emir had decided that his sons, the two crown princes, should spend their summer holidays studying in London. Would Her Britannic Majesty's representatives kindly make the requisite arrangements?

'Not bloody likely,' retorted my boss, the emirate's Political Agent. 'What if they do a runner? Mess around with drugs? Get themselves mugged? Could be a frightful hooha. Anyway it's more your corner, don't you think?' he asked the consul, his number two.

The consul thought not. His brief, as he would often rather tediously repeat, was the welfare of the emirate's British subjects. We were too diplomatic to point out that the latter all worked for multinationals far better equipped than he was to cater for their welfare. His consequent contribution to our workload was of an insignificance he vigorously defended.

As Arabist factotum in our desert outpost I had raised the emir's request in the weekly office meeting. Another of my jobs was to keep an ear on the broadcasts from Baghdad, Cairo and Damascus which rather flatteringly lambasted the three of us as a hotbed of British imperialism.

'Has the emir been naughty at all?' I wondered out loud. 'Any political pegs we could hang a refusal on?'

Apparently not. Relations were, I was told, ticketyboo.

'Not even a hunting raid over the border machine-gunning gazelle? No retaking slaves we've manumitted? What about the Queen's Birthday, wasn't the twenty-one-gun salute one short?'

'You know very well they ran out of dummy ammo,' smirked the consul. 'Used a live round and hit the regimental camel.'

'Well I can't just go back to the palace and tell His Highness no dice,' I objected, and played a few limp cards about moulding future emirate opinion. Shouldn't we keep relations ticketyboo too?

Under such intense low-level pressure the head of post capitulated. If I wanted to let two teenage Arab princes loose on London, then I could but off my own bat if I liked, which I didn't.

He opened a file, closing the meeting.

'Just don't blame me if it's a shambles,' he warned.

I was miffed by his even considering the possibility of any such disloy-alty. Unthinkable. No, I'd naturally let London take the blame. And for-warded the emir's request to Whitehall by our new telex machine.

The speed with which they responded rather nullified the benefits of modern communication. 'Is there any equivalent here of our mañana?' a Spanish visitor to the emirate once asked. 'Plenty,' he was told. 'But none expressing quite the same degree of urgency.'

Whitehall seemed to have gone native in this respect; there was weeks of stalling at the palace before I could rush over with a reply just received from London and, with other work pressing, unread.

The *majlis* or 'sitting-place' was a hall of the palace where the emir held audience daily – a designer hangar with marble floors from Italy, Louis XV furniture made in Jaipur, and serried sofas from Heals. First-time visitors were mostly struck by its soaring columns and roaring air conditioners.

I was ushered in and crossed the crowded hall giving the standard loud, bold greeting: '*Salaamu 'alaikum*'.

'*Wa 'alaikum as-salaam*' came back, choir-led by the emir and chorused by the rest.

The majlis that day was full house. Dressed to a man in full-length dish-dashas, with black *ghutra*s around white *kaffia*s on their heads, the favour-seekers were seated in a horseshoe with the emir in the centre. Half the horseshoe rose and shuffled down a seat to make space on the emir's right. After the usual polite enquiries as to his health, his sons, his hawks and the bustard-hunting season I began translating London's long-awaited reply:

'Classes of no more than twenty pupils. Accommodation with an approved host-family at the special price of fourteen pounds a week (No Weekend Meals). Fortnightly coach outings . . . '

The emir was known for a boisterous if mercurial sense of humour; I sensed it lapsing as I read on. 'Or perhaps the young gentlemen would prefer to share? Seventeen pounds weekly for a double en suite. And sub-sidised travel by London Transport on production of a Student Union card . . . '

I stopped: London had blundered, I realised too late. The emir's sparkling eyes were glazed, his usual smile almost a frown. The assembled majlis was silent. I tried an apologetic grin. At this the emir guffawed. What he said is probably best translated as 'You are a one!'

'It's a joke,' he announced to the still bemused assembly.

'A joke' was solemnly repeated down the line.

'Now,' said the emir in a joke-over tone. 'They'll need an apartment in that, what's it called, Playfair place, by Hyde Park Lane. And a cook, and a driver. Our UK exporter can handle a car for them. Anything else?'

'Flat in Mayfair, near Park Lane,' I checked my notes. 'Yes Highness, May God give you long life. There is just one thing. If their Excellencies are to study, may I suggest a tutor?'

The emir agreed one might be useful and, summoning his secretary, told him in a loud whisper to pay whatever it cost. That was my cue to leave.

Asked by telex to raise his sights, my opposite number in Whitehall replied that his sights didn't go that high. He proposed recruiting consultants if the emir would pay. The latter's secretary concurred. The opposite number also proposed that the consultants and I liaise direct: he was subtler than my boss had been in passing the buck and ducking out.

The educational agency consulted asked for details. The dates of birth prompted a query: only two months between the brothers? Polygamy, I explained. They then asked for copies of the princes' school reports. 'Sorry,' I telexed back. 'They don't attend school. Shall I have a word with their private tutor?'

This last was a Dickensian Palestinian, a worried and humble academic whose hang-dog air and furrowed brow suggested that job satisfaction might be lacking. He looked even more worried by my request, but the palace had authorized the talk.

'They know some,' he said guardedly when asked about the boys' English.

'No doubt the agency will assess them on arrival. Could you tell us a bit about their character? It'll help the agency make the right arrangements, recruit suitable staff and so on.'

The tutor closed his eyes as though signing his own death-sentence. 'What to say? They are different. Let me give you a specimen.'

The elder son, the tutor specified, if he was sitting in his room and a fly bothered him, would take his machine-gun and spray the room with bullets till he'd killed the fly. But his brother wasn't like that at all. No, he would get some halwa, or sugar or honey. Then hold it and sit quietly until the fly landed. Then pull it apart with his hands and smash the pieces. Reporting this to the educational agency meant a rather tricky précis.

Unperturbed, and obscenely paid, they completed the arrangements. The princes flew off to their five-bedroomed rental in Mayfair. They regularly telephoned happily. I was called to be thanked by an equally happy emir. 'You know what?' he beamed. 'They're studying so hard they've asked for a second tutor!'

I left for home leave a short while later and in London looked up the princes. Never at their flat, they could, the hall porter said, be found playing football in Hyde Park. This they did apparently each livelong summer's day. With cook, driver and just one tutor, sides had been uneven. But the extra tutor made it nicely three a side.

On the topic of hospitality the unevenness was not so easily resolved. The emir was famously open-handed; there were frequent banquets at his palace. To reciprocate at my parents' semi-detached in North London? 'Why not?' thought my father. 'I'll invite the lads to tea. They can only say No.'

They didn't. They duly arrived on the appointed day in a white limousine of an opulence and length rarely seen in those parts then or now. The chauffeur parked it outside our house and much of our next-door neighbour's too.

The princes were ushered in and seated on the settee. My parents and teenage sister were introduced, pleasantries exchanged and translated. Being for the first time in an English home, the Arabs were clearly taken aback by my mother's brazen effrontery in sitting and joking with us men. Then amazed by my father's offering to fetch tea. 'He likes to supervise the staff' was the best I could manage as a conversation-saver.

He failed to supervise our puppy. It escaped from the kitchen and lolloped excitedly into the lounge, sloppily licking at ankles and hands and trying to leap into laps. This did not prompt the customary Anglo-Saxon reaction. While the gun-toting prince visibly suppressed an instinctive kick, his brother recoiled horrified and cringed back in the settee. I forget which of them later became Supreme Commander of the emirate's Armed Forces.

Whether, once this reached the emir's ears, relations would continue to be ticketyboo I rather doubted. The princes however still accepted the occasional evening out – I thought the première of *Lawrence of Arabia* appropriate – and their departure date approached without any bomb-shells from my boss.

My home leave was shortly due to end too when one morning the limousine reappeared outside. The chauffeur rang the door-bell. 'Mr T.? The emir's sent word to give you the car. The papers' been put in your name, and so's the insurance.' He handed over the documents and car keys, then stood hesitating. Expecting a tip? I wasn't sure what the going rate for a limousine might be. But knew I couldn't afford it. 'Would you like a lift to the Tube?' I asked instead. He showed me how to handle the limo as we drove around the houses. The lesson was worth a tip: he disappeared down the escalator carless but content.

The Foreign Office has alas rules about such things: keeping the car was not an option. Nor, ironically, was giving it back. Declining gifts from Arab potentates was scarcely politick. During Britain's Gulf years HM Residency in Bahrain maintained what was known as a Toshana Fund for gifts such as this which could neither be accepted nor declined – against the day when a serving officer was required to reciprocate with a suitable present that neither he nor HMG could afford. It was a governmental version of Unwanted Christmas Gifts, and required the same careful record-keeping of who had given/got what.

There was nothing for it but to drive the limo back – through Belgium, Germany and Austria, from *Autobahn* on to the Yugoslav *autoput*, via northern Greece, Turkey, Syria and Jordan, then across Arabia proper along the pipe-line roads – and hand it in. Travel Section had no objection: petrol allowance and *per diem* would cost the taxpayer less than the airfare.

Something occurred to me and I telephoned the princes before leaving. But thank you, no, the emir was sending his jet. They didn't need a lift home.

MICHAEL TOMKINSON

Going Dutch

The telephone rang in my office in Amsterdam. For a moment I did not recognise the voice. 'It's Ted. From Washington. You remember? Sure, it's been a long time. You're still in Holland. Your Dutch must be fantastic.'

Ted's law firm was leading the American side in a Sarajevo project and he was looking for a Dutch specialist in gas contract negotiation. I just about fitted the bill but my British passport made me an unconvincing Dutchman. Ted had spent several years working for an oil company in dangerous places and never allowed small matters of detail to get in his way. He was in a hurry and interpreted his terms of reference liberally. The firm's partner had to be a Dutch speaker with the required expertise, but no one had said anything about Dutch nationality. He arranged a transatlantic telephone call with someone he was working with in the Dutch embassy and I spoke in Dutch. Ted called me back.

'Congratulations, you passed the language test. So you're in then? Good. Give me your fax number and I'll send you an outline of the work. Well actually it's a pretty long outline so you'd better check your supply of fax paper.' There was a gurgling sound at the other end of the line. Ted was amused.

The facts behind the Netherlands' involvement in ex-Yugoslavia were more complex. Dutch soldiers under UN command had failed to protect a group of seven thousand Bosnians, young men and old, at Srebrenica: their massacre by Serbian troops had shocked the Dutch public. For many the event triggered memories of Europe's darker past. When the war ended soon after, and with it the four-year-long siege of Sarajevo, a Dutch government representative instructed the embassy in Washington to develop jointly with the Americans a programme of emergency assistance to Bosnia. A key task was to restore the electricity supply. Power cuts kept much of the city in darkness at night and would cause hardship in the sub-zero temperatures of the coming winter. Two specialists would be provided to assist the embryonic Federation Government in securing from the Russians new supplies of gas to generate electricity in Sarajevo. One of the advisers had to be American, the other Dutch. But not exactly.

My arrival in Sarajevo was dramatic enough. There were no civilian air-craft, only military flights carrying troops, police and casually dressed aid workers. Sarajevo Airport was a small group of buildings that had been hurriedly constructed by the United Nations' peacekeeeping troops at the edge of a dense forest. From their uniforms I could see that the blue-bereted UN troops who checked my papers were French. Standing in the heat in a dark suit, I waited for my driver to appear and looked around. The airstrip was short, set in a flat wilderness, with barbed-wire perimeter fencing and beyond, at the end of the valley, some spectacular mountains. Later I learned that the scrub around the airfield was thick with mines left from the war. They had not yet been cleared.

The drive into the city was over an uneven, dusty road. The wheels ground slowly and noisily over the pebble and grit surface, then lurched and turned like a safari rally car's as the driver tried to avoid craters made by mortar shells. On either side of the road the buildings looked like sets from a film about Beirut in the Seventies or Berlin in 1945. Most were in various stages of collapse, sinking into the rubble of broken glass, brick, concrete and paving-stones that lay everywhere. Among the debris were objects that hinted at a story: a sink ripped from a kitchen wall, a bath with one of its taps missing, a battered and dirty mattress and one half of a suit-case. 'Keep away from here,' the driver warned. He waved his arm at the derelict buildings. 'Mines. Traps. Danger.' The car lurched onward.

At the Hotel Bosnia I was shown to a small room, decorated in insipid colours and shaped in an oddly angular manner that suggested it was the product of a hurried conversion. While unpacking, I heard a knock on the door and went to open it, noticing a small hole in the wall beside the door. Ted had arrived. 'Welcome to Bosnia,' he greeted me as he walked straight in, bubbling with enthusiasm. He looked around and noted the various holes in the window, the walls and even the bathroom door. His eyes widened. 'Good Grief! Bullets. Your room's seen some action then.'

The next day began with a rendezvous at the ministry where Ted and I met the Bosnian team we would be working with. Our mandate was to prepare them for the negotiations with the Russian suppliers, whose rep-resentatives were scheduled to arrive in three weeks. The Bosnian con-tracts for gas purchase all dated from the Yugoslav era, their terms and conditions reflecting the mindset of Soviet-style central planning. While the siege had lasted, the outside world (including the Russians) had embraced the idea of a market economy *en masse*. In Central and Eastern Europe the contracts for gas purchase had taken on a harder, Western edge, linking production with consumption. Our first task was to help the Bosnians design new contracts that made sense in this new market-oriented environment.

The second problem was delicate and concerned money. Payments for gas had now to be made in hard currency. That meant dollars. Although these were in short supply in Sarajevo, a package of international aid was available. The problem lay in deciding first how much to pay the Russians, who were claiming huge unpaid bills for gas that had left Russia. When gas bound for Sarajevo made its way by pipe-line through Hungary, transit fees were levied by the astute Hungarians. They took payment in gas instead of waiting for dollars. Once the gas left Hungary, it had to cross territory now controlled by Serbian nationalists, who appropriated further quantities for their own use. What was left belonged to the government of the newly formed state of Bosnia-Herzegovina, an uneasy federation of Muslims, Croatians and Serbs.

The Russians wanted them to pay for all this gas, including what it never received. Ted and I knew that our hosts needed urgently a master class in business. They had to learn quickly if they were not to be taken to the cleaners by the Russians, who well knew that some of the gas had never arrived but hoped that the Bosnians could be persuaded to pay with international aid money. A complicating factor was that the negotiations would have to be carried out in parallel with those involving the Serbian nationalists, based in their fortress-like enclave within the Bosnian Federation. Relations between our hosts and their neighbours were evidently strained. Happily for me, this aspect was to be Ted's job.

By the end of the afternoon a series of meetings had run their course, leaving us exhausted but without any obvious effects upon our hosts' stamina. A work-programme and timetable had been agreed and we seemed to have the basis for a good working relationship. It was time to go back to the hotel. I began forcing bundles of contracts and documents into my briefcase.

'They want to tell you something,' the interpreter said. 'They have a message.' Our hosts were still seated round the circular table. No one had stood up to leave. The silence continued, uncomfortably for me. Ted seemed relaxed, as if he knew what was going to happen. Like participants in a group-therapy session, they began to talk one by one about their experiences during the war and the years in which the city was besieged. Each of them spoke through the interpreter, telling stories, anecdotes, making observations about life in the city, sometimes adding sentences in broken English.

'We thought that everyone had forgotten us,' one began. 'No one could understand why the world did not help.'

Another was bitter: 'Some of our people left before the war, or during it. It's difficult for us to talk to them about it.'

A woman told how her husband had been wounded in the head and she had walked for five hours to find water to care for him. It was always a problem to find water for cooking; everywhere, she added, there was dirt.

The leader of the team, a middle-aged man who looked much older, told how his daughter had been a baby when the siege began. When it ended, he took her to the Adriatic. She had never seen the sea before. In a restaurant there she looked puzzled at the sight of an orange, not knowing how to peel it. He described how he had bought her the first bar of chocolate she had ever had.

A silver-haired engineer who appeared to be the oldest among them began: 'You should have seen our city before. It was so beautiful'. His voice broke, and the interpreter put her hand on his shoulder. The emotion was intense.

Ted and I walked back through the town and along the Miljacka River. It was getting dark but we both needed the walk and the bracing effects of the fresh air, now turned icy cold. We passed the shell of the town library, its roof collapsed and its interior burned and crushed by Serbian mortars, then the place on the old town bridge where the Serbian nationalist supposedly fired the shot that killed the Archduke Franz Ferdinand and so triggered the First World War. Along much of the route were tall, solid apartment blocks, their walls pock-marked by shrapnel and bullet-holes.

Ted broke the silence. 'He was a psychiatrist,' he said quietly, a cloud of smoke puffing from his mouth as he spoke.

'Who?' I asked.

'Karadzic. The Serbian leader in Bosnia. He was a kind of disciple of Milosevic, who started the whole nationalist thing. The point is, he knew what he was doing with the siege. The targets were picked carefully from the hills up there. Buildings like the library. Old people. Children. The memory of the past. And the future.' I looked up at the hills above the city and felt vulnerable.

Three weeks later the Russians arrived. Dressed in dapper suits, white shirts and dark ties, they looked every inch a disciplined team. The leader wore a trilby-style hat and seemed younger than the rest. They spoke to each other in low voices. The hierarchy among them was clear. I remembered that the gas company had been called a state within a state in the new Russia and that it benefited from the protection of the prime minister. They were preceded by a reputation as fierce negotiators. 'They are like wolves,' one of our Bosnian colleagues hissed. The contrast with our casual, disorganised hosts was impossible to miss.

The Russians appeared to know exactly what they wanted. The Bosnian response was to invite them to have coffee after their long journey, and to discuss pleasantries with them. After coffee came lunch, an afternoon break for 'leg-stretching' and in the evening a banquet. Try as they would to commence detailed discussions on business matters, the Russians were constrained at every turn by the social priorities of our hosts. Given the stakes involved, I was baffled by this behaviour. Ted was quicker off the mark. 'Our hosts have started to negotiate,' he whispered.

After several days an interim deal was struck. The Russians compromised, although the deal would be signed in Moscow at a follow-up meeting. In celebratory mood, the Bosnians organised a dinner for us. The work had gone well, at least for this first phase. The Russians left early and excused themselves from the dinner. Bad weather between Sarajevo and Zagreb prevented them from flying out, they said, so they had had to hire a car for the long journey.

The evening air was cool after the day's heat, if a little heavy. The dinner was held in the garden of a restaurant that all claimed was the best in the city. Cloths were spread over white plastic tables. The paving-stones were cracked. We were the only customers. Our hosts thanked us for our work and made gracious speeches, ending in toasts to the success of the partnership in the months ahead. The leader of the Bosnian team leaned over and confided in me: 'You speak English very clearly. We understood everything'. The compliment was a little surprising but I accepted it with good grace. 'All of your people speak good English,' the interpreter added. This sounded a little peculiar, even to a Scotsman. Ted was smiling. He started to say something, with an impish look on his face, but I kicked him under the table. The Bosnian began again, telling his guests how several doctors and nurses from the Netherlands had stayed in the city throughout the siege. 'They were heroes. They could have left, but they stayed. And they would not accept compliments.' The others nodded earnestly. Our interpreter contributed her assessment, furrowing her brow a little, looking for a word. 'Modest, very modest,' she said. Belatedly I realised that they had all been assuming I was Dutch. Unsure how to react, I lowered my eyes and nodded in what I hoped was a modestly heroic manner.

PETER DUNCANSON CAMERON

An Unwelcome Visitor

When I was Private Secretary to the ambassador in Moscow, I had the privilege of living in a flat in the stable-block at the bottom of the garden. The splendid residence was and still is beside the Moskva River with breath-taking views of the Kremlin.

One Sunday afternoon I was in the flat when I had a hysterical 'phone call from the embassy's security guard on the main door saying that a gunman had burst in and run upstairs to the ambassador's quarters. I did not then know whether the latter was at home. The guard did not tell me, and I did not learn until later, that the intruder had already shot one of the Russian guards at the embassy gate.

I ran to the main building and was joined by another British security guard named Grey. We ran up the grand staircase. I remember throwing off my coat on the stairs and wondering if I would ever see it again. On the landing Grey and I were confronted by a young Russian who pointed a gun at us and said: 'You English?' I was not sure what the correct answer was to this question, so Grey and I leapt at him and took the gun before he could fire.

We bundled him down the staircase to the Chancery below. He then lucidly explained that he had heard of the practice of granting political asylum. He said that he came to warn us of Soviet intelligence intentions to the West.

We were joined by another member of the embassy staff who made a sketch, which I still have, of the gun. It was home-made, but each of the bullets had been carved with a cross at the end to ensure maximum harm.

I explained to the intruder that there was no chance of us giving him political asylum and that I had no alternative but to hand him over to the Soviet authorities. I advised him that it would be best if this were done as quietly as possible. His response was to bite both of his wrists, which resulted in a great deal of sluggish blood and a considerable mess.

At this point the ambassador, Sir William Hayter, and his wife returned home from skiing in the outskirts of Moscow. I reported on the situation and he agreed that we had no choice but to hand the intruder over. I told the Russian of the ambassador's decision and advised him to come calmly to the embassy gates. He agreed. However, when we reached the door of the embassy he tried to open the veins in his neck with his hands. Much to my surprise, he partially succeeded and there was yet more blood.

By then we had had more than enough and my colleagues and I carried him to the gates, where a group of Soviet policemen were waiting impassively. They grabbed him, threw him into the back of a car and drove away at high speed.

The incident attracted front-page attention in the British press. The *Evening Moscow* had one line: 'Mentally ill person enters British Embassy'. The *News Chronicle* of 15 March 1955 published a cartoon, of which I still have the original, with an imperturbable ambassador saying: 'Tell Faucet I would like a word with him when he has finished struggling with that gunman'. I do not think I looked a bit like Faucet.

JOHN MORGAN

The View from Ho Chi Minh Street

I had just returned from a posting in the Gulf and was enjoying wide-eyed a bachelor life in London when a telephone call brought my gilded new existence to an abrupt end.

'We need you to go to Aden,' said someone in Personnel, 'as soon as possible.' Aden? Unquestionably the worst posting in the Middle East, if not the world.

Aden was then the capital of the People's Democratic Republic of Yemen, a suspicious title which immediately suggested a system of government that had little to do with the people and even less to do with democracy. The PDRY was ruled by a radical group of former gunmen who had seized power five years earlier, following the ignominious British withdrawal after almost 130 years of colonial rule.

The unlovely group ran the country on pseudo-Marxist lines, with the enthusiastic support of the Russians and East Germans. In those five short years the prosperous former colony had become a wasteland and all expatriates had fled, apart from a handful of British workers literally incarcerated in nearby Little Aden, where they tried to maintain the decaying BP refinery. The British Embassy had been removed from its strategically sensitive site overlooking the harbour and banished to Ho Chi Minh Street in Lenin Quarter, an area behind Aden town that had housed RAF families.

It transpired that HMG had recently expelled the First Secretary of the PDRY embassy in London for activities 'incompatible with his status'. In retaliation the PDRY had expelled the First Secretary of our embassy in Aden. Hence the 'phone call from Personnel Department.

In darkest gloom at the prospect of this posting I sought out our First Secretary who had just returned. 'Tell me, Henry,' I said. 'Tell me that life in Aden is not as unspeakably awful as it seems.'

'Why no,' he replied. 'It's quite good really. On Monday nights there is fish and chips and a film on the embassy roof and on Thursdays you can go over to Little Aden and play darts with the riggers.'

I felt physically sick. Ye gods! Was this to be the sum of my social life? Henry was a civilised man. Surely he must realise how bleak his words sounded? But if he did he showed no awareness of it. I made a silent vow that whatever else I did in Aden I would never go to fish-&-chip night at the embassy and never, ever, play darts with the riggers at the refinery.

In the midst of all this darkness there was one ray of light. I knew that Henry had had a rather nice PA, the only female of my sort of age in the mission, and thought that, fate having thrown us together, we might, in one way or another, be able to comfort each other and so offset the bleakness around. Indeed, that very bleakness might enhance the romanticism of it and – who knows? – love might even flourish in those unlikely surroundings. Tentatively I asked my predecessor about her.

'She's absolutely delightful,' he replied. 'In fact so much so that we've got engaged and she's leaving the embassy and coming back to London next week!'

In desperation I rang Personnel Department and asked whom they had in mind to replace her.

'Aden is now classified as unsuitable for children,' was the reply, 'and we've decided that conditions there aren't suitable for young female PAs either. So we're sending out an old warhorse – a splendid lady with plenty of experience of hardship posts. It's her last posting before retirement.' My morale, never high where this posting was concerned, finally collapsed.

I arrived in Aden a week or so later. It was much as anticipated: the stark and arid setting of Aden town (a volcanic crater which Kipling described as 'an old barrack stove that no one has lit for years') matched the stark and arid life-style imposed on all by Marxism. For three months I held firm to my vow not to go to the fish-&-chip night on the embassy roof or, God help us, the darts night at Little Aden. But then I gave in. There was after all absolutely nothing else. Six months later I found myself carefully noting these occasions in my diary; a year, and I was looking forward to them for days ahead.

Some diplomats in overseas posts take pride in achievements such as evacuating an embassy under fire or negotiating the definitive bilateral defence treaty. For me the high point of my tour in Aden was winning one game of darts against a pot-bellied rigger called Dave who could usually hit a treble twenty with his eyes shut.

GEOFFREY TANTUM

Fighting in Dhofar

The sad truth about peacetime tank manœuvres was that the officers who shone more brightly were those who played by the book. There was no place for individual brilliance or initiative, largely because in the 1960s we were expecting and training for a short, sharp nuclear war.

After three years in tanks I volunteered to join the SAS regiment fighting in the Borneo jungle. On the day I received my SAS wings I became the youngest captain in the British Army but, a few months later, I was demoted to lieutenant and sent back to the Scots Greys. My crime was to have used army explosives to blow up a Twentieth Century-Fox film-set in Dorset which an old friend of mine objected to environmentally. This was an initiative which neither the SAS nor the Army Board approved of, and my lifelong aspiration to command the Greys suffered a severe set-back.

This was in 1967 and, at the age of twenty-three, I felt as if I was getting nowhere fast. Officers who had joined the regiment two years after me were in more senior positions, which was not a good omen for my making it to CO.

A Greys captain serving in Arabia sent me a letter with a colourful stamp. 'Come and join me,' he suggested. 'No tanks, no mud and good pay.' He failed to mention that the Sultan of Oman, his boss, was involved in an escalating war with Marxist revolutionaries.

My application for the posting was approved and, after a quick London course in Arabic (which I failed), I was sent to Muscat in Oman. The sultan's senior officers included many relics of the Raj, the headquarters was a Beau Geste-style fortress with crenellated keeps and cannon, and our rifles were Second World War, bolt-action left-overs.

I was sent south to the war zone of Dhofar and soon savoured my baptism of fire. The Marxist terrorists, at home in the jungle-clad ravines, had received their training and automatic weapons from the Soviets. Their numbers far exceeded our puny Sultanate forces and they gained control of the mountains in Western Dhofar during my first summer there.

There were no helicopters. The sultan's entire air force consisted of two antiquated Piston Provost fighters flown by ex-RAF pilots. Our navy was a simple wooden dhow. Richard John, the Scots Greys officer whose letter had attracted me to Arabia, was shot through the shoulder in an ambush. His painful evacuation on the back of a mule took eight hours.

Back in Muscat, I was introduced by my new colonel to the reconnaissance platoon I was to lead, a rag-tag band of fifteen men and five dilapidated, open Land Rovers. Half the unit were volunteer Omanis; the other half (whom the first half hated) came from Baluchistan, a country which the sultan had recently sold to Pakistan for one million pounds.

Unlike the rest of the regiment's three infantry companies, the 'recce' platoon traditionally travelled in vehicles, and the colonel had decided I should command it. His logic was clear: I knew how to work with tanks, so I could surely cope with Land Rovers.

The rationale of my fifteen men in joining the recce platoon was equally straightforward. The infantry companies had no vehicles so, down in Dhofar, they would have to walk everywhere. Furthermore, the most dangerous region was the mountains, where vehicles could not travel. Recce was clearly the best choice for any sane man. The thought of entering the war zone with this motley bunch of back-seaters filled me with horror.

My recent initiation to being shot at and the sphincter-tightening experience of driving through mine-fields had quickly dissipated the lust for excitement which had drawn me to Oman. I now needed a just cause to work for if I was to stick my neck out and do a good job in Dhofar. A mercenary captain, Peter Southward-Heyton, supplied the information needed to stiffen my spine.

'In Germany, Ran, you were a tiny cog in the vast NATO wheel, but here you can personally make a difference to history. I'm not exaggerating. The Soviets desperately need to control the Oman coast and thus block eighty per cent of the free world's oil. Now they've taken Aden, Dhofar will be next. They will have a brief window of opportunity when that will be easy. This year and next. Why? Because all Oman wants freedom from the sultan. He is undeniably reactionary. No schools, no hospitals. But soon, maybe in a year, his son Qaboos, who is half-Dhofari, will take over. He will be progressive and the people will love him. This will jerk the enemy's propaganda platform from under their feet.'

'So,' he continued, 'they must move now in Dhofar. They know that. Great quantities of arms, ammunition and trained cadres are infiltrating as

we speak. We will have only one infantry regiment and your mobile platoon in the whole region. Anything you can do this year to delay the
enemy's consolidation, and their preparations to expel the sultan, will be
vital.'

Peter died not long afterwards, but his advice gave me the boost I
needed.

I blitzed the platoon, sacking the 'rotten apples' and replacing them
with good soldiers I tempted away from the other three companies when
their officers were on leave. I raised the platoon strength to thirty, including five good drivers who rejuvenated our vehicles. I 'borrowed' eight
extra light machine-guns, a mortar, grenades and better clothing from a
friendly quartermaster. With some difficulty I formed six sections of mixed
race and made a strong point of never showing favour to either Omani or
Baluch.

We patrolled into little-known wadis in the Sharqiya province, the fiefdom of Shaikh Mohammed al-Harthi who hated the sultan. We practised
tactical vehicle movement through rough scrubland, repairing the vehicles
quietly by night, and communicating via code on radios which I had also
scrounged. Then I was summoned by the colonel. News from Dhofar was
all bad, including a rocket ambush that had wiped out the vehicles and
many men of the recce platoon whose patrol sector I was to take over.

'You must train your men immediately,' the colonel told me, 'to operate on foot as well as in your Land Rovers.'

For two months, in the heat of the Omani summer, we trained on foot
by day and by night, both on the gravel plains and in the dense scrub of
the Jabal Akhdar at ten thousand feet above sea-level. Many of the men,
exhausted, transferred back to their companies. I found replacements of a
tougher disposition.

My training methods were not, so far as I knew, present in any military
textbook. They stemmed from common-sense reactions to the emergency
situations likely to occur in Dhofar. I remembered from SAS days that
movement by night is usually preferable, silence is vital, unpredictability
essential, and small units a bonus. We practised night movement and hand
signals repeatedly, ambush reactions daily, and accurate shooting with live
rounds weekly. I read various guerilla-warfare manuals, sent by mail order,
and found Chairman Mao's advice the most sensible and easy to follow. At

the end of the date-harvest we took our leave of Northern Oman and drove the five Land Rovers five hundred miles south.

The Rub' al-Khali, or Empty Quarter, is the second greatest sand desert in the world and stretches for a thousand miles from the Oman coast into Saudi Arabia. In it there is nothing permanent. The eastern fingers of the sands, through which we travelled, stretched flat and grey to the sea with a surface of black gravel and yellow pans of gypsum.

For a while we patrolled only to the north of the Qara Mountains which stretch the length of Dhofar, separating the arid northern desert from the fertile plain of Salala to the south. In Salala village the sultan lived in a whitewashed palace overlooking the Arabian Sea.

White sand and oases of palms led away east and west from the palace as far as the eye could see. The Marxist-controlled mountains rose sheer from the plain only eight miles to the north of the palace. The mountains themselves, though hundreds of miles in length, were but ten miles across between southern plain and northern desert.

Army strength in Dhofar numbered fewer than three hundred men, whereas some four thousand armed terrorists held the mountains. To drive over the only vehicle track across the Qara was a lethal experience involving mines and ambush, but we were lucky. Once on Salala plain, we began a series of ambushes, moving only by night to hide in caves and deep forest. We could usually carry enough ammunition and water for four days.

We killed many of the enemy, had many near scrapes, and lived in constant fear of mines – both the tank mines that could throw a Land Rover thirty yards and the anti-personnel devices which blew your foot through your stomach and removed your face. There were snakes everywhere. The carpet viper's venomous bite could render a strong man brain-dead in seconds. Seven-inch camel-spiders and the even bulkier, poison-fanged wolf-spiders were common.

Hyænas and wolves roamed the foot-hills, leopards and wild cats snarled from caves, and ticks, whose bite paralysed or poisoned, dropped from foliage onto passers-by. Twelve-inch centipedes, great scorpions and giant lizards scuttled about as we lay 'doggo' in ambush hides.

At night the stars were huge as we advanced in a long, silent file, sometimes with a guide but more often using highly inaccurate maps. Patrick Brook, an old army friend, was ambushed in the hills one day and a bullet smashed the flask he carried on his right hip. Another drilled through his left arm. The soldiers immediately ahead of and behind him were killed. His guardian angel was on top form that day.

I always led from the front, mainly because I knew where I wanted to go and how fast a pace I needed to set. I found it impossible to convey these wishes to anyone else.

Some officers wore comfortable clothes and shaved. They stood out like sore thumbs – prime targets for enemy snipers. Nearly all my men wore standard army camouflage. I tried to dress exactly like them in order to increase my chances of survival.

In exchange for information about enemy movements we gave food and medicine to the goatherds in the valleys. They would ask when we would next visit so they could tell other sick people. Suspecting they might tell the enemy, we laid ambushes in readiness for any would-be ambushers. But sometimes we grew tired and careless. On two such occasions we nearly paid with our lives.

Early in 1969 our colonel changed tactics as the enemy brought in bigger and better weapons. He installed a north-south blocking line at key points across the mountains in an attempt to disrupt this lethal inflow. My unit was to patrol the ancient Dehedoba camel trails in the rugged country immediately north of the Qara Mountains and up to the Yemen border.

For months we lived on the move in the scorching gravel deserts, dodging enemy traps, suffering ulcerating desert sores, straying many miles over the Yemen border and never developing a routine. The fear of mines, the ever-present tension and the day-long irritations of flies and dust affected everyone. One of the companies mutinied. The officer was a Royal Marine captain with an impatient nature. He would throw stones at soldiers lagging behind. Royal Marines may have put up with this but the Arabs found it distressing. His gung-ho approach to the enemy had ended in a serious ambush and several casualties. After the mutiny he was replaced by an officer more capable of compromise and subtlety.

I could sense when the men were on edge, though they seldom complained. Hardest was the month of Ramadhan, when no Muslim should eat or drink during daylight hours. When we needed to move rapidly by day, with heavy loads in the searing heat, it was doubly wearisome to fast.

I decided to follow the same rules as the men. That way I could ask more from them without fear of the attitude: 'It's all right for him, he's not fasting'. Experiencing the privations of Ramadhan for myself also greatly increased my already considerable respect for the toughness of the men.

After Dhofar I knew never to ask for more than I was prepared to give. But not every salutary lesson I learned from the Arabs worked with European soldiers or expedition colleagues. A big bonus for officers dealing with awkward enquiries from their Muslim charges – such as the query: 'My pay will be increased next year, won't it?' – was the ability to respond with a sincere *Insh'allah*, 'God willing'. This closed the matter with the Muslims but not with the Scots Greys.

Although I killed people in Dhofar, my conscience did not disturb me because I rarely saw the bodies and I knew that the individuals concerned had been trying to kill me. Most fire-fights took place at a distance of at least a hundred yards in thick bush or broken rock outcrops. Once, however, we killed three women in error. The fact that they were active terrorists did not soften the blow when I realised what we had done. Soon afterwards, I aborted bringing artillery shells down on a village sheltering a heavily armed enemy patrol because I heard children playing in the huts.

Overall I was lucky that I never received orders to do anything I was morally against. I hope that I would have had the courage of my convictions if this had happened. I will never know, since the nearest I came to it was an order to sow anti-personnel mines along the Dehedoba trails which we were blocking. Innocent *bedu* sometimes used these ancient camel routes, as well as the enemy, so I hedged my bets by laying the mines as ordered but then placing barbed wire all around them.

Because the sultan's army had no mines, ours were manufactured from Coca-Cola cans, torch batteries and plastic explosive. Nevertheless, they were fully capable of amputating a leg below the knee or blinding their victims with shrapnel. When I finally left Dhofar I removed each and every mine that I had laid and came within an ace of kneeling on one. A suitable epitaph would have been: 'Hoist with his own petard'.

As 1969 came to a close we realised that our blocking tactics had been only partially successful. The enemy had still managed to infiltrate huge amounts of war materials in readiness to wipe out the sultan's army, and soon they would be able to block his government's only resupply route over the mountains. They already controlled ninety per cent of Dhofar. The colonel ordered me to locate an alternate route to the western mountains, so for three months we explored the labyrinthine valleys and high, giddy ridges of the gravel Nejd region between the Qara and the Empty Quarter. Eventually we identified, and then engineered, a vertiginous new trail which enabled the army to reach the western mountains without fear of ambush.

In October 1969 I was summoned by the sultan's Intelligence Officer to penetrate deep into the enemy's eastern heartland and kidnap two key political commissars. The operation was the most hazardous of my army life but it made up in a small way for my failure to achieve my life's dream, the command of the Royal Scots Greys.

Our ambush was a success but, to avoid being shot at close range myself, I had to kill both the commissars. We removed all the documents they carried, from which Intelligence learned a great deal about the enemy's organisation. Many names and ranks of their leaders were revealed along with their intended policy.

More importantly, the death of the two commissars deep within their own stronghold had far-reaching effects on enemy morale at a key period. Tribesmen hitherto cowed by the Marxists fled for the first time to government safe havens, took up arms against the Marxists and asserted themselves as anti-Communist Muslims. The enemy switched their focus to brutally suppressing defection, but were wrongfooted at the crucial moment when, a few months after our operation, the sultan was overthrown with British complicity and his progressive son Qaboos took over. It was during those key months prior to the coup, when both Dhofar and Northern Oman were ripe for revolution, that the enemy could have struck with force and sparked off a general uprising.

That they did not seize the opportunity was largely due to their uncertainty as to the mountain tribesmen's loyalty, an uncertainty first promoted by the informers who led us to the commissars.

The day that I left the men of the recce platoon, somewhere in the wilderness of the Dehedoba trails, was one I shall never forget. I counted many of them as true friends.

RANULPH FIENNES

Ghosts on Socotra

In 1956 I joined the Oxford University Expedition to Socotra. This was to be the first scientific expedition to visit the island in the twentieth century. Although only two hundred miles from the Arabian Peninsula and even closer to the Horn of Africa, it was protected by the ferocity of the prevailing winds and preserved all the mystery of the 'Island of the Terraces of Incense' or 'Island of the Dragon's Blood'. The granite Haghier Mountains which formed the backbone of the island rose to five thousand feet and were reckoned to be one of the oldest land-masses in the world. They contained not only 250 indigenous species of plant but also a population of mainly troglodytes. It was to be my function, and my joy, to travel up and down these magical mountains and study this fascinating people.

I was at the time a final-year medical student at St Thomas's Hospital and the fact that I had received my pre-clinical training at the younger university didn't seem to be a problem. We were taken by ship to Aden and from there were flown on to an airstrip on Socotra's coastal plain by the RAF – who were only too glad to fly away from this windswept place. 'Imperial progressions' with the full panoply of camera-man, botanist and archæologist, camels and camel-drivers were fascinating but frustrating. Of our six-man team three members travelled on the coastal plains looking, with the archæologist, for evidence of Portuguese occupation. Marco Polo may even have been a visitor. Meanwhile the remaining three of us, including the botanist, travelled into the mountains with a Somali cook and a small caravan of camels.

As we climbed, the temperature dropped, cloud swirled around and the air was full of the fragrance of myrtle. The mountains were indeed terraced and there were indeed aloes and frankincense. We found a terrace at about two thousand feet for our camp. Beside it was a pool which made an excellent bath if one didn't mind sharing it with little orange crabs. And in a cave a few terraces up lived a local troglodyte with his wives and children, a poor relation, his goats and quantities of fleas. Our Somali cook had grandiose ideas about Englishmen on safari and insisted on a table-cloth which was no match for the incessant wind. He could however make the most marvellous bread and inventive meals on a single, smouldering log. It was an idyllic spot.

My brief was to make contact with the troglodytes, assess their main medical problems, gain some idea of their mortality rate and take blood for grouping. Simple ABO groups I planned to do 'on the hoof', while larger samples of blood were to be taken home for more detailed analysis at the Blood Group Reference Laboratory in London. All this by a medical student who spoke no language but English among a people very few of whom had ever seen a white man let alone a needle and syringe.

They were curious and friendly and began to bring me a bizarre selection of ailments, at first to our camp on the terrace. Then, as their confidence and mine increased, I would travel further and further afield on domiciliary visits. They had no idea about time and when asked to see one old sick man 'just over the hill' I might be away for nine or ten hours and see twenty. I sometimes travelled alone but usually with a young local, Ali, who had appeared the first day with a load of little oranges. The smaller the party the more chance I had of winning the confidence of the troglodytes before I assaulted them, vampire-like, with my blood-letting plans.

These mountain trips were pure joy. Up through ever more fragrant trees; oranges glowing 'like golden lamps in a green night'; crocuses, mushrooms, pomegranates, aloes and aubrietia; yellow hibiscus with its itchy leaves. At least they closely resembled such things to an untutored gardener if not a botanist. Then we might drop down to an arid valley with a floor of sharp red gravel and thorny scrub; Dragon's Blood trees like great umbrellas which exuded a blood-red sap; pink-flowering adenium-trees with grotesque bulbous trunks, and cucumber-trees which bore what looked like cucumbers. Up again into the fragrant coolness of the high ground and the little troglodyte villages, caves on terraces, stone houses in goat-pens, tiny fields and cows no bigger than large dogs.

Staying the night was an adventure in itself. The locals' staple diet was a porridge of maize. This they would cook in a clay pot stirred with a palm-frond. The worst of the goat droppings would be brushed with the back of a hand off a suitably flat stone and the thick porridge poured on and piled up. Into the middle of this would be poured sour milk and we would all sit round and eat with our fingers. Just occasionally a goat would be slaughtered with considerable ceremony into the setting sun. I learned not to accept the hospitality of a cave or a hut. The fleas made sleep impossible. Sometimes I would accept a goatskin 'on the veranda'. This I always turned upside down and sprinkled liberally with DDT. I would then sprinkle another dose up my trouser legs and down my shirt, stoke up a smoky fire and, as I mentioned in my diary, 'the place was quite like home'. This subsequently appeared in print much to my mother's dismay.

The locals' idea of medicine mainly consisted of covering the offending area with mud or cauterising it with a smouldering twig. It was not too difficult to see who had toothache though I was dismayed to see the abdomens of quite small children treated in this way. My own ministrations were revolutionary. A couple of aspirin worked wonders once the locals had been persuaded that pills should be swallowed and not suspended over the offending pain. And a single shot of penicillin cured persistent chest problems overnight. And so the needle developed into a cult craving and opened the way to further assaults for scientific purposes. Children were brought with immense malarial spleens, and my assessment of graveyards as I travelled over the mountains suggested an infant mortality of around sixty per cent.

On one of these trips a Socotran approached me with a human skull and asked if I was interested. I was of course intrigued and wanted to know where it came from and to whom it belonged. It belonged, he said, to the 'Zamaan', a people who lived a very long time ago (the word in fact means 'long ago') and who had no connection with the present population. There were plenty more skulls and bones where this came from, he told me, and pointed further up into the mountains. Ali, who was with me, said he knew the place and would take me. I asked if they minded if I disturbed the bones. 'Not a bit, why should we?' he replied. Modern bedu buried their own dead underground, but these bones could be found in caves and belonged to a different people of a different era. Maybe, I thought, it was this ancient people that had built the stone walls, constructed the terraces and developed the trade in aloes, Dragon's Blood and frankincense, none of which were of interest to the present-day Socotrans.

A few days later Ali and I and a donkey set off to find the bone caves. Higher and more precipitous than we had travelled so far, our route commanded the most spectacular views of the Arabian Sea two or three thousand feet below. We came to three caves on a terrace and each one was walled up. It was not difficult to dismantle the dry-stone wall and look inside and there sure enough were very large quantities of human bones. We were rather closer to our base camp than I had been led to believe, and the plains' party had come up to join us for a little mountain air. This was too good a find not to share. Ali and I returned the next day with camera-man and archæologist. I totally dismantled one cave and removed skulls, ribs and limb bones to make up about a dozen skeletons. There was no question of bodies being laid out intact: this must have been some form of charnel house. The only objects of slight archæological interest were some ivory jars which looked as though they may have contained antimony. The camera-man and the archæologist returned to camp while I got dustier and dustier in the bone-dry atmosphere of the cave. All the bones were taken out and arranged in some sort of order on the terrace. Ali remained indifferent to the whole operation throughout the day but as evening approached he said he would like to get back to his cave and his wife and anyway he was not going to spend the night with those bones. Off he went with the donkey down the mountain.

I had the mountain to myself. I made a little fire and some supper and settled down for the night on the terrace immediately below the bones. I had acquired a blanket, I think for two shillings, from a local woman who wove them. Woven in strips from goat's wool and dyed with vegetable dyes, which were fixed in camel's urine, it was colourful, almost completely waterproof and smelled richly of Harris tweed when wet. This was my constant companion when travelling (and now forty-five years later does good service from the boot of my car). Wrapped in this I settled down for the night by the embers and soon fell asleep. I was woken by stones falling on me. The fire was now dead but the moon was full in a starry sky and the sea looked magnificent far below. But not a sign of life could I see on the moonlit mountain, just my row of skulls looking balefully from the terrace above.

I settled down again but no sooner was I asleep than stones fell on me again. Nothing to be seen but the moonlight and the bones of the ancients. After this had happened three times I gave up the unequal struggle, relit my fire and waited for dawn.

Ali and the donkey arrived on cue. I boxed up the bones and wrapped what were left over in my blanket and we returned to camp. Here I re-arranged, cleaned and photographed my finds and boxed them up in old champagne crates (victualling had been done in Oxford at the end of the ball season) ready for transport to England. During the rest of the trip I managed to extract a quantity of blood samples from unsuspecting patients. These had to be sent by runner daily to the capital, Hadibo, where we had a paraffin 'fridge' which worked better upside down.

Back in London, the Blood Group Reference Laboratory established that the current population of Socotra is closely related to pure Yemenite Jews. I delivered my precious bones to the British Museum where they were greeted with enthusiasm but have not, so far as I know, surfaced since. The pages of my diary which record this little adventure have faded so as to be almost unreadable, and none of the pictures on the spool I devoted to bones came out. Perhaps the 'Zamaan' of Socotra resented an intrusion after so many centuries and their ghosts retain their integrity.

NEIL ORR

The Ambassador's Advice

I was by way of fulfilling a mad and long-held ambition to cross the southern Sahara from west to east – from Dakar to Port Sudan in several stages – taking whatever transport was available, be it bus, truck or train but not camel. (Thesiger had not been entirely approving when first told of my plan thirty years ago.) The longest sector, from Dakar to Chad, was behind me; all that remained was the seventeen hundred miles from Ndjamena, the capital of Chad, east to Khartoum and Port Sudan. I had attempted this two years earlier but been thwarted by illness and visas.

Now, in 1997, it appeared that I had a better chance of completing the crossing by attempting this final leg in reverse. Sudanese visas for entry by air and exit by road were (through the good offices of a kindly hote-lier) more readily issued in Khartoum than elsewhere. Visas for Chad had to be obtained in Paris; this was easy but expensive. A purist might not have approved of my completing the Saharan crossing backwards but I was not seeking a purist's advice. It was the advice of HM Ambassador in Khartoum that I was after, and which I ignored to my cost.

How safe would it be, I had asked him, to travel through Kordofan and Darfur to Chad? His elegant answer had been: 'I have no doubt that you would be received by the Sudanese with their usual courtesy and hospitality. But Darfur is more than usually plagued with tribal disputes at present . . . My advice would therefore be to postpone your journey'. I bounced this later off a former British ambassador to Chad over lunch in Oxford: 'Oh, he's just covering his backside. Ignore it'.

So I ignored the advice and set off. My kindly hotelier eased my way with Grecian skill through Khartoum and I was soon on the bus westward to El-Obeid. But how to continue from there? The train to Nyala had not run for ages, and there were no westbound buses. I need not have worried. My neighbour on the bus, a local businessman, had me to stay in his house when we reached El-Obeid, and arranged for me to leave the next morning for El-Fasher – on a heavily laden truck. It took three days but we arrived safely, though we heard there had been shooting in Kutum, north-west of El-Fasher.

The truck-driver found me a seat (but no legroom) in the bus on to Nyala, where a fellow-passenger duly helped with a hotel. There was a hiccough the next morning when the car I had booked to take me to the bus station early never arrived, but the hotel porter waylaid a passing van. It being Friday, the only bus to Zalingei, my next port of call, was already full to overflowing. So I persuaded the van-driver to help not just with a lift to the bus station but all 130 miles to Zalingei. He needed provisions for this unexpected journey, plus a jack, spare wheel, water and bedding. And the Nyala police needed a little persuasion to let us through.

Off we set and reached Zalingei that afternoon. The driver relayed me to another friend, who was busy that evening gathering passengers for the trip to El-Geneina. He gave us all supper and a bed for the night. We set off early the next morning in a Toyota truck with three or four people in the driver's cabin and about twenty of us crammed into the back. Progress was slow as there was a problem understandably with the suspension and with one of the wheels. In mid-afternoon another truck stopped to help as we were conducting yet another repair.

It had set off with a headstart of perhaps five minutes when we suddenly heard shooting ahead – or those of us on the back did. Our driver in his cabin carried on oblivious. We banged for all we were worth and he duly stopped. We drove back a little way and hid among some thorn-bushes. The shooting was clearly audible a few hundred yards ahead; my heart was pounding. I remember fussing about two ridiculous things: some chocolate I had with me was melting in the heat and my water-bottle was leaking.

The shooting died down, but we waited in the thorn-bushes for an hour or so more. Two other trucks caught up with us and we decided to carry on in convoy. As we passed the spot where the first truck had been shot up, my hat blew off. I would have been very happy to wave it good-bye but my Sudanese companions would not hear of it and the driver turned back to retrieve it. We reached El-Geneina safely after nightfall.

What happened to the unfortunate occupants of the other truck we never discovered, but we feared the worst and assumed that brigands had hijacked the vehicle and disposed of them. But for our running repairs it might well have been us and not them. The police in El-Geneina, who had heard such stories often before, showed little interest and even less inclination to venture into the bush and investigate.

My travelling companions found me a truck leaving the next day for Chad and, with their help and some patience, I found my way through the labyrinth of security, passport and Customs offices on the Sudanese border. The driver then volunteered typically to take me all the way to Ndjamena: I had 'completed' my crossing of the southern Sahara.

The ambassador in Khartoum had been right in both respects. I had witnessed the insecurity in Darfur all too closely, but had also enjoyed astonishing Sudanese courtesy and hospitality. Unarmed, my companions had been powerless to assist the hapless passengers in the other truck but they, like all other Sudanese with whom I travelled, had seen to it that the Englishman was given every conceivable assistance on his way.

It is unlikely that I shall ever have the chance of introducing them to the Travellers Club. I was happy, however, to put my name down for the ambassador from Khartoum when he was proposed a year or two later.

FRANCIS WITTS

Shooting Pig

To commemorate the death in August 2003 of Sir Wilfred Thesiger, a member of the Travellers for over seventy years, the Club published some months later a tribute entitled The Ultimate Traveller. *A close friend and former Club chairman, George Webb, selected for it the following excerpts from* The Marsh Arabs.

'Have you ever shot pig?' asked Falih. 'Watch out, they are dangerous. Only last week one attacked and killed a man near here while he was looking at his crops.'

Falih, accompanied by a throng of armed retainers, came to fetch me for the promised pig shoot. After they had all drunk coffee, I got into the same canoe as Falih and his son . . . a beautiful craft that could carry as many as twelve people. Thirty-six feet long but only three and a half feet at her widest beam. . . . The front swept forwards and upwards in a perfect curve to form a long, thin, tapering stem; the stern too rose in a graceful sweep. . . . Four men punted the canoe, two in the stern and two in the bows, moving rhythmically in time as they drove their poles into the water. . . . They had laid their rifles in the canoe beside them and had taken off their cloaks. Each wore a bandolier filled with cartridges and a curved, narrow-bladed dagger in the front of his belt. . . . Dogs raced along the bank above and stopped every ten or fifteen yards to bark at us in a sort of gibbering frenzy, their lips drawn back over their teeth. Each group of dogs handed us over at its boundary to a fresh lot. Children watched silently and women, none of them veiled, looked out from the houses. There seemed to be few men about. We drew into the bank under a large house and one of Falih's retainers shouted: 'Zair Mahaisin!' An elderly man came out fastening his headcloth. 'Welcome! Welcome *Ya Muhafadh*! Come in! Come in!' Falih refused, although the man pressed us to drink coffee. Falih asked: 'Have you sent the men down to the marsh in their canoes?'

'Yes, *Muhafadh*, they are all there and waiting for you at the mouth of the stream.'

'Are there any pigs in the reeds?'

'Yes, but very scattered. The water is too low for them to have collect-ed on the reed islands.'

'Come on, in you get,' and Zair Mahaisin climbed neatly into the canoe.

The channel which we were following had little water in it and the canoe-men kept the *tarada* moving with difficulty. The earth banks were lower and by sitting up straight I could see over them. On either side a couple of hundred yards of weed-carpeted mud glistened in the sun, and past them lay the reedbeds. A small flock of cattle-egrets showed up snow-white against this background; two buff-backed herons sat, humped and brooding, on the edge of a small ditch, and some pied crows quarrelled noisily round a piece of garbage. Falih remarked: 'This is where they plant their rice; they will start clearing the fields soon'.

Ahead of us I could see a large number of men and canoes. When we were near them . . . a few old men, better dressed than the others, waded through the mud and water, to greet Falih and to kiss his hand. The rest, many of them boys, sat or stood in their canoes a short way off. . . . Some had coarse black or brown cloaks wrapped round their waists but were otherwise naked; the rest wore the long Arab shirt, tucked high up round their thighs; two, who were pulling a canoe through shallow water, lifted their shirts up under their armpits, exposing their nakedness with com-plete unconcern.

Many of the men punted their canoes with fish-spears, the butt end in the water. These spears were formidable-looking weapons with bamboo shafts as long as twelve feet, and five-pronged heads like giant toasting forks, but with each prong barbed.

Falih had suggested that I should arm myself with my shotgun, as it would be dangerous to use a rifle with so many people about. Now I was glad to see that only his four canoemen carried rifles, though in fact the villagers possessed plenty of firearms. During the First World War the local tribesmen had acquired a large number of British and Turkish rifles picked up on the battlefields, and afterwards had never been disarmed.

Falih had been listening to an involved complaint about the distribution of some rice-land. . . . When someone else came forward with another complaint, Falih said: 'Enough. Come, show us the pig. I wish to see how the Englishman shoots.' To me he said: 'You go in that *mashuf*. Be careful how you move about in it. This man will paddle you.'

I climbed into a small canoe which had been drawn up at my feet. Falih and his son each got into another, and we started towards the reedbeds, followed by the rest. When the water deepened, each man laid down the pole or fishing spear with which he had been punting, settled himself in the canoe and started to paddle with short quick strokes. When more than one person was in a boat, they dipped in time together on the same side.

The haze of the previous day had disappeared and the sky was a pale luminous blue, touched here and there with semi-transparent wisps of cirrus cloud. The paddles dug a succession of tiny whirlpools and the sparkling drops fell back into the clear water which looked very cold. We had left the muddy flow from the stream's mouth behind us, among the beds of grey, battered bulrushes that grew in the shallows. Now we were among the *qasab* (*Phragmites communis*) which covered most of the permanent marsh. This giant grass, which looked like a bamboo, grew in the dense reedbeds to a height of more than twenty-five feet. The stems, each terminating in a tasselled head of palest buff, were so thick that the marshmen used them as punt-poles. At this season the reedbeds bordering the narrow waterways were light and airy. Relics of the past year, they were pale gold and silvery grey, except at their base where the new growth, as yet only a few feet high, was very green. Small parties of coot scuttered along the water ahead of us to the shelter of the reedbeds; pigmy cormorants and darters, sitting with their dark wings spread out to dry on reed stumps, white with droppings, took fright and dived into the water. . . . The canoes, of which there must have been at least forty, jostled and bumped as they crowded down the narrow lanes, or spread out on the more open stretches, the crews racing each other with shouts and laughter. . . . Suddenly we were out of the reeds and on to a small sheltered lagoon. Mallard rose quacking and flew back high over our heads. Many small islands, some only a few yards across, others covering an acre or more, enclosed the far end of the lagoon. . . .

At one of these islands Falih's canoe drew alongside mine. 'This is the place,' he said and shouted to the others: 'Come on, get into it and see if there is anything there.' Several men stepped ashore holding their spears in front of them. They drew blank, so they tried another island and then a third. I was watching two warblers, hopping about among the reeds, when I was startled by several loud crashes, followed by shouts. 'There he is! Quick! Look out! By God! Four of them.' Then a splash and silence.

'Where have they gone?' asked another voice.

'They have taken to the water. One got up right under my feet, by God! As big as a donkey, by Abbas!'

Someone else cried: 'I threw my spear and just missed; a sow with three young.'

More shouts, 'They have gone in here. Get round quick and cut them off.'

We were wedged in a narrow passage between two islands, but my canoeman backed out hurriedly into the open water where several more canoes joined us. The hunt had moved on to another island and as we hastened towards it, there was more excitement. Then a piercing squeal cut off short, a laugh and a man shouting: 'I've got it; one of the small ones; I have speared it. It was in the water; I am drowning it.'

Falih's canoe went past. He had taken off his cloak and was himself paddling. 'Where has the big one gone, Manati?' he asked a vigorous old man who had led the hunt so far.

'Into the large island over there, I think, *Ya Muhafadh.* . . . Yes, here are its tracks. Come on. Let's get it out!'

Manati plunged out of sight into the jungle of reeds followed by two others. I could hear them moving about. One of them called, 'It has not gone this way,' and a little later Manati shouted, 'Here are its tracks.'

Nothing happened, however, and I thought they must have lost it when a series of splintering crashes came from the far side and a voice screamed, 'It is killing me! It is killing me!'

Someone shouted, 'It has got Manati. Come on lads. Quick! Where are the warriors?'

Many people answered his call, splashing through the reeds.

Falih, I and some others paddled frantically to the far side of the island where we found Manati being helped into one of the larger canoes. His shirt, covered with blood, was torn half off and he lay with his eyes closed. There was a hole in his right buttock I could have put my fist in. Falih leant over him and asked anxiously, 'How are you, Manati?' The old man opened his eyes and whispered, 'I am all right, *Ya Muhafadh*'. Falih gave orders to go back at once to the mouth of the Khirr, which was not far.

As we paddled back, a boy said, 'It was a sow that bit him. A boar would have slashed him with its tushes and killed him.'

Someone else said, 'It was a good thing he managed to fall on his stomach. I saw a man two years ago in the Al bu Bakhit country after he had been killed by a sow. She had dragged out half his guts.'

Another said, 'The boar that killed the young *Sayid* last year in the wheat cultivation cut him to pieces. He was alone and unarmed and must have trodden on it. . . . He crawled back towards the village but died before he got out of the field.'

A boy asked, 'Do you remember when Hashim rode the pig?'

'Yes, by God,' answered my canoeman, 'he and his brother were inspecting their barley when they saw a boar, an old one, grey-coloured. Hashim's brother wanted to shoot it. He had just bought a rifle from the Feraigat. Hashim tried to stop him but he fired and wounded it in the stomach.'

'Yes,' interrupted another man, 'he is a very bad shot.'

My canoeman continued, 'The pig charged and knocked him down; it slashed his arm badly. Hashim got behind it and stabbed it in the shoulder with his dagger. When it turned on him, he dropped the dagger and jumped on its back. The pig made off with him riding it. He held on to its ears. It took him all the way to Sayid Ali's garden and collapsed trying to cross the big ditch. Hashim said he never wanted to ride a pig again!' and the audience laughed.

'Pigs, they are the foe,' said an older man. 'They eat our crops and kill our men. God destroy them! Look at Manati; he will never be any use again. That sow has finished him.'

We arrived at the stream's mouth. Falih's *tarada* with a small crowd was waiting for us where the embankment was high and fairly wide. We landed and drew up the canoe with Manati in it. He was lying on his side, a man supporting his head and shoulders. He seemed to have bled very little for the water in the bottom of the boat was only tinged with pink, but the wound was a ghastly looking mess, the torn ends of muscles sticking out from the oozing flesh. Manati moved slightly to look at his injury but said nothing.

In my boxes at Falih's village was a large supply of drugs. I was not qualified as a doctor, but after twenty years in wild places, where everyone assumed, as a matter of course, that I would treat their sick and injured, I had acquired some experience of medicine. Furthermore, I had always taken every opportunity to go round wards of hospitals and to watch operations and in that way had picked up quite a bit of surgical knowledge. I was to acquire a great deal more during the years I spent in the Marshes.

Now I said to Falih: 'We had better get him back as quickly as we can to your *mudhif*, where I can give him morphia and try to patch him up, not that there is much I can do for him. We must send him to hospital in Amara'.

'Don't send me to hospital,' Manati pleaded, 'not hospital. Let me stay in my village. Ask the Englishman to doctor me.'

I said, 'Let's get him back anyway to your village,' but Falih insisted that the meal was ready. 'Let us first eat and then go.'

I was getting angry when Manati smiled at me and said, 'Eat, Sahib, eat; I am all right,' and added, 'Anyway I am hungry. I want some food myself before I go any farther.'

I gave in and walked over to where the food was spread out on a reed mat. There was a great dish of rice and joints of mutton, as well as roast chickens and dishes of stew. I found it impossible to eat and rose quickly, hoping that now we could be off, but the others sat down in turn until everyone had fed; after that there was coffee and tea. Unable any longer to conceal my irritation... I walked over to Manati. He was holding a mutton bone. I wondered whether he had really eaten... He looked ghastly.

Back at Falih's village Manati begged again not to be sent to hospital, but Falih eventually persuaded him to go. The pig appeared to have bitten a great lump out of his buttock. I gave him an injection of morphia, washed his wound and sprinkled it thickly with sulphonamide powder. Then we made him as comfortable as we could in a canoe and sent him off to Majar al Kabir on his way to Amara.

I met him again a year later when I lunched in his village and was horrified to find him permanently crippled, unable to move unless he supported himself on a pole. I asked how long he had been in hospital and he answered, 'When I got there they wouldn't let me in, so I came back. Thanks be to God, your medicine cured me. It was all I had.'

I suspected, however, that he had never been near the hospital but had returned to his village from Falih's *mudhif.*

A marsh near Falih's uncle Muhammad's house was at certain seasons a favourite haunt of pig, which devastated the rice-fields at night. Falih and I stalked them in small canoes along the ditches intersecting the reed-beds. One day I shot forty-seven and on another forty-two. These pig were of the same species as the European and Indian wild boar, but ran to an exceptional size. I measured two that were average, and both were thirty-seven inches at the shoulder. I regret that I never measured a really big one. By day they lay up on sodden nests, usually built on the low banks that bordered these ditches. The nests, sometimes six feet across, were great heaps of rushes which they must have bitten off and carried in their mouths, often for yards. When the floods were high the pig moved out of the marshes and lay up in the date gardens, mostly jungles of untended palms and close-growing thorn scrub, in one of which I also saw a wolf and three cubs. Falih and I either walked the pig up, which was exciting, but usually unrewarding, or we had them driven out into the open, when we rode them down on horses and shot them from the saddle.

I had left in the last week of July 1952 and it was now an early afternoon in February. Seven months later; it seemed longer. In that time I had crossed high passes through the snows of the Hindu Kush to the cold blue lake of Korombar where the Chitral river rises; I had looked out over Wakand from the Borogil Pass, and seen in the distance a glint that was the Oxus; I had slept on the glaciers at the foot of Tirich Mir, and in dark, verminous houses among mulberry orchards, where the last of the Black Kafirs lived on the borders of Nuristan. Now, back once more in Falih's *mudhif* on the edge of the Marshes, I felt that I had come home.

Abd ar Ridha bustled in, gap-toothed and rather bent. 'Falih was talking about you only last night, wondering when you would be back. Sadam was here the other day from Qabab, and he too enquired after you. Welcome, welcome. Today is a feast day.' We sat down round the hearth to coffee. Then everyone rose as Falih came in. He embraced me, kissed me on the cheek and asked how I was. 'Why have you been so long? We have been expecting you for the past month. Is that not so, Abd ar Ridha? Anyway it is good to see you back now.'

We were now among the Sudan, one of the nicest of the tribes and the most unfortunate. In the past they had been powerful and prosperous, but now they were scattered and their land was largely derelict. . . .

On the way I had counted sixty pig feeding outside one reedbed. The Sudan implored me to shoot them as they were devastating their small crops of wheat and barley that were nearly ripe. Pig seldom entered barley if there was wheat nearby. At this season they fed in the fields at night and lay up in them by day. In places the corn was four feet high, which made hunting extremely dangerous. . . . I had been knocked down by a boar under similar circumstances the year before.

On that occasion I had already shot a dozen or so, kicking them out of bramble thickets along abandoned ditches, and shooting them as they broke across the open. A boy brought me news of a pig he had found in some nearby wheat and pointed out the exact spot. The hollow in the corn was obvious even from a distance, but the corn was breast high and I could not see into it until less than a yard away. Suddenly an ear flicked, and the pig was there, lying in the shadow with its back to me. I shot it in the neck and it never moved. 'Come on, let's return: we have a long way to go.'. . .

As we were leaving, the boy ran up again with the news of another pig. 'Come and shoot it, Sahib, it is destroying all my crop.'

My host tried to dissuade me, but I said, 'Just this one and then I will be with you'. Again I stalked the hollow which the boy indicated and peered over the top of the corn straight into the eyes of a big boar – I still remember the white glint of its tushes. Before I could aim I was on my back, yards from where I had been standing, the rifle going off as I went down. Then the pig was on me again. I felt its weight on my thighs, saw its long snout and small angry eyes above me, and felt its breath on my face. It drove at my chest with its tushes, and instinctively I blocked the swipe with the butt of my rifle. Then the pig was gone. I sat up and looked at my rifle; there was a great gouge in the stock, and one of my fingers, slashed to the bone as by a razor, was pouring blood. I reloaded and got to my feet. The boar, a big one, was walking away on the edge of the cornfield. I shouted, it swung round, and I aimed at its chest. It dropped where it stood.

WILFRED THESIGER

The Parade that went with a Bang

The art of success – in diplomacy as in many other professions (though perhaps not in the oldest) – lies not so much in what you achieve yourself as in what you effectively delegate to others. This thought was clearly in the minds of most heads of mission in Baghdad in September 1987, when an invitation arrived from the Iraqi Ministry of Foreign Affairs to attend the annual Orange Festival in Ba'quba, a town about fifty miles east of the capital, in what has since become known as the Sunni Triangle.

Iraq in September is still uncomfortably hot, and those few excellencies who had returned from leave had little hesitation in passing on the invitation to their deputies. After all, diplomatic travel outside Saddam's Baghdad usually required written permission in advance from a slow-moving, suspicious and unpredictable MFA, so a visit to Ba'quba was a treat not to be missed – at least by the deputies.

My own ambassador, Terry Clarke, was himself an effective delegator (and was in any case due to play tennis that afternoon with some ambassadorial colleagues). So it was that I – newly arrived the previous April, just two months after my wedding – found myself seated in a dusty government coach with my wife and about fifty of my fellow-number twos and threes plus spouses, bound for Ba'quba.

We arrived there in the late afternoon and took our places on the VIP grandstand on assorted seats and armchairs (and in our case behind a sofa – of which more later). In the front row, with their black berets and olive-green uniforms, were the party bosses, including of course the local governor and the Minister of Local Government. To back up the minders from Protocol were squads of well-armed military police. In front of us, in the opposite grandstand, schoolchildren were holding reversible placards to form mosaics of Saddam or the Iraqi flag.

The parade began. For once it was essentially a civilian affair, featuring regional arts, crafts and traditions but with a mock-up of an Iraqi missile to remind us that the Enemy was only forty miles away to the east, and that the war with Iran (which had already lasted seven years) was still far from over.

I cannot claim it was a riveting spectacle and after an hour or so, when the schoolchildren had displayed their mosaics for the fifth time, my thoughts began to wander: the latest telegram about the tanker war in the Gulf . . . Was all prepared for my next visit to our two long-term British prisoners in Abu Ghraib jail . . . Could we deploy Weapons of Mass Destruction (DDT) against the termites infesting our villa in Mansour? I also idly cast my mind back to a day in October 1981 when in a hotel room in Miami I had watched with fascinated horror the TV coverage of Anwar Sadat's assassination during a parade on a grandstand packed with foreign diplomats . . .

At which point the parade suddenly became a good deal livelier.

What sounded like a few pops from some fireworks was instantly answered by a fusillade, both from our MP guards and from elsewhere. The diplomatic corps at once threw themselves on the floor – in our case, my wife behind the sofa and I behind her (just in case the attack developed from behind – at least that's what I told her afterwards). The shooting lasted a couple of minutes at the most, but felt a good deal longer for those lying on the ground.

Finally it stopped. We cautiously rose to our feet and assessed the damage. None to the diplomats, but several wounded (at least) amongst the officials in front of us. Worse, in the grandstand opposite, the schoolchildren had understandably panicked and stampeded: casualties, we heard afterwards were heavy.

The shaken Protocol officers hurriedly ushered us off the grandstand (jumping down from the back, after removing the canvas flaps) and into our buses for the return trip to Baghdad. To our repeated requests for an explanation they not surprisingly had little to offer: 'Just a silly mistake . . . a wedding-party getting out of hand . . .'. They then handed out large quantities of oranges – designed presumably to put an end to our questions if not our curiosity.

So ended our trip to Ba'quba. Nothing, of course, appeared in the local media and the only report, so far as I know, was in the *Financial Times* several weeks later. The most likely explanation was that four members of the Iraqi military police had deserted a few weeks earlier with their uniforms and weapons, and that they had infiltrated the parade in order to assassinate whichever senior officials or ministers they could get in their sights. They were inevitably shot down, but not before a good many innocent bystanders had been killed or injured in the cross-fire.

Set against the violent events since 2003, in which Ba'quba featured all too often, this was a relatively minor skirmish. But it was frightening enough at the time. As one of the taller members of the FCO (and a good foot taller than Michael Weir who was on the grandstand with Sadat), I was at least relieved to find out that, when practising horizontal diplomacy (as it were), a tall diplomat presents no greater target than one built on lesser lines. Or as Dorothy Parker might have put it: 'If all the diplomats at this parade were laid end to end, I wouldn't be at all surprised'.

ROBIN KEALY

An Ethiopian Birthday

We all remember our birthdays. It is the one day when members of the family send cards and generally a celebratory meal is involved. I was explaining this to Alemayehu as we bumped along a windy track in northern Tigray, approaching his home town of Mek'ele. He had not been home for four years, since I had adopted him and paid for him to go to the General Wingate School in Addis Ababa. I say pay, but it did not cost me much. It was part of a government-backed project to give bright peasant boys a chance for further education. Haile Selassie had presented Alemayehu with his leaving certificate a few weeks earlier and now he was training to be a public health officer in Gondar.

It happened to be the Ethiopian Christmas Day as we passed through Bahir Dar, and Alemayehu decided to call upon a distant relative whom he had never met. I felt embarrassed by our intrusion. The relative lived in a new house not far from the Tissisiat Falls, and could speak some English. As an honoured guest I was made to sit down and eat a special Christmas delicacy: raw lamb coated in rancid butter. No drink was offered, and I had to eat in front of a roomful of smiling Ethiopians and excited children.

I don't really know how I did it; one mouthful would have been possible, like taking an odious pill in one swallow, but perched on my knee was a large saucer of the stuff! I had to chew on, realising that I was eating their Christmas dinner, and trying not to retch. Sweat broke out on my brow and my forced smile of enjoyment must have been jaded by the end.

As soon as we left, I stopped the car and asked Alemayehu for a bottle of Fanta, which he opened, as usual, with his teeth. Food was beginning to become an obsession with me. Already I had sampled a variety of *injera* and *wot* sauces. The fermented pancake had not agreed with me and I had an upset stomach. I dreamed of the whole curried eggs which Princess Tournesh had given me for dinner one evening in Addis Ababa: I had offended her by eating the lot. You must always leave some of the dish for the children, Alemayehu told me afterwards.

Whilst we were travelling to Mek'ele, he mentioned a wonderful hotel built by an Italian count on the outskirts of town. That is where Europeans stay and that was the thought on my mind as we worked our way down, past the site of the battle of Adowa, towards the lower ground. I had spent several nights in Ethiopian hotels, very cheap, with little choice of food and by most standards very dirty!

When we arrived, Alemayehu said I must come and see his house and meet his family. We drove into a shanty town with stony streets down which water ran haphazardly. It was a maze of houses; people stared at the car. Suddenly Alemayehu rolled down the window and started waving at people. A crowd quickly gathered and I had to slow down, then stop. 'This is my home.' He pointed to a one-room shack. 'And here is my mother.' A woman emerged with a baby at her breast, wrapped in a *shamma*. She was very surprised at the return of her eldest son with a mysterious European. She bowed and I held out my hand.

Everyone began talking excitedly in Tigrayan, giving furtive glances at me. I was ushered into the only room, in which there was a stone bench round the wall, a bed without a mattress, and a vat from which the mother sold her Tej beer. I declined the drink and asked Alemayehu to get another Fanta from the car. He then said I should meet his other fathers. Three men had shuffled into the room and we all sat down on the bench. Food was being prepared outside. I whispered to Alemayehu: 'I want nothing to eat'. He smiled. 'Mother's roasting nuts.'

There was a long silence whilst the food was prepared. I realised that I had become the senior father, so decided to say some sort of grace. '*Benedicat, Benedicatur*' rang more true than 'For what we are about to receive'. The other fathers bowed their heads. Munching nuts was comparatively painless.

Outside, more relatives had turned up. I took photographs, bid farewell and bumped out of town to the hotel. What bliss it was to lie in a hot bath and, amazingly, find a copy of *Gloucestershire Life* with spring daffodils on its cover. The three-course, European meal, with good Italian wines, was lovely; my hunger quickly faded. I was excited for tomorrow was my birthday and I had promised Alemayehu a good dinner in Dese.

The following morning was beautifully clear and I lazed around the hotel until Alemayehu arrived, having run all the way from home with his younger brother Meselle. I never worked out how many half-siblings he has from his mother's three marriages. Most of them are only partly literate, so great hopes were pinned on the eldest son.

We drove back into town, where he wanted to buy my youngest son an Ethiopian silver cross, as I had asked him to be godfather. The camels coming in from the Danakil Desert laden with salt were an impressive sight. We followed their route a little way out of town, then drove on sticking to the Italian-built roads.

At Korem it came as a sudden shock to see lots of people sitting by the roadside in the intense midday heat. At first I thought they must be waiting for a bus. What were they doing, I asked Alemayehu. 'They must be refugees from the famine,' he replied. I slowed down but was beckoned on by a soldier brandishing a rifle. We passed what seemed to be an endless queue, mostly young women with babies and old ladies in shawls. I had a strong urge to help but could do nothing. We had no food and only the odd bottle of Fanta left. Eerily, there was no movement amongst the people and very little sound, just a sea of bodies barely alive, waiting.

'We must move on,' Alemayehu said. He did not seem as concerned as I was. 'It just happens,' he shrugged. He had seen it before.

The memory was still seared on my mind as we drove on to Dese. The bleak and arid mountains seemed empty of people. It was nightfall as we approached the town, guided by lots of little lights. We headed for the only European hotel, looking forward to my birthday dinner.

There was no room. There was no food. The hotel was bustling with Europeans, aid workers arriving to tackle the famine. We drove disconsolately into town. Only one shop was open.

'You can't go in there,' Alemayehu said. 'It's for Muslims.'

'Don't be ridiculous,' I said, and I went in and bought a couple of rather sickly-looking cakes. It was food. I also bought a bottle of Ethiopian brandy, which was awful, and celebrated the remains of my birthday.

The next day I woke hungry, but with such vivid memories that I dared not complain. We drove on to Kembolcha. There we filled up with petrol, which had doubled in price that day. I wandered into a nearby market looking for food. There was none. A beggar woman came up and asked for money. I shook my head and she screamed at me. I did not know what she said; some stallholders looked up smiling and Alemayehu was embarrassed that someone should insult his father.

The corollary of this journey is that the famine spread and became headline news. Haile Selassie was overthrown and murdered. Alemayehu resumed his studies for a short while then was arrested. He spent five years in prison, where he was tortured because of his politics. I tried to help him through Amnesty International, but was told it was too dangerous. I visited him shortly after he was released. He was emaciated and very asthmatic.

His story does however have a happy ending. He came to the UK as a political refugee, and now teaches mathematics in a South London comprehensive. He is ambivalent about returning to Ethiopia. His mother now lives in Mekele in a house with four bedrooms but no husband!

TIMOTHY THORNTON

A Gift Horse

Although I knew that Haile Selassie, Conquering Lion of Judah, Elect of God, Emperor of Ethiopia was an autocrat I had no idea until I reached Addis Ababa in December 1959 of the extent of his powers and the awe in which he was held. The smallest details had to go to him for a decision.

As he passed in the street all other cars were expected to stop and their occupants, including ambassadors, jump out, doff their hats and bow. Equestrians dismounted and bystanders often prostrated themselves – indeed they did as much for me in the mistaken belief that the impressive cavalry escort that preceded my car as I was driven slowly to the palace to present my credentials heralded the coming of the emperor.

Not surprisingly, perhaps, the Crown Prince Assefa Wossen, then in his late forties, was allowed no public rôle by his father. He had, however, his followers, particularly among the younger generation who hoped that one day he would lead his backward country into the twentieth century. Among them was the engaging and impish Minister for Public Health, Ato Abebe Retta, who had somehow survived fathering a child by one of the emperor's daughters during his exile with the Ethiopian royal family in England after the Italian occupation in 1936. Encouraged by Abebe Retta and others to help bring the crown prince more into the public eye, I asked the emperor to let me present a large British Council gift of books for the National Library to the crown prince at a time when I knew that he himself would be abroad on a series of state visits to West Africa and South America. Rather to my surprise, he agreed.

Thus it was that in the late afternoon of Tuesday, 13 December 1960, just a year after my arrival in Addis Ababa, in a short ceremony at the National Library I made the presentation to the crown prince who was accompanied by his influential cousin, His Imperial Highness Dejazmatch Asrate Kassa, and two ministers. By 5.30 p.m. the proceedings were over and we each went our own way, little aware of the high drama in which all of us would be involved a few hours later.

Early next morning, while my wife and I were still in bed, our head Ethiopian servant entered the bedroom, woke me and handed me Asrate Kassa's visiting-card (which I still possess) on which was scribbled *Can I see you it is very urgent.* I went in my pyjamas to find Kassa in the sitting-room with the Minister of Education and the deputy mayor of Addis Ababa. Kassa, who spoke excellent English – having been educated at Monkton Combe School near Bath while in exile with the royal family, told me the startling news that the empress, the crown prince and other members of the royal family had all been arrested during the night by the Imperial Bodyguard by whom they were now held prisoner. He asked me to telegraph urgently and secretly his report of the situation to the emperor, then in Brazil. I did this after getting Kassa to dictate to me an English version of his message for encypherment and dispatch by the embassy's diplomatic wireless.

Kassa and his two companions then left in the small, inconspicuous car in which they had come, making for the army's 1. Division Headquarters on the edge of town. A little later, two Imperial Bodyguard sentries were posted at the embassy gates where they refused entry to non-Europeans; our telephones and electricity were cut and a night curfew declared. Shortly after midday the crown prince went on the air – with or without a pistol at his head was never known – to announce to the nation that he was now the head of a new and more liberal government, making no mention of his father. Shortly afterwards, a Foreign Ministry messenger delivered an official Note signed by the Vice-Minister for Foreign Affairs informing me of this new government. Some hours later, with the telephone still out of action, a junior official called to invite me to the ministry where a more senior official asked me to obtain my government's recognition of the new government. We learnt later that the vice-minister had by this time been arrested. He was subsequently shot.

Although as yet there had been no shooting, the atmosphere was tense as the news got around. As a precaution I decided to bring all embassy families living outside into our large compound; meanwhile my wife and others went shopping to stock up their larders in case of need.

The next day, Thursday 15 December, shooting began and continued with varying degrees of intensity for the next three days. We hurriedly erected all our tents, of which we had a good stock left over from World War II, and let it be known that any British or Commonwealth subjects so wishing could take refuge in the embassy. In the event over one hundred and thirty did so, including thirty students – boys and girls – from East and West Africa. They must have enjoyed themselves as we had some difficulty in persuading them to return to their separate hostels when the fighting was over.

The emperor was in São Paulo when Kassa's message reached our ambassador in Rio de Janiero. It so happened that the civil airline was on strike that day. However, Sir Geoffrey Wallinger persuaded the Brazilian authorities to fly him in one of their air force jets to São Paulo where, on reading Kassa's report and my own account of the situation, Haile Selassie decided to return home immediately. For one reason or another he reached Addis Ababa only in the afternoon of Saturday 17 December, by which time the shooting had all but stopped, the rebels having been defeated by the combined efforts of the army and the air force at a cost of several hundred lives and many wounded, but luckily none from Britain or the Commonwealth. It had been a close shave until the army got reinforcements from near Addis Ababa and the air force belatedly joined them.

On his way back the emperor landed at Khartoum where our ambassador, Sir Edwin Chapman Andrews (who had served with him in the Ethiopian Campaign and knew him well), briefed him with my latest news of the situation and was asked to send me the following message.

'I thank you very much for what you have done to help us during these difficult days. The British Ambassador at Rio journeyed to São Paulo to see me and deliver the message you sent me. I thank you both and would wish you to convey to HM the Queen an expression of my gratitude for this help at a time when trouble-makers have caused us annoyance. I renew my confidence in the friendship towards us of HM the Queen and the British people.'

Three days after his return I was summoned to the palace and again thanked by the emperor, a sad little figure wearing a black tie with his customary khaki uniform. I offered my condolences on the loss of a number of his closest advisers and ministers, held prisoner by the rebels and brutally murdered by them when they saw their game was up.

Some months later Haile Selassie again demonstrated his gratitude by sending his Master of the Imperial Horse, a dapper Armenian colonel (several Armenian families had settled in Ethiopia after the massacres in Ottoman Turkey), together with a groom leading a splendid bay horse from the royal stables to replace mine, killed in an accident when I was home on leave. He had heard of the tragedy from one of his grand-daughters with whom my wife and I sometimes went riding.

Mindful of the strict Foreign Office rule about expensive gifts I wrote, tongue in cheek, asking for instructions. The reply was short and to the point: *Don't look a gift horse in the mouth.*

DENIS WRIGHT

The War on Terror

We were just inside Brazil. A mile or so down the road was Argentina. A mile or so the other way was Paraguay. From the air this area looks like a huge T-junction of jungle, river and the frothing, white waters of the Iguaçu Falls. On the ground it is a confluence of porous frontiers, under-paid Customs officers and policemen with modern weapons and old uniforms, soaked with sweat and the latest tropical downpour.

It is called the Triple Border. And has been described by the CIA as the most dangerous focal point in Latin America for Islamist terrorism.

The rain came down in a sheet, bouncing off the golden roof of the mosque, splashing into the tiny guard-house where we were sheltering, then shorting the electrics so the automatic gate to the compound would not open and we could not get out.

On the other side of the fence, umbrella raised then blown out by the tropical wind, was Jeffrey Hessler from Iowa, a small, rotund, bespectacled man who represented the local American Chamber of Commerce. He showed us a way through the railings and drove us to his home. Dried off, he explained he did not like what we had come to talk to him about. But being a dutiful American, he obliged.

'I suppose there is a concentration of religious activity,' he started cautiously, 'and a lot of money is changing hands. But it's difficult to say where it all goes.' He shifted uncomfortably in his chair, tapping restlessly on the arm. This was not a topic into which he wanted to be drawn.

'The feeling among businessmen,' he continued after some time, 'is that if this sort of thing does exist, it should be taken care of. But you have to decide whether Hezbollah and Hamas are political or religious.'

'Barakat,' I ventured, as the steaming Brazilian coffee arrived and the rain started up again, loud on the roof. 'Do you know him? Was he a member of the Chamber of Commerce?'

Hessler shook his head and adjusted his glasses. 'No. I've heard of the man but I don't know him.'

Assad Ahmad Barakat, Lebanese immigrant, father of three and Hezbollah sympathizer, is one of the many wanted names around the world in the war on terror. He used to run an electronics business in the damp, paint-peeled town of Ciudad del Este in Paraguay. Just across the Parana River from Brazil, this distant and little-known region has in the last generation become a magnet for those disrupted by the upheavals of the Middle East. Once no more than a riverside shanty town, Ciudad del Este has sprouted high-rise apartment blocks, mosques and security firms. Its economy has boomed with the business of thousands of Arabs, many just wanting a quiet life, others actively involved in drugs, smuggling and funding terror.

We left Mr Hessler and headed into Paraguay, across a road and footbridge spanning a high river gorge. In Ciudad del Este, ducking from another squall, we sprinted through the razor-wired compound of the honorary consul for Syria. I asked him if he knew how to find Barakat.

'Barakat?' asked Consul Bazaz, a tall, urbane man who not only represented the Syrian government but was also the local salesman for Givenchy.

'Mr Barakat is in Brazil right now. I don't think Brazil would defend him if he were a criminal.'

He paused, looking around his perfumes as though they could rescue him from the thin ice we were treading. He rubbed his hand down his roughly-shaven chin, then looked straight at me, his eyes ablaze with conviction.

'What is happening is completely unfair. Intelligence agents from the US and Israel are here and so far they haven't been able to find any proof. Schoolchildren are treated like terrorists just because they're Arabs.' After that brief outburst he pressed boxes of perfume into our hands and ushered us to the door.

Ernesto Iruni, the young mayor of Ciudad del Este, had another view. An aspiring presidential candidate and a heavy-weight from the ruling party, he was sent here to clean up the place and rid it of any links with terror. With him came the black-uniformed special police seen around town in four-wheel drives with tinted windows, automatic pistols strapped to their thighs.

'If Barakat was here we would have him locked up,' said the mayor, slapping a newspaper cutting with the back of his hand. 'This man is our Enemy Number One. He would not escape.'

Except that he had.

While I was with the mayor, my fixer had been working the coffee-shops. She introduced me to a man who described himself as a garment trader. He must have been in his mid-thirties and was more smartly dressed than most in Ciudad del Este, with a whiff of one of Consul Bazaz's products about him. We followed his jeep through the evening rush-hour traffic, back to the town of Foz do Iguaçu. No passport or papers were required.

Just inside Brazil, down a side-street of low-rise, middle-class houses, he flashed his hazard lights, tooted his horn, pointed to a house and sped off. Mr Barakat, all smiles and confidence, opened his front door to us.

We walked through a patio where garden chairs were stacked by a swimming-pool, through the carport with two vehicles in it, and into the living-room. We sat on big sofas, Barakat with his eight-month-old son on his lap. He was a tall, broad-shouldered man with thick, dark hair and a moustache. As with many people who suddenly find themselves dislodged, there was an unsettled atmosphere about him.

'So you are a terrorist?' I asked. He laughed.

'I came here in 1985, when I was a student.' He leaned forward, one arm round his son and the other stretched out to a pile of newspaper cuttings he wanted to show me. 'I never took part in any war and have no military training. Of course we are sympathizers of Hezbollah because they fought the invaders who entered Lebanon. All Lebanese people everywhere are sympathizers.'

'But the mayor of Ciudad del Este says you're Enemy Number One.'

He handed the boy to his wife and paused for a moment in thought. 'Listen,' he said. 'Paraguay is so poor it pretends it is chasing terrorists just to get American aid. Brazil thinks it's so big it can give two fingers to the gringos. As for men like the mayor, supporting the US by accusing us is good for their careers. They get more aid money and more for their pockets.

'Whether anyone's a terrorist or not doesn't matter at all,' we were told. 'It's just a big political game.'

HUMPHREY HAWKSLEY

The Headless Security Risk

The summer of '63 in London was piquantly dramatic. On May 8, at the Court of Session in Edinburgh, Lord Wheatley delivered his 65,000-word judgment granting a divorce to the Duke of Argyll. His Lordship referred to photographs of Margaret, Duchess of Argyll, wearing a three-string pearl necklace and engaged in fellatio with an unknown 'headless man'. One of the candidates for the latter rôle was Duncan Sandys, then Minister of Defence.

In June the Profumo crisis erupted – it had been simmering for a few months. John Profumo, Secretary of State for War, resigned for having lied about his relationship with a call girl, Christine Keeler. She had also given her sexual favours to an air attaché at the Soviet Embassy and, in those security-sensitive days, a crisis ensued. Lord Denning, then Master of the Rolls, was charged with conducting an Inquiry into it all, including Duncan Sandys' involvement. Margaret Argyll had thus become a possible security risk too.

In mid-June I was about to begin a long vacation and wanted to work in Italy. There appeared in *The Times*, on page one in those days, a notice for a governess/tutor in Latin, on Elba, for a boy of nine. I wrote to the given box number and received a reply from a Mrs Mathilda Mortimer of Strachur in Argyll. She stated that her youngest son was going to Summerfields and was down for Eton; the appointee would be expected to spend some two-three months preparing him and tutoring his twin brothers aged fourteen. I was duly invited to Claridge's for lunch where I met the charming and intelligent Mrs Mortimer, then in her thirties. We discussed everything except the appointment, and after lunch she invited me to her suite for coffee and brandy. I was enjoying her company when in walked the Duke of Argyll, whom I instantly recognised. In the course of the conversation Mrs Mortimer turned to him to say that I would be going with them to Elba.

I duly went to Paris to meet the boy and took him to Elba by train and ferry. Disembarking, we were met by a chauffeur who looked exactly like Pope Pius XII, and taken to the splendid Villa Rosa near Marciana Marina.

Mrs Mortimer and the duke greeted us on arrival, and over dinner I was told in great confidence that they were married, a fact not made public until August. I have since learned that even the former duchess was taken by surprise. I was in effect with them on their honeymoon and was treated at all times as part of the family.

Whilst still on Elba the duke was startled to be summoned to London to appear before Lord Denning and his Inquiry. The duke was one of the hundred and sixty witnesses interviewed: in particular he was asked about the headless photographs and the consequent security risk. I well remember that he was very apprehensive and asked me (a law student of twenty-two!) if I knew Lord Denning. I am afraid I did not. Returning after a day or two, he told me about his encounter: 'Denning! What a man!' he said. 'He's as smooth as a billiard ball.'

Lord Denning's conclusions about the duke's involvement are set out in his report on the Profumo Affair. It would have read like a great novel had its characters not been real and so well known.

ROGER DAVIES

My First Serious Fee

Starting out in accountancy, I was naturally aware of professional liability, but the sums involved with my first clients were rarely such as to warrant liability cover.

One of the assignments undertaken as a result of my policy of doing anything for a crust was the investigation of a Costa Rican shoe factory. It came about through my being ushered into the presence of a charming, elegant and handsome earl in his extensive Lowndes Square home. He was about twenty-five years old and his personal income was, I was told, then about a million a month. He wanted to make this investment (costing merely a few months' income) and I was to report upon the business.

A day or two later I flew to Miami with the two Italians who owned the factory and who were immaculately mannered and spoke fairly good English. (I could not speak Italian or Spanish.) At Miami we were due to take a further flight on to San José, Costa Rica's capital. We were just about to board when one of the Italians was held back by Immigration. So we sat around for six hours until he re-emerged, rather irritably pointing out that they had got the wrong man.

At San José we were met by a strongly built chauffeur at the wheel of a Mercedes 600. He had once been personal bodyguard to General Somoza, the president of Nicaragua, who had needed a bodyguard if anybody ever did – he was assassinated in Paraguay in 1980.

The Mercedes swept towards central San José through a Graham Greene setting of decrepit and overloaded lorries. It then thrust up a hill and, at the click of the chauffeur's control switch, the gates of a vast hacienda swung open. Several servants emerged to handle our baggage and we were led up to a magnificent drawing-room with panorama windows looking out over the city.

I was introduced to the Secretary of the National Assembly. He was modest and unassuming and I presumed that he was the equivalent of our Clerk to the House of Commons. He was actually the equivalent of prime minister. He explained that there was no corruption in Costa Rica. If this was so I was at a loss to explain how a man on twenty thousand dollars per annum, as he claimed, could afford to live in this style.

After a superb dinner I crawled exhausted into bed at about 2.30 a.m. One of the Italians and the ever-attentive chauffeur made off into San José to sample some nightlife. However, I was determined to hit the ground running and had agreed to visit the factory at 7.30 a.m. So you can imagine my surprise when the chauffeur was on hand at that time; I doubt if he had had any sleep to speak of. He buckled on his shoulder holster. This struck me as slightly disconcerting since I had not realised that armed robbery was all the rage in Central America. More than once, lying awake at night, I heard shots – and they were not that far away. So either Costa Ricans just like nocturnal target practice or burgling is a pretty risky business.

My assignment had started simply on the assumption that I would review the factory's accounts and extrapolate using common sense. But I was able to strengthen my presentation greatly by recruiting a study-mate from my time at Rugby. He specialized in shoe-making machinery and flew in from the States a day later.

Costa Rica's national debt was at that time something like two billion US dollars. There was no chance of its repaying more than a tiny fraction because there were only two million Costa Ricans and their average monthly wage was in the order of thirty dollars.

One effect however was that Costa Rica enjoyed preferential export opportunities to the US, which was then very concerned to see that Communism did not spread through Central America. Washington was determined to sponsor local employment and industry. The shoes produced could therefore be theoretically sold into the Southern States at around six dollars a pair. Furthermore, Costa Rican cow-hide had by law to be offered for sale first to the shoe factory. So I took the view that all essential supplies of materials and labour and the company's markets were secure. My expert schoolfriend also advised that the machinery was in good working order.

However, from here matters tended to unravel. The business was heavily in debt and the machinery seemed far more expensive than expected. This proved to be not surprising, because it had first been sold to associates of the P2 Masonic Lodge in Italy and uplifted by about one hundred per cent before Italian overseas aid, financed through the Banco Ambrosiano, provided for its installation in Costa Rica. It has been my unvarying experience that corrupt businessmen make bad business managers: they always take their eye off the ball.

As we finally left Costa Rica, the management thrust six pairs of shoes into our hands as parting gifts. This was a mistake since they were subsequently analysed: it was determined that they would last ten days at most, and only as long as conditions were dry. It is utterly astonishing to me that this sort of overseas aid is ever extended by anybody.

I see a photograph of the earl from time to time in tabloid 'diaries' – usually à propos his latest marriage. The Italian who was detained at Miami Airport was declared a wanted man over Costa Rican radio a few months later – he was reportedly associated with the Red Brigades in Italy. With the airports blocked, I think he got out over the border into Nicaragua. I doubt if he is in the shoe business these days. And I got four thousand pounds for ten days' work, my first serious fee.

SIMON CAWKWELL

Kidnapped!

In 1956 Adrian Cowell led an Oxford & Cambridge University expedition driving three new Land Rovers from London to Singapore. I believe that this was the first and last time such a journey has succeeded, but I await refutation.

A year later I set off with an Irish friend, Johnny Clements, in a bullet-scarred World War II jeep, which I had bought for one hundred pounds, to drive to Ceylon. Johnny was the ideal travelling companion since he had but two passions in life, motor vehicles and horses, both of which he knew a great deal about. Since our jeep spent much of its time broken down and needing extensive, on-the-spot repairs, he was happy and I was free, without any sense of urgency, to dream my way through the Middle East, musing on the towers of Trebizond, wandering about the ruins of Persepolis at dawn and haggling in the markets of Tabas or Meshed or wherever we had broken down.

After crossing Afghanistan and reaching Kabul, we decided to make a side-trip over the Koh-i-Baba Mountains to the Band-i-Amir Lakes and the Bamian Buddhas and on into the edge of the Hindu Kush. The British Embassy, which in those days welcomed the occasional traveller with generous hospitality, strongly advised us against going. The terrain would be impassable since the tracks were designed for camels and, shortly before, an American and his Swedish girlfriend had disappeared there. It was feared that he had been killed and she had been taken into a harem and would not be seen again.

We followed the ridges, teetering along razor edges with sheer drops on either side, before winding down impossible slopes to camp in little green strips of valleys where poplars grew, their autumn leaves bright yellow beside the icy water. We slept in crumbling, deserted forts, huddled against the bitter cold, and sometimes in fortified farms.

In Kabul I had bought in the market a superior fishing-rod and a case of flies left behind a decade before by a British officer on leave. I was determined to catch some of the big trout I could see in the clear streams that coursed down each valley floor. One afternoon I left Johnny working underneath the jeep and wandered out of sight to an open meadow where the silence was absolute. I became absorbed and oblivious.

A sound like distant thunder made me look up at the rich blue, cloudless sky before I turned to see twenty wild horsemen in turbans and flowing robes bearing down on me. They carried long-barrelled rifles and had daggers in their belts. Beside their spirited horses loped large, hairy hounds. With their Genghis Khan moustaches and fine, aquiline noses they were almost caricatures of the bandits we had been warned about. I should have been frightened but all I could think was that if I had to go I could not have found a more romantic end.

Forming a perfect half-circle between me and escape, the horses reared as they came to a halt and then stood with heaving sides as their riders watched me reel in my line. With my very few words of Persian I greeted them while they stared at me in stony silence. Bowing towards the water, I indicated that the horses might like to drink and that the fish were not biting anyway. Failing to break the ice, I dismantled the rod and walked along the line patting the horses' necks and expressing exaggerated admiration. Suddenly the tension broke and loud guffaws shattered the silence. The undoubted chief, so swathed in bandoliers of ammunition that bullets fired at him would have bounced off, reached down and grabbed my hand. Thinking innocently that he wanted to shake it, I gave it to him freely, only to find it lashed with a leather thong and clamped between the stirrup and his foot as he spurred his horse into a gallop.

I flew beside him, taking giant strides so as not to fall, until we came upon the jeep, from the underneath of which Johnny's feet poked out. Nothing ever surprised Johnny and the possible danger of the situation never occurred to him. But he knew a good horse when he saw one and, heading straight for the finest stallion, he began to admire its finer points. Horse language is universal and he was immediately recognised as an expert and therefore, unlike me, a man to be reckoned with. My hand was released and his was shaken all round.

They played with us for a while, charging at us in two battle-lines to see if our nerves held, and showing how they could lean right out of the saddle to pluck things from the ground. Their rifles were mostly Russian: the frontier, marked by what used to be called the Oxus River (now the Amudarya), lay not far to the north.

There were two teenage boys in the group who rode wild little ponies and grinned with pure happiness as they dashed about. They seemed to know that their lives were the envy of their contemporaries throughout the world and I thought they looked on us with pity. God knows what has happened to them as, over the following forty years, their country degenerated into civil war and the land became strewn with mines.

ROBIN HANBURY-TENISON

The Last Wali of Swat

It was a bright day in January 1974. The Wali had sent his driver and a large four-wheel-drive vehicle for the journey from Peshawar to his remote kingdom far up in the tribal areas of the North-West Frontier of what is now Pakistan.

His Highness Miangul Gulshahzada Sayed Abdul Haq Jahan Zeb, Badshah and Wali of Swat and Buner – king, to put it more simply – had become ruler of this Shangri-La of a state in 1949 on the abdication of his remarkable father. It had originally been governed by religious leaders or Akhunds. (We all remember Edward Lear's rhyme 'Who or why or which or what is the Akhund of Swat'.) The Wali's ancestors were Sufi saints and mystics but also very warlike. The British never conquered Swat; instead they recognized the kingdom in 1926, seeing in the Wali's father an astute, effective and charismatic ruler who was content to let the British rush around the North-West Frontier provided they left him well alone. The whole area bordering on Afghanistan and being extremely unstable, it was a great advantage to have such a man on your side. Little has changed.

We set off early to travel the one hundred and fifty-odd miles, along very bad roads with alarmingly deep, mountainous drops, passing through villages and small towns, narrowly missing the hundreds of gaily painted trucks and buses which are the main means of transportation in this region. The road roughly followed the Swat River, that poured its melt-waters down to the great Indus. The Wali's driver, a man of about fifty and of very grave countenance and few words, was fully aware of the impor-tance of his office. With the conviction that everyone would bow to the Wali's absolute right of way in all situations, even outside Swat, he drove down the centre of the road refusing to swerve or give way, even to on-coming trucks driven by qat-chewing, desperate men who had probably been driving for days. Qat or *paani* is the drug of choice for such knights of the road.

The friend I was travelling with, who was married to one of the Wali's grand-daughters and had been the initiator of my invitation, said that we were going to stop at Mardan to attend a local khan's wedding-party for his son. Our other passenger was my friend's unmarried sister.

Presently we came upon a large estate and house. On the lawns were vast tents of red, blue and white cloth; people were swarming around; wonderful smells wafted in our direction, and there were sounds of tribal music. The men and women were of course separated so I was taken to the men's pavilion where everyone was wearing their most refined clothes and generally having a good time. They were very friendly and welcoming to this complete stranger. Tea was served, then plate after plate of won-derful Frontier food. An orchestra and a famous singer had been brought from Kabul to entertain the guests. They had been playing for two days now.

The singer, an old lady wrinkled and slightly bowed, continually played her hand-pumped harmonium and wailed with a good deal of feeling: rather sad I thought for a wedding. Occasionally she would slow up, the harmonium would become even more dirge-like and she would cry out in Pashto to be allowed to stop. But everyone would start shouting and urg-ing her on, throwing large quantities of money. This seemed to revive her spirits.

However, we had to press on to get to Swat before nightfall. We said our goodbyes to our fellow wedding-guests, who of course begged us to stay, offering accommodation for the night, or indeed several nights. We paid our respects to the bridegroom's father and congratulated the alarm-ingly young bridegroom, collected our driver who had been similarly fed and watered, and continued our unswerving progress towards Swat.

Two thirds of the journey had been completed and soon we were approaching the border. Here we stopped again at a large wooden house, built up a hillside but very comfortable and in a beautiful setting. The faded grandeur of the building extended to its owner, a remarkable gentleman of about eighty years, dressed completely in white cotton of the finest sort with a long, white beard and turban to match. Glasses of hot, sweet tea were served together with bowls of almonds and white, translucent honey. Our venerable host was, I was given to understand, a local holy man, a Sufi saint of good family. I told him that I had never tasted such delicious honey before. This pleased him and he pointed to a mud wall in which there were a number of holes, in and out of which there was a continuous traffic of industrious bees.

There was another purpose to this stop at the border. Besides the driver, we were two men and a woman to whom I was neither married nor related. She could not continue into Swat in the same vehicle. It would not be seemly. What happened in Pakistan was different. Swat was Swat. Another car was found into which my friend's sister was decanted, destined for the women's quarters which stood behind the palace in the Wali's capital. I began to realize that things from now on would be very different and I would not be seeing my delightful lady friend again for a while. In fact I would not be seeing any women at all.

We began the last part of our journey and suddenly the world changed. The roads were now well kept and orderly. Each village we passed through was well maintained, with its own dispensary, school and police station. The essentials of civilization were all here: the chaos of Pakistan was left behind. Health, education, public order and good communications were, I was to learn, a large feature of the Wali's absolute rule.

As we crossed the border into Swat, our driver broke his silence for the second time. Thrusting his arm across the bridge of my nose and pointing out of the window, he shouted: 'Winston Churchill'. Momentarily confused but following his finger, I saw a very small, hillside building on which was daubed the name in question. My friend explained that this was where Churchill had commanded a small group of men when the British were trying to take Malakand. This was as far as they got.

Swat's capital, Saidu, came into sight, hilly with low, level buildings and good lighting. But before I narrate our arrival at the palace, I have to tell you that the Swat Valley is one of the most agreeable and beautiful places on Earth. Surrounded by permanently snow-capped peaks, its verdant rice-fields are watered by endless rocky streams over which, from the roof of the world, tumbles the sweetest water. Apricots, pears and cumquats bloom everywhere; scent is in the velvet air; the climate is kind and moderate.

The Wali's palace stands in the centre of Saidu on a hill in a beautiful walled garden. It is not gigantic but stylish, and very reminiscent of a comfortable and manageable English country house with touches of the Dorchester or the Savoy.

As our car drew up, about twenty barefoot servants dressed in black *shalwar* chemises came down the steps of the palace. Amongst them was a man who was obviously in authority – the Wali's major-domo who greeted me most warmly. He announced that the Wali was at prayer and that my bags would be taken to my room. This last was large and comfortable, again with a sort of country-house feel about it – solid Western furniture – but with also an oriental touch in the lattice-doors which opened onto a small private courtyard.

As I began to unpack, there was a knock at the door and another servant entered, again all in black, and said: 'Allow me, Sir'. Completing the onerous task of unpacking, he proceeded to the bathroom and began to fill an extremely large bath, testing the water from time to time. The bathroom itself was entirely of marble with Western taps and fittings of solid chrome, art déco style. I really could have been in the Savoy. The servant announced that my bath was ready but made no attempt to leave. What now, I thought? Taking all my dusty clothes off and getting into the bath was the right decision: the servant smiled, gathered up my clothes, bowed and left. The clothes appeared some hours later, still warm from their careful washing and neat pressing.

After the bath I put on a collar and tie and changed into a suit, opened the French windows and lay on the bed smoking and enjoying the evening breeze. It was now about six o'clock and there was a knock at the door. It was my friend, come to tell me that the Wali would receive me now.

From what I had so far seen of Swat, I somehow knew the man I was going to meet. The Ruler was the State, and the State was the Ruler. I was shown into a long, narrow reception room. Along each side were rows of comfortable lounge chairs, separated by low tables on which I observed silver cigarette boxes, lighters and ashtrays. All very elegant and Western.

Sitting in a chair at the end, a large window behind him, was His Highness, the fabled Wali and architect of everything here. I walked towards him and he stood up. He was of medium height, with a strong military bearing, immaculately turned out in grey Astrakhan hat, silk tie, striped shirt, well-tailored check jacket, V-necked woollen pullover and grey flannel trousers. The Wali evidently got his clothes from Savile Row and his cigarettes from Burlington Arcade.

'You are most welcome,' he said. 'Come and sit by me.' He gestured to a chair on his right and we sat down. He had immense authority, did not smile, but was not forbidding. He was so relaxed that I immediately relaxed too, but remained aware that this man had absolute power. It was however an absoluteness tempered by genuine concern and interest. He looked at me intently and unhurriedly through tinted glasses: I felt that he could see into the innermost recesses of my soul.

He lit a cigarette. Asked if I might do likewise, he gestured to the nearest cigarette box. He then proceeded to ask me about every detail of my journey and also about my reflections on all that I had seen. This was not mere politeness: he really wanted to know. He was pleased with what I had to say; I felt I could be totally honest and candid in my replies.

He rose and asked if I would like to walk on the terrace and observe the mountains before it got too chilly and dark. As we left, the Wali took off his Astrakhan hat and took a brown trilby from the hands of a waiting servant. We progressed up and down the terrace as he told me about Swat and how much he wanted me to see. All the time we were followed by two servants, one with a small table, the other with two chairs, which were immediately put into position if the Wali stopped for a moment. It began to dawn on me that this was absolutism in action.

At his suggestion I retired to my room for a rest before dinner. The Wali had said that he normally ate English food – Mulligatawny soup, roast beef and apple and custard were regularly on the palace's menu – but suggested that I might like to try some local food. At the appointed time I was taken to the drawing-room where I found my friend waiting, looking suitably respectful. The Wali enquired if I would like a drink and I said whisky; this was before the days when we all have to pretend that Muslims do not drink. A servant duly appeared with a silver tray on which there were at least twenty varieties of the said drink. I was asked which one

I would like. I knew already that the Wali's favourite was Black Dog. My choice was greeted with approval and we both had several. My friend did not fare so well. He had become infected by the new fashion of 'I'm more Muslim than you' and, despite being quite Westernized, would not drink with the Wali. This was not objected to but no other drink was offered. A slight rebuke, I thought, but it made an important point.

We talked and talked as we were to do on many subsequent occasions. There followed a splendid meal of delicately flavoured meats and pilaus, rather in the Persian or Moghul style, followed by fresh and crystallized fruits and sweetmeats. As is the custom with Muslims, the end of eating signified the end of the occasion, and I went to my bed to sleep soundly.

Many days of adventure followed in which I explored the stunningly beautiful Swat Valley and the surrounding hills. I was escorted by eight of the Wali's armed guard who were excellent and amusing company although they spoke no English and I no Pashto. Despite being manly and warlike, they had a fatal interest in their coiffures, which were very elaborate and resembled those seen on classical Greek statues. Each carried a small, round tin, with a mirror in the lid, in which was kept *paani* for chewing. So there was much crimping of the hair whenever we would rest or stop and the machine-guns were put down. Where had these hair-styles come from, these bundles of ringlets to the side of the head? Indeed, where had these fair skins, fair hair and even blue eyes, on occasion, come into the picture? The Wali himself had the skin of an English colonial. Were these people mixed with the descendants of Alexander's army as legend would have us believe? The Greeks had been here in great numbers, had even passed through and gone as far as Kabul. The faces and bone structures were also unlike those of southern Pakistan, and not Central Asian or oriental as one encounters in parts of Afghanistan and beyond.

A ruler like the Wali must always act in the interests of the state. He had to cut down power-crazed khans, stem the hand of avaricious landowners and personally adjudicate the cases brought before him without sentimentality or partiality. He could owe no one a favour. I saw all this with my own eyes when I was there. The schools, roads, bridges, dispensaries, police stations and the administration of the law spoke for themselves.

The Wali always said that you cannot fight the uncontrollable. He was running a small, traditional state and at the same time having to keep at bay a modern, chaotic neighbour: Pakistan. Swat was eventually absorbed into Pakistan in 1969. The Wali, seeing the inevitable, co-operated, took neither land nor money for himself and remained in his palace amongst his people until his death in 1985. The great sadness of his last years was to see Swat begin to fall into the disintegrated and corrupt state of Pakistan as a whole. There are not many absolute rulers who can relinquish their throne and continue to live with honour and respect in their own land. The Wali was such a man.

PETER GWYNVAY HOPKINS

Among the Heart-hunters

It was the drums that did it. Drove every thought from my head. Perhaps it was better that way.

Facing thirteen hundred upturned faces, men on the left, women on the right, children packed into the gallery ahead of me, I knew it was right that the dull subordinate clauses of Anglican discourse should disappear. There was nothing they didn't know about the Epiphany because in the parish of Bethlehem, Aizawl, Mizoram, north-east India, in this year of grace 2001, every child attends Sunday school and every adult attends church, sometimes several times a day.

This was Sunday evensong and they were all there, watching the pantomime of a six-foot Englishman trying to adjust a microphone firmly fixed at five foot two. Every few sentences I stopped and smiled benevolently while a Church elder translated my words into Mizo. I said that I had noticed thirteen hundred people in church that morning, and that in pagan Paddington where I exercised my Anglican ministry there were churches that would be thrilled at an attendance of thirty-five souls unless it was raining, in which case expectations would be lowered. The decline of the West, the rising star in the East, Epiphany, this parish of Bethlehem, we missioned you, now you could mission us, you get my drift. Having only had an hour's notice, I thought I had acquitted myself quite well. I sat down.

The drumming started again, but slower, and there arose the sound of the electronic equivalent of timbrel and harp. We accelerated into Guide Me O Thou Great Redeemer. I sang along phonetically in Mizo:

Aw Lalpa, i malsawmna hlu, Kan engkim chungah a lang.

It began to dawn on me that nobody had believed me, that my intimations of secularisation and decline, which I took so seriously, had been dismissed as politeness, a veiled compliment paid to Third-World faith. They knew that England was exactly as shown on the calendars I had given them, a secure world of cathedrals and thatched cottages, grenadiers and beefeaters, a wonderful land full of English men and women who never give up, who never tell a lie, and who go to church on Sunday.

Intrepid Welsh Presbyterian missionaries had followed the flag into these Lushai Hills in the late 1890s. Conversions followed on a massive scale. As I was told many times in Mizoram, head-hunters became heart-hunters, and in the hills above Hindu India was created under the Presbyterian Church a fiercely protective theocracy which persists to this day.

Geography assists this isolation. Nobody knows where Mizoram is. It is in the little bit of India squashed between Bangladesh and Burma. To the north lies Assam. A running battle between the Indian army and the local insurgents and nationalists means that Mizoram is, in every possible way, a restricted area. You have to be invited before you can apply for a visa, and you have then to travel in a party of six. There are ways and means, although it is a little strange to be welcomed into the state in the company of James Bond, Donald Duck and John F. Kennedy.

Only recently have direct flights from Calcutta been introduced. There are no back-packers. There are no hotels and no restaurants because there is no tourism. In Aizawl the children play in the streets because there is nowhere else to play, and they jump out of the way as the cars leap the potholes. The houses reach out to each other across the streets. There are no electric tools, so a constant hammering persists. It took me a little while to make the right comparison but I may have glimpsed Reformation Europe.

I woke early in Bethlehem and heard what sounded like the muezzin. But no, it was Christians calling themselves to prayer. In each household there is a television, but the machine is switched off for daily family prayers, a psalm or a bible reading. The church and the family provide all the entertainment there is. For delinquents, the church and family mete out justice.

Tourism can be a drearily passive affair, the comfortable input of impressions through the coach window, the safe grazing of the cultural menu turistico. The traveller has a different approach. Having made my contribution to evensong, I looked forward to an adventurous holiday planned by the family who had invited me. But in the Lushai Hills other plans were afoot. Ancient telephones purred, a delegation arrived. There was to be a vast gathering at a place called ChhingChhip, where several parishes were staging a mission. Mizoram's leading Gospel singer would be present. Would I consent to be a guest preacher?

Clutching a hat and the Book of Common Prayer, I found there was plenty of time for imploring divine aid as the little Japanese taxi bounced from one sheer drop to the next. If four wheels cannot get round a landslide, try two. No officious signs announced an imminent Viewpoint. On every side were stupendous hillscapes under a sky so blue that it hurt. At times we were vertical, seeing only sky. From shacks by the road people waved then stared and pointed incredulously, shouting 'Sahib, Sahib' at the neo-Victorian missionary disappearing in a cloud of dust. Most had never seen a European. I have never met such friendliness and charm, never seen such light in children's eyes. A whole village would pile into one house for a conversazione with this strange being, the head of the household present me with a beautiful miniature woven basket and announce that he never thought he would live to see the day when a sahib from the land of the Great White Queen across the water would bestow a blessing on his humble home. I got quite carried away and named an unborn child after myself, remembering to provide male and female alternatives.

After another day's journey, atop a mountain, and fuelled possibly by a bottle of black-market whisky obtained from the Assam Rifles, I had a little epiphany of my own because the silence was so tangible and the Creator of all this beauty so obvious. And because nothing had changed since Colonel Roberts, later Earl Roberts of Kandahar, received a CB for organizing the transport for the Lushai Hills Expedition of 1872.

At dusk the next day the first-ever Western missionary to ChhingChhip rode into town. The local pastor and his fellows, in crisp double-breasted suits, were waiting. I was, through an accident of laundry, dressed for lunch at the Travellers, although the following morning, after a night in a jungle rest house, I was, in the words of the antiquarian book trade, slightly creased. I was presented with a red rosette. So it was as a Labour candidate, or perhaps a prize heifer being led to sacrifice, that I ascended to a vast concrete church with open, cruciform windows. In green neon letters on a red background above the double-decker pulpit was written 'ChhingChhip K.T.P. Conference Vawi 33-Na, ISAIAH 60.1'. Which in any language, but particularly that of the Authorised Version, reads: 'Arise, shine; for thy light is come, and the glory of the Lord is risen upon thee'.

In the church were at least two thousand locals in their multicoloured Sunday best. The Mizos are wonderful at public performance. There were choirs, and junior choirs, and youth groups, and elders, in lettered sashes and matching lungis. Pride in group performance overcame any shyness. The drumming began; lesson followed hymn and an hour or two later, when I felt as though I'd been pressed like a flower in a book in the Club Library, there was a pause and a hush. Our famous singer, in a brown jacket and shimmering ankle-length skirt, stepped forward to the microphone and began a slow and emotional rendering of Nearer, my God, to Thee.

Murmurs and sniffles were audible. The deck began to slip beneath me. My cue to mount the pulpit was verse three: 'There let the way appear, Steps unto heaven'. The content of my sermon was academic because nobody understood a word. But they knew what I was doing and they were so pleased that I had come. I ditched all modern apologies and liberal ho-hums; I spared them the patronising pluralist cant of modern England and preached the Gospel as neat as a tot of Assam Rifles whisky, as braver men would have done a century before me. Rise 'n shine.

After all this there were photo-calls innumerable with choirs and elders and preachers and readers. Mothers pushed their children forward, and my favourite photograph shows twenty-five children and among them, just visible, myself with the mountains of Mizoram beyond. I was a hundred years late, but perhaps just a little nearer to God, as we sang, in Mizo, the valedictory.

JULIAN BROWNING

On Not Being Harry Potter

The first school I attended was situated in a small Cheshire village. There were two teachers only. Recently I received a letter from that school inviting me to return after an absence of almost sixty years as they wanted me to open an extension. On arrival I discovered that little had changed. There were still two teachers (not the same two of course). The air-raid shelter had disappeared and the War-time allotments had been turned into a playing field but otherwise it was as I remembered it.

A sizeable group of villagers had gathered for the grand opening of the modest extension. A pink ribbon had been strategically placed across the doorway and I was handed a pair of scissors with which to cut it. The pupils were assembled and everyone waited for my speech. I leaned across to the head teacher.

'Wouldn't it be good if the youngest member of the school joined me in cutting the tape?' I whispered.

She nodded, stepped forward and took the hand of a very small fellow not more than four years old. He was so small I picked him up.

'What is your name?' I asked.

To my surprise he whispered reluctantly into my ear: 'Harry Potter'! Indeed it was. Afterwards his mother told me that he could not understand why it was that whenever he was taken into a bookshop his name was displayed everywhere. Later, a newspaper carried the headline: 'Harry Potter opens school assisted by Terry Waite'. Such is celebrity status.

It was the American comedian Fred Allen who once said: 'A celebrity is one who works hard all his life to become well known and then goes through the streets wearing dark glasses so that he won't be recognised'.

I lay no claim whatsoever to celebrity status but having been in and out of the news for some twenty or more years and being six foot seven and bearded, I am inevitably recognised wherever I go. Also, I don't much care for wearing dark glasses.

On visits to New York I always made a point of calling at the Tall Man's Shop to buy a shirt that wouldn't expose my waistline as soon as I raised my arms, or a pair of trousers that didn't appear to be Bermuda shorts when I put them on. On one such visit, to my surprise, my familiar supplier had simply disappeared. I stood in the street wondering if senility was beginning to take over when suddenly an NYPD car screeched to a halt. A cop thrust his florid face through the window.

'Hi Terry,' he said cheerfully. 'You look lost. Jump in and we'll take you where you wanna go.'

Needless to say, I wasn't wearing dark glasses and, as the police delivered me to the outfitter's new premises within a few moments, I was glad to be without them.

Cape Town delivered an even greater surprise. Walking along the street with a colleague I saw several characters lingering in an empty shop doorway. They were drinking heartily. As we passed by one fellow with hair like a frozen mop stared at me.

'Terry Waite!' he exclaimed. 'What are you doing in South Africa?'

One might have thought that on the remote island of St Helena, accessible only by a four-day sea journey, dark glasses would hardly be required. Not so. Early one morning I stepped ashore and began to walk through the small dockyard into town. Alas, I was cornered.

'You've arrived just at the right time,' said a charming lady who gave the impression that she had been expecting me all along.

'Today is the official opening of my new shop. The bishop will bless it and you will open it, won't you?'

Open it I did and my impromptu speech was well reported in the local paper.

For many years I had the pleasure of travelling throughout the world as an advisor to the late Archbishop of Canterbury, Robert Runcie. From time to time we had to attend a church conference. Anyone who has been present at such an event will know it is not the most stimulating of occasions and at the end of the day a good dose of fresh air is usually called for. On one occasion we were attending a conference in a small town in Scotland. The archbishop was in the chair and throughout the day I sat by his side ensuring that he received his documents in the correct order. As evening approached and the last speech of the day had been delivered, the arch-bishop gave a long yawn.

'Come on,' he said. 'Let's take a walk along the main street.'

He changed into his favourite rust-coloured sweater and off we set. We had just got into our pace when in the distance we saw a wee Scots-man approaching. We assumed he was Scottish as he was wearing the kilt. When he got within hailing distance he stopped and stared at us both. We stopped. He approached and looked directly at me.

'Mr Waite,' he exclaimed. 'I dinna expect to see ye in Scotland. Come and have a wee dram and bring your friend along too.'

The archbishop took it in good part; he was a modest and good-humoured man. We had had a similar experience in East Africa when none other than a missionary picked me out and totally ignored His Grace. The missionary did not offer us a wee dram.

Mercifully, however, one is not always recognised. My wife and I were disembarking from a ship in Madeira and were being helped with our lug-gage by a young Asian porter who clearly had not the faintest idea who I was. Why should he? We waited on the dockside for our car and he kind-ly waited with us. I have an aversion to wearing glasses of any description and consequently passers-by stopped and exchanged a civil word or two. The porter looked on in amazement. Finally, when there was a lull, he turned to me.

'Excuse me, sir,' he said politely. 'Are you by any chance an author?'

'Well I have written one or two books in my time.'

At this his face lit up. 'You're not by any chance Mr Harry Potter, are you?'

'Alas,' I replied, 'I am not. But I have met him!'

TERRY WAITE

The Riots in Kandy

When the anti-Tamil riots broke out in Kandy, the old capital of Sri Lanka, on Tuesday, 26 July 1983, my friend Meyrick Horton and I were out of town visiting some up-country temples. Because the tracks leading to these temples were quite narrow we had decided to go by motor cycle and, as we rode back into Kandy down Trincomalee Street in the late afternoon, we were surprised to find ourselves riding down an avenue of fire. A mob was burning Tamil businesses on both sides of the road. It was not behaving quite as I had imagined a mob would behave. As far as we were concerned, the rioters seemed friendly enough. Smiling young men proudly showed us the Molotov cocktails they were carrying. Policemen lounged around sharing cigarettes and jokes with the rioters. The only sign of animation on the part of the police was when we took some photographs, and they insisted on exposing the film. Protecting the rioters' identity seemed more of a priority for them than stopping the riot.

We were staying in a small and inexpensive hotel much favoured by indigent academics. It had a first-floor veranda furnished with 'planters' chairs', which had such essentials as extendable arm-rests so that one could put one's feet up, and also a round hole into which one slotted the tumbler containing one's 'chota peg'. As night descended and the rioters spread their activities across the town, this veranda proved a sort of dress circle from where to observe the unfolding drama. Sipping orange juice laced with double-distilled arak, we watched Kandy burn, feeling a bit like the Emperor Nero. Two paint shops burned fiercely. Another shop had a stock of Chinese fireworks, the popping explosions of which provoked an echoing burst of gunfire from the nervous police posts. From time to time firemen would drop into the hotel for something to quench their thirst. We wondered if they were intending to piss on the fire.

By morning the fires had burned themselves out and, except for the black gaps in the townscape, there was an appearance of normality. We went about our business, and as night fell we again took our places on the veranda, like veteran theatre-goers. Another regular was a British medical student called Richard Quinton; we had met a few days earlier and become firm friends. Sure enough, the trouble started up again and this time it seemed to be getting closer. Shops only a few doors away were being targeted, and we were acutely aware that our hotel, which was largely made of wood and had only one entrance, was a natural fire-trap. Despite this I was feeling very tired, having had little sleep the previous night, and around midnight decided to go to bed.

The next thing I remember was having this dream. I was trapped in a room, and someone outside was trying to jemmy open the shutters. Suddenly I was wide awake. It was not a dream. Somebody really was fiddling with the windows.

The great thing about an English public school education is that it teaches you to dress fast. All those years of nearly missed roll-calls and chapel had knocked the last millisecond off the time it takes one's right foot to get into a shoe while one's left arm is simultaneously fighting its way into a shirt. In no time at all I was dressed, packed and out in the corridor. Some other Westerners were also there, mostly women. I could see no sign of Richard and Meyrick and assumed they must have gone on ahead. We decided that the best thing to do was to make a dash for the Queen's, the doyen of Kandy hotels, which occupied a larger and much better-protected building than the one we were in. We set off at a fine pace carrying our suitcases, but when we arrived we found that a large metal grill was blocking the entrance and the night porter showed little inclination to raise it. 'But we have been ordered here by the police,' we lied. 'All foreigners to the Queen's Hotel.' Very reluctantly he agreed to let us in.

It was now clear that Richard and Meyrick had not gone on ahead, and my leaving them was beginning to seem less than heroic. I kept peering through the grill hoping to see them come pounding down the street. Meanwhile I tried to get a room.

'Sorry, all rooms are taken.'

'Damn!'

'We are having a suit.'

'I'm sorry?'

'Honeymoon suit is available.'

'Great! I'll take it.'

Suddenly Richard and Meyrick were outside. Somehow they had obtained a car. There was furthermore inside the car a Sri Lankan family including two very small children. Breathlessly my friends explained that this was a Tamil family whom the Sinhalese owner of our former hotel had been bravely hiding, and that it was they rather than us who were the rioters' potential target. By now a rather supercilious manager in a dressing-gown had appeared, and I begged him to raise the grill quickly so that they could all get inside before being seen. But he too had realised that the family were Tamils and adamantly refused to let them in. Nothing I could say would persuade him to change his mind, and he was equally suspicious of the two Europeans. Who did he think they were, I asked: Israeli para-troopers? I was left raging incoherently. I would report him to the president, to the Queen of England, to the Pope. Sadly he seemed able to live with this prospect, and I groped wildly for a more effective line of attack. Then I had an idea. Was this not an Oberoi Hotel, I asked, one of the Indian chain? What did he think they were going to say in India when they learned that an Oberoi Hotel let Tamil children be killed on its doorstep? This was well below the belt, but I could see that it had gone home. The manager picked up the 'phone and talked for a couple of minutes. Then he said: 'They can all go to the Hotel Suisse on the other side of the lake. They are expected'. This turned out to be untrue, and in any case it was a less than generous offer since by now there was a curfew and anyone breaking it was at risk not just from the rioters but also from the trigger-happy security forces. But it was the only game in town so we had little alternative but to accept his suggestion.

Now let Richard, who was at the sharp end of this situation, give his side of the story.

Whilst Henry and Meyrick were on their motor-cycle expedition I spent the day at the Peradeniya Botanic Gardens, wandering around in a peace-ful reverie broken only by the sounds of what I took to be firecrackers in the distance. Walking back into town, I was surprised to see fire-damaged and looted shops and to encounter groups of clearly ill-intentioned men and squads of khaki-clad policemen armed with Lee-Enfield rifles. Both were warily giving each other a broad berth. I naively assumed that some kind of minor civil disturbance had been nipped in the bud with the time-ly arrival of the security forces, but later I heard Henry and Meyrick's account of the more widespread looting, arson and police indifference they had encountered. The violence was directed against ethnic Tamils, their homes and businesses. However, fire is an unselective weapon and, when one or two units in a terraced parade of shops is set alight, any possible jubilation experienced by neighbouring Sinhalese shopkeepers at the demise of a business rival was destined to be short-lived.

As we waited for dusk to fall, I was particularly struck by the concerned expression of our hotel-owner. He was a bearded man, strikingly big by Sri Lankan standards, and this, together with the broad, teak-decked veranda he paced along, endowed him with the air of a ship's captain awaiting the coming storm. The police were no longer to be seen, leaving the stage to the rioters. I had always assumed that rioting was something done by faceless mobs but, looking down from our well-appointed viewpoint, I was able to recognise several faces among those dexterously concealing petrol bombs under their lungis. This was all the more surprising as I had only been in Kandy for a few days. One of the rioters looked up, gave me a broad smile, waved in recognition and invited me to join the affray. Shaking my head in the European negative (itself an ambiguous gesture in South Asia), I found myself foolishly waving back. The previous day he had struck up a conversation in the Devon Restaurant, culminating in a proposal for me to smuggle two kilos of heroin back into the UK packed inside Sinhalese devil masks. For a full twenty-four hours (prior to his subsequent shouted suggestion for me to partake in a little fire-bombing and ethnic cleansing), my polite refusal had represented the easiest decision I had ever made.

The following night Meyrick and I, who had rooms in the basement, were woken up by a knock on the door and advised to gather up our belongings and evacuate the hotel because of the fire risk. Fortunately, the kind of loose cotton trousers with draw-strings affected by young travellers are highly interchangeable with pyjamas so, despite having missed out on the delights of boarding school, we too made a lightning appearance upstairs. We found the other guests already gone and the owner directing his remaining loyal staff to pour water from the topmost windows onto an adjacent rooftop in danger from sparks from nearby burning buildings. In the absence of a better plan, we found ourselves helping to shift things onto a small green in front of the hotel. Our first instinct was to rescue our beloved planters' chairs, greatly to the bemusement of the staff who had clearly prioritized the crates of beer and soft drinks. Once this process was completed, we were rewarded with a bottle of beer each and sat back on the chairs wondering where Henry had got to. At this point the situation rapidly evolved beyond our control as a handful of the staff ran off into the warm and smoky night, exchanging recriminations with the owner. Shortly afterwards he arranged for his most loyal retainers to watch over the pile of goods overnight, sent the remainder of the staff home, padlocked the hotel, and brought the Tamil family to our attention. He explained that all the other guests had checked into the Queen's Hotel and that we should likewise go there, along with our new-found travelling companions whose safety he could no longer guarantee.

Although the Queen's Hotel was only round the corner, a car was produced, and it was suggested that we drive right up to the entrance with the Tamil family lying in the back. On arrival, the security grill was down. We argued fruitlessly in the all-too-well-lit doorway while our companions became increasingly nervous. Fortunately we caught the attention of Henry in the lobby, who immediately sought redress further up the administrative chain. Henry's exclamation to the manager, who commented that he couldn't be sure exactly what sort of people Meyrick and I might be, still rings in my ears twenty years later: 'Who do you think they are, Israeli paratroopers?'

It began to rain heavily, which initially added to our misery, but it fortunately also cleared the streets, dampening the flames of Kandy both literally and metaphorically. Our Tamil companions then unwittingly began the most dangerous part of their journey, with an English teenager behind the wheel of an unfamiliar vehicle, a bottle or two of beer in his empty stomach, and a driving test passed at the third attempt only a few months before. Having wrestled in vain with the stick-shift, I gave up and slowly ground the protesting car around in second gear.

The Hotel Suisse was a modern top-end establishment set in lush gardens on the opposite side of the lake. The duty manager had not been expecting us and was not at all pleased to have a pair of bedraggled, bottom-end Europeans and a family of Tamil refugees cluttering his immaculate lobby. Nevertheless, this time we had two priceless advantages. First, the open-plan nature of the hotel meant that we were already inside, and second, we were geographically far enough removed from the town-centre mayhem. Meyrick, moreover, recently the author of a prize-winning dissertation on 'Human Aggression', had managed to make himself seem seriously threatening as he fulminated at the duty manager. We finally began to spread out our belongings as if to bed down for the night in the lobby. That clinched it: we were immediately assigned the honeymoon suite at ruinous expense – met by Henry, who now takes up the story again.

The next day we all held a council of war. The Tamil family came from Jaffna in the north. They were trying to get to Colombo and there was nothing to keep them in Kandy. The question was whether it was safe for them to travel. Meyrick and I also wanted to go to Colombo. Since there was little evidence of violence directed against foreigners, we felt fairly safe. Going with the Tamil family in their car would get us there faster, and perhaps our presence might afford them some sort of protection.

Before finalising this plan, we decided to seek the advice of my only contact in Kandy, a former ambassador. His brother was a cabinet minister and – much more important as far as Kandyans were concerned – was also the current *Diyawadana Nilame*, the Lay Guardian of the Buddha's Tooth Relic. The distinguished man's advice was highly practical. 'You must leave at 5 a.m. when the curfew is lifted. That way, anyone who has been up all night will be feeling tired and the people who have just woken up will still be sleepy. Fill the petrol tank the day before as there are long queues at the pumps and you won't be able to keep a secret that long. Henry should drive. Invent Muslim names for your Tamil friends and get the lady to wear her sari over her hair in the Muslim manner. Give the children a mild sedative so that they don't start talking Tamil at the wrong moment. Drive fast enough that you can't be stopped except at a road block, but not so fast as to draw attention to yourselves.'

We followed all this advice, and 6 a.m. the next day saw us speeding down the Colombo road. We passed Kegalla, rumoured to be a trouble-spot. We drove on through burned-out villages, including one where even at that early hour a small band of scavengers was picking like crows at the carcasses of two overturned lorries. Our spirits lifted as we reached the outskirts of Colombo. The Tamils were intending to stay with a family of evangelical preachers who lived in an area called Borella. The trouble was that they were not sure of the address. Also, what none of us had appreciated was that Borella had seen some of the worst violence. The Tamil-owned biscuit factory where half of Borella worked was a gutted shell. We drove round the streets looking for a clue. Suddenly there it was – a sign in English: 'I am the Way, the Truth and the Life, saith the Lord'. The preachers greeted us with warm smiles, their arms moving like semaphores as they told us their story. They had prayed night and day for our safety. They had had a dream. They had known we would come. Unfortunately their dream had not told them we could stay. Looking around, we could see they had a point: the house was wide open to the street and already a group of very unfriendly-looking people were staring at us through the window.

So it was back to the car. Our next target was a block of flats which turned out to have been gutted. At our third stop a malevolent old crone scuttled away to alert the neighbours to our arrival. Rajan, the Tamil father, tactfully pointed out that our presence in the car was making them conspicuous. Besides, an all-weekend curfew was due to come into force at nightfall, and we had to find ourselves a hotel. So we decided that it was time to part company. They were going to try two other friends and then head for the refugee camp. Before leaving, Rajan tried a small joke. In the past, he said, tourists who came to Sri Lanka to see its ruins had to go all the way to the ancient city of Pollonaruwa, but now the ruins were right here in the middle of Colombo.

Life under curfew is not a lot of fun so we decided to try India until things had calmed down. There was however a Catch 22. Tickets could only be obtained at the airport, which one was not allowed to enter without a ticket. The only way round this was to 'phone the airline, but the number was perpetually engaged. We 'phoned at fifteen-minute intervals throughout the morning and paid someone else to 'phone throughout the afternoon. Eventually we got lucky and the next day we were airborne.

We found Madras in a very emotional state. Every auto-rickshaw was flying a black flag. Every wall seemed to bear a slogan saying 'INVADE LANKA. SEND ARMY NOW'. As some of the first neutral observers to come out, we found that we were celebrities. Meyrick was cross-examined by a man from Indian Intelligence, and I got so bored with repeating the same story that I decided to write an article for the respected South Indian daily *The Hindu*. This was intended to be balanced and non-sensational, but the effect was rather spoiled when my anodyne title was changed into 'When the Police Turned a Blind Eye to Arson'. The only other change was that the 'Oberoi Group' was altered to 'an Indian hotel group'. But it was pretty clear which one I was talking about and I hoped that there would be a few uncomfortable questions at the AGM.

A week or so later we returned to Kandy. It had always been our plan to see the Perahera, one of the great festivals of Asia, when the Buddha's Tooth Relic is processed through the town by singers, dancers, thirty caparisoned elephants and a supporting cast of thousands. At the Hotel Suisse we received a mixed reception. Some of the staff came up and shook our hands while others were clearly less than pleased to see us. I had one odd experience. A walk round the town brought me to former Brownrigg Street. Originally named after a kinsman of mine, the street had long since been renamed but two of the old metal street-signs had survived and one was now projecting from the ruins of a shop. It seemed to be souvenir time. I tugged at the sign but it snagged on something. Inevitably a little crowd came to watch. Then a policeman appeared and I remembered firstly that looters were being shot on sight and secondly that Kandy police station would just have had time to receive its copy of 'When the Police Turned a Blind Eye to Arson'. Discretion seemed to have the edge over valour. Flashing the policeman a smile, I beat an undignified retreat.

The riots of July 1983 turned out to be the start of the long, cruel insurgency which only now seems at last to be coming to a negotiated conclusion. The fighting was concentrated in Tamil-majority areas in the north and east of the island. Kandy was largely spared from this trouble, and over the years I made several further visits. On each occasion I renewed my acquaintance with the hotelier who hid the Tamil family and with the helpful ex-ambassador. Back in Britain, Richard and I kept in touch as he established a distinguished medical career. Many years later I had the very great pleasure of proposing him for membership of the Travellers Club.

HENRY BROWNRIGG & RICHARD QUINTON

Look no Farther than Barking

The streets were jammed so a cab was pointless. I was already late. A hastily organised evening appointment in Mayfair, which seemed like a good idea when the arrangement was made, was looking distinctly inauspicious. But perhaps all was not lost. It was a fine day and, accepting the fact that occasionally I should take a little exercise, I considered a brisk walk through the back-streets from Covent Garden a sensible solution.

Having hardly set out, though, I came across a Buddhist monk sitting by the railings in Leicester Square. He had cropped, grey hair, little round glasses and a trim, grey robe. He sat cross-legged on the pavement with a huge banner behind him: 'The Supreme Enlightened Being, Hathagata, can answer all your questions. Know the Secrets of Future Medicine, Future Events, Future Technology'.

The Supreme Enlightened Being to answer all of your questions, now that was an offer. In my distant past I had been offered a place at medical school and, although I had taken a different path in life, I remained interested in medical solutions of all kinds. I hesitated, I was late, but what did I have to lose? I stopped and walked up to the meagre monk and asked him to tell me about the future of medicine, half expecting some yarn built around the correct use of ectoplasm or marijuana.

'Oh no! I am not Hathagata, I am his disciple. He is a man, and I am a woman.' Could this be why I have such poor luck with the fair sex, I wondered. They always look so much more obvious in the magazines. To be fair, one monk's crew cut looks much the same as the next. 'That is what I meant,' I offered diplomatically. She did not look convinced.

'Hathagata has reached the highest level of enlightenment, and he can answer anything you ask of him,' she told me with an earnest look. It appeared that the master never pounded the beat, but did offer his information freely to those who made it to his ashram in Barking. I was given an address and told that he accepted audiences on Fridays at seven p.m. A little disappointed that illumination was not as instant as the poster suggested, I made my excuses and left, just as an unwieldy pack of giggling schoolgirls descended on the monk to ask where the Spice Girls would be in next week's charts. How shallow, I thought. Mind you . . . 'Will answer all of your questions about the future' . . . I tried to remember what races were running that week, perhaps the lottery numbers or . . . I walked on and made my appointment in Mayfair with minutes to spare.

Unfortunately I was born with an insane curiosity that lies dormant for long periods but, once roused, is very hard to quench unless the object of interest has been explained, visited or viewed. A little trip it would have to be. Otherwise, how could I live with myself if the Supreme Enlightened Being had really returned to walk amongst the dark Satanic mills of Barking.

I set off after work on Friday armed with a gift of food as a peace offering and a list of questions that I had been preparing. A sinking feeling settled on me as the train rattled on, the carriages emptied and we headed to what seemed like the fringes of nowhere. I alighted at Barking with the sun just starting to fade in a pale blue sky – always a sign of foreboding in a 'B' movie. I stepped into the street trying to look inconspicuous, which is hard when you are carrying a briefcase and wearing a grey suit with a jolly handkerchief blossoming from the pocket, and the people hanging around on street-corners in slightly sinister groups aren't. Purposefully I headed for the Hathagata Centre, which proved to be harder to find than I had expected, not least because it was nothing more than a terraced house with a tiny brass plaque declaring the true holy nature of the place.

A cute Korean girl in her early twenties answered the door. 'Come in, we have been expecting you,' she said in slightly stilted English. She declared that she was my translator for the evening and that I should wait a few minutes while Hathagata prepared himself for the audience.

Finally I was ushered into what looked remarkably like a suburban sitting-room with a large, green sofa placed in the bay-window. In the centre of the sofa sat a tall man in the lotus position – hands on knees, thumb and middle finger forming a circle in the classic posture of the enlightened eastern guru. He was perhaps in his mid-sixties, with short-cropped hair and a detached look that I felt was a little too studied. Beams of light from the disappearing sun poured through the net curtains and formed a soft halo round his body. His hands caught my attention: they were enormously long, with long, fine fingers, and almost disturbingly out of proportion to his body.

I presented my peace offering to break the ice. Hathagata spoke in Korean and the girl settled demurely in a seat beside me to translate. 'Hathagata says Thank you!' And so the audience began. The Enlightened One pondered his next statement, staring mistily into one corner of the room, then into the corner opposite, at the same time working his jaw as if he were battling with a stubborn, invisible toffee – a pattern he would follow before every statement or answer. He started to explain the history of his life and the hardships that he had endured – grinding poverty in rural Korea, lack of education, violence – and how he had overcome these adversities to receive total illumination that descended on him one day like a beam of light while he prayed. He had realised that no one had been so illuminated. This new-found gift allowed him to comprehend more than anyone alive, and foresee the future.

As I listened to the broken translation of Hathagata's words, the door opened and the monk from Leicester Square appeared.

'Hello,' she said. 'I would have called to give you directions, but I knew it would be unnecessary because I dreamed that you would be here.' Then she promptly glided away. It was the last I saw of her.

Soon Hathagata had broadened his autobiographical scope to include the translator sat beside me. He explained how she had worked in a dead-end waitressing job in a Chinese restaurant until she had discovered him. He had changed her life and filled it with a new direction.

Then we moved to the purpose of my visit, to receive some insight into the future of medicine, the techniques that will be employed to provide universal relief from disease. I asked my questions of the ex-waitress, who would think for a second as she tried to find the right words, then spout a staccato stream of Korean. Occasionally she would shoot an uncertain glance in my direction, which made me wonder about the accuracy of the translation. A little disappointing that divine illumination does not provide for understanding languages as well. My question on medical advancement was pondered and, after a quick bout of phantom chewing, the answer came.

'Hathagata says that he comprehends how to heal the body through manipulation of its own invisible energies. He can explain everything to you, but you would not understand because your consciousness is not as expanded as his.'

'Perhaps he could explain in simple terms?'

'Hathagata says that what he understands is beyond your comprehension, because he is illuminated and you are not.' So much for answering all questions on all subjects.

The Supreme Enlightened Being continued. He assured me that his great knowledge allowed him to cure many people of diseases that doctors had declared incurable. He cited several examples: how he had tried to help the president of Korea, who was very ill, but had been ignored, so the man had died. My knowledge of the recent history of Korea was not up to speed, so I could not determine the veracity of this statement or the accuracy of the neophyte's translation.

I pressed for more detail. I wanted to go away with at least some idea of what he was peddling. Hathagata replied that whilst I, as a normal human being, was too restricted spiritually to understand how he healed people, he could teach me in simple terms but it would take several years because I could learn only by studying his techniques as an apprentice at his elbow. To do this I would have to leave my material world and become his disciple.

Whilst my curiosity might extend to a couple of hours on a Friday evening, it did not run to taking that sort of leap of faith. I ignored the comment. Hathagata looked disappointed.

'Take any of the greatest minds and pit them against me in competition,' he continued. 'I will be able to answer fully when they are not able to answer at all. Take any professor from Oxford or Cambridge and ask them questions and they will not be able to compete with me because they are working from worldly knowledge which is limited but I, having been illuminated, comprehend everything.'

An image passed through my mind: Oxbridge dons versus the Supreme Being in a heavy-weight play-off. Black robes and mortar boards on one side, saffron on the other. Perfect for TV.

Hathagata had just launched into a critique of those dark souls that sought to undermine the magnitude of his illumination when another Korean girl glided in and asked if we all wanted tea.

While this was being made and Hathagata preached on and the redeemed waitress translated, I watched the sky outside become an ever darker shade of blue tinged with fiery blades of red from the setting sun.

I was becoming mindful that I would have to make my way back to the station, running the gauntlet of suspicious characters perhaps emboldened by the darkness. The more the sun set, the greater the flight of my imagination.

As I held the bowl the tea-girl had brought, wondering how soon I could edge away, Hathagata returned to the subject of my giving up earthly bondage for a life of illumination under his patronage. He said that whilst he had gathered a few disciples in Britain, they were of a low order viz. the ex-waitress, which I thought a bit harsh since she was translating. He said that a person of my calibre, if I joined him, could end up as head of the British division of his worldwide network. Chief British Monk. It did have a ring to it.

Then a sly look passed across Hathagata's face and he mumbled something the ex-waitress did not translate. But the way she eyed me implied that accommodation was limited and the Supreme Enlightened Being had just suggested whose room I might end up in. She smiled at me warmly.

As I raised the tea to my lips, they seemed to slide to the edge of their seats in anticipation, then froze when I stopped and asked another question. They looked disappointed. Perhaps it was an issue of Oriental courtesy but it did bring Boris Karloff to mind. The sun had almost disappeared – I seemed to hear the howl of a wolf outside! I raised the bowl to my lips again. 'Drink, drink,' Hathagata said. Both he and the translator almost collapsed off their seats, eyes wide and intense. Time for a sharp exit, I thought. Better to be rude than wake up woozily sporting a bald head and a saffron robe.

The train clacked away overland before diving underground for the centre of town, leaving behind the dark blue evening sky of Barking. What an interesting encounter, I thought. Right, where to next?

MARK BRETT-WARBURTON

Going up to Oxford

Port Meadow is Oxford's oldest monument, given by King Alfred to the Freemen of the City, recorded in the Domesday Book and never since built upon or ploughed. Described by the Countryside Commission as 'magnificent', it is a Site of Special Scientific Interest, a Scheduled Ancient Monument and a Special Area of Conservation.

It is also four hundred bleak and treeless acres of thistles, weeds, cow-pats and cattle-trampled mud. First-time picnickers lose their appetite try-ing to find a salubrious square yard. Joggers stick gingerly to its few beat-en paths. Its hummocks and tufts are nurtured daily by the dogs whose owners unleash them then look away, whistling. Once a year the sheriff and his entourage process in full regalia around the Meadow's three-mile perimeter. They are Taking Stock, and feature on a quiet day in the local press. Once a year, a day or two before, a team of cleaners precedes them with heavy-duty poop-scoops.

The Thames redeems this famed but unlovely wasteland. Here the river is no longer the dignified Isis, the broad, straight stretch that borders Christ Church Meadow, where couples stroll along summer towpaths, the college boat-houses stand impressive (and the derelict college barges sank), where punters pushing in from the Cherwell misjudge the depth and lose their pole. This is the Thames upstream of Folly Bridge reverting to its mellow rural self. The No Mooring signs grow less aggressive; wash-ing is strung to dry on gaily painted narrow boats; towpaths dwindle into tracks where hawthorns cling and nettles sting. A part-time boat yard or two, the backs of factories, then the river curves tranquil and expansive along the length of Port Meadow. In exceptionally wet winters it bursts its banks, usefully sluicing *le tout*. Freezing, this becomes a smooth, white wonderland that puts the Oxford Ice Rink temporarily out of business.

Here was the solution to a personal problem. Recently divorced and in consequence impoverished, I would live here cheaply afloat. From Walton Well Road a track leads to a boat station with walkways and jetties for mooring. I would turn my stern on Port Meadow's dung and mud, and eat, sleep and work to the lapping and sway of the waves. Birds would perch unfearing on my prow. I would bring the bow round and have a different river vista every day.

The only piece missing in this idyll was the boat. It had to be high-roofed and roomy: not for me the constant stooping and inevitably bumped head of the lowly narrow boat. Also, my filing system meant spreading piles of papers *passim*. Weeks of scouring glossy magazines and Thames Valley marinas produced finally the ideal floating home, a forty-two-foot Princess. With the Free Marine Mortgage Guidance came much unsolicited advice, such as: 'Lovely job, go to sea in her you could'. Seafaring had not originally figured in my thinking, but why not? Would it be wise, though, with the Princess' one engine? The ever-helpful mariners consulted in boat yards and bars were as one: I would, they agreed, want my blinking brains testing, putting to sea single-screwed. So I dropped the Princess and set off again in search of a roomy, high-roofed, twin-screwed craft. One marina I enquired at happened to be busy.

'What are you planning on,' shouted the salesman. 'Cross-channel or transatlantic?'

'Well, to start with I'll be mooring her in Oxford and just pootling up and down the river a bit.' I noticed a sudden stunned hush before the salesroom burst into laughter.

There is for pleasure craft on the Thames a walking-pace speed limit dictated by one's wash. Or rather not dictated: one mustn't make one. Eights in training aim to exceed it so are, exceptionally, exempt. Even the Princess would have been over-powered, and twin screws ludicrous.

I took to asking round, humbly, for a large boat with a little engine. A familiar figure in marina salesrooms by now, I sensed the salesmen growing less deferential. 'Tried the Mekong Delta?' grinned one. 'Sorry but we're right out of royal barges,' said another.

Salvation came in the shape of the Aleutian, a thirty-four-foot beauty comfortably broad in the beam and drawing only three feet. She was lying at Staines but nearer Monte Carlo in the suave, white sweep of her lines. Seduced by this, I was attracted also by the prow berths for my children and the king-sized bed astern. With her massive fuel tank and slow, chugging consumption, fuel would probably have gone up by the time the boat needed refilling. She was unique, the only one of her kind ever made, according to the liquidator of the boat yard where I bought her. Sailing into a lock days later, I learned why.

'Isn't that the Aleutian?' The lock-keeper seemed quite excited. 'Never thought I'd see it afloat.' Gratified by the recognition, if less so by the comment, I was told the vessel's story. Her Norfolk manufacturers had invested heavily in a revolutionary design, and just as heavily in promoting it in readiness for an imminent London Boat Show. Full-page advertisements in the trade press; potential buyers flown in from abroad; journalists and VIPs invited to Earls Court for the champagne-lubricated launch. Amidst yards of red carpet, with bikini-clad sales aids draped over the rails, the managing director had mounted the dais to welcome all those gathered there to witness this milestone in riverboat design. As he cleared his throat to speak, an oath came from below. Loud banging followed, then more cussing. The MD's mike was turned up, and the next few minutes saw the assembly entertained by a smooth PR-speech delivered full blast but drowned out by cursing workmen from within. Mottled interestingly black with anger and red with embarrassment, the MD mounted the gangplank. His guests followed hard behind. The beauties in bikinis smiled dutifully on as VIPs, journalists and ex-potential buyers stepped down into the chaos of the uncompleted cabins.

'They was still sticking cladding on the walls,' continued the lock-keeper, 'trying to glue it on quick with their dirty hands they was. The papers had a ball the next day, laughed the boat off the Show.'

Back in Staines, the marine mortgage guidance had been taken and the balance paid by my bank (where the usually unenthusing manager had become another man since borrowing rates topped twenty per cent). Armed with Thames Water licence and insurance certificate, provisions, bedding and not a clue about boats, I was dropped off at Staines in teeming rain.

'Shouldn't try another test-run in this muck,' said the caretaker.

'Test-run be damned. This is showtime, I'm off.' Taking the keys, I shuttled my stuff through the deluge. The last words I heard shouted from the shelter of his doorway were something about red Caution signs being up on the river. As if anyone would want to swim in this weather!

I stowed the food first, if only because the sodden cartons were collapsing. Then wiped the bed dry, and the berths. Drying the worktops and control console took another towel. As daylight faded I switched on the neon strips and saw the condensation thick on walls and windows. Condensation on the ceiling was dripping stalactitically back onto the bed. Wiping and rewiping the cabin and its contents took my last two towels, three rugger shirts brought on as substitutes, and the best part of an hour. At least with the windows cleared I would be able to see outside. Or would have done had night not fallen unnoticed in the meantime.

I started the engine to charge the batteries sufficiently for a few hours' light, then hunkered down for a first inglorious night. Shortly after day-break came a knocking on the hull: 'Oi you in there, there's no sleeping in the yard'.

'Not to worry, I didn't get a wink.'

'That's all right then. But the boss said to tell you the river's running at seven knots.'

'He told me she could do eight so what's the problem?'

The voice vanished – probably not for want of a withering answer but because heavy rain was falling again.

Starting the engine and releasing the mooring lines, I reversed clear of the neighbouring berths in what is best described as a bump-start. Only to be blown back again broadside on to the davit of a yacht. Trying to accel-erate away would mean scraping both boats so, remembering a six-foot pole on deck, I braved the rain, checked no one was looking, then com-mitted the waterman's cardinal sin of pushing off from another vessel.

Would the headwind, I wondered, wipe out my one-knot advantage over the fast-running river? No. It reduced it to half a knot or so. At this giddy pace, making scarcely a ripple let alone a wash, I edged into the fair-way and up river. Roaring along at full throttle was not unlike revving a vehicle *in vacuo* when it's bogged down in the desert. The raincloud lift-ed and revealed trees and buildings on each bank; the same trees and buildings remained in view for an uncomfortably long time. By mid-morning viz. a mile or two further I was cold, bored and numbed – from nervousness, I realised. If the engine failed, Old Father Thames would just roll me along, maybe not down to the mighty sea but certainly past Eton and Kew. The embarrassment if godsons or botanical acquaintances hap-pened to be watching! Drifting helplessly through Chelsea would be even more humiliating. Would the Thames Barrier help? Or would I fetch up off Southend or even Ostend, washed away with not so much as a single screw?

I decided it was time to moor at some welcoming riverside inn. Crossing, eventually, from bank to bank, all I found on the lawned waterfronts of highly desirable properties was large warnings: No Mooring. Not all were so bluntly offputting. Some were more explicitly so: Mooring here is Prohibited. By Order. Very well, I was willing to forego the friendly inn and simply settle for somewhere to stop. Men were working on a jetty up ahead; I was one of the boating fraternity now; a friend in need . . . As I nosed in with a cheery wave one of them grabbed a pole and pushed me off. Perhaps it was just as well I misheard what he shouted, scowling.

After another eternity, or maybe a mile, I saw a stretch of bank free of workmen, mansions and No Mooring signs. I drew in close, went on deck and jumped ashore with a mooring line in my hand. Then slipped over on the wet grass and was pulled along bodily as the boat sailed blithely on. Saved by a tree, which I threw the rope round fast, I made a mental note to manœuvre in neutral next time. But still regretted forgetting to enquire about the brakes.

Over bun break on the bank I read the river guide. The next obstacle would be locks – there were, I learned, to be twenty-eight of them from Staines to Osney Bridge. I racked my brains for facts about locks but all I came up with was a vague memory of a Sunday afternoon spent with a maiden aunt admiring the flower-beds of what the signs said was the Best Kept in Britain. But *nil desperandum*: I remembered also the cosy lock-keeper's cottage; at each lock a friendly face would no doubt appear, to open and close the lock-gates for me and perhaps pass the time of day before waving me on my way.

I sailed on, heeding the river guide's warning about the first lock coming, very slowly, into view. Keep to the Marked Channel and Form an Orderly Queue at the Lay-by Moorings, it said. On no account Drift near the Weir. Forming an orderly queue, I came alongside, caught a mooring-ring with the hook of my pole and climbed ashore to tie up with a deftness that surprised me. Then waited for the lock-keeper. None came. I climbed up the bank beside the downstream gates. There was no one around. But there was a rainswept cottage and flooded flower-beds. Locks were operated electrically, I had read, or failing that hydraulically, by hand. So assuming this was the lock-keeper's day off, I found what was clearly the manual control and gave its massive wheel a tentative turn. The gates gave an ear-splitting creak, followed by what sounded like a hundred flushing cisterns. I looked down: the gates were ajar and through them was pouring a torrent of roaring water. I was emptying the lock-chamber! I looked around guiltily: no alarms were sounding or warning lights flashing. So I turned the wheel further: the maelstrom below became an onslaught of water that must surely carry the gates away. Outside, the boat was bobbing like a cork. Until, with the gates wide open, the turmoil subsided as suddenly as it had started. The level inside the lock was at one with the river below.

I returned to the boat and steered into the chamber, but too fast. With the current blocked and the water unwontedly calm, I over-revved and went careening towards the gates up stream. Remembering neutral, I jumped out with the mooring line. And slipped over on the lockside. I was dragged along again, but felt I was improving as a human anchor. I hoped no one had noticed.

They had. 'Don't you know about reversing?' yelled the lock-keeper, brought out by the commotion.

'Well yes, but I'm going forwards, up stream.'

'Not with my lock-gates in the way you're not. You reverse engines to stop, then come ashore and tie up.'

'Er yes, thanks.' That explained about the brakes.

He left me to wind the tail gates shut: closing lock-gates against the flow entails rather more effort than opening them with it. Then he pressed a button and the head gates parted, electrically; we were now on the receiving end of the incoming torrent. Aboard as the lock-chamber refilled, I enjoyed the novel experience of feeling my five tons of boat rise beneath me. Until with a jerk the bow dipped dramatically. The stern was still rising; plates were falling from shelves, papers sliding down the floor which was now at a Titanic angle. I staggered to the deck. The lock-keeper was trying to untie the bow-rope: it was short and very taut from holding down five tons.

'Could you try remembering to leave some slack?' He waited unsmiling for me to leave. He did not wave me on my way.

The next lock was manned more affably. Despite the drizzle the lock-keeper came out to operate the gates and enquire where I was bound. Not having any flower-beds with which to win awards, he seemed to welcome the distraction. He was curious about Port Meadow. 'Not planning on overnighting there, are you?'

'Overnighting, overweeking, overmonthing. I may even put up a name-plate *Dunroamin*.'

'So what about the Council?'

'What Council?'

'The Oxford lot. You know they've stopped issuing residential permits? You can moor for a maximum two nights but anything over that and they'll be on you.'

I was dumbfounded. My vision of bliss was vanishing; had my long search for a floating home been in vain? But *Port* Meadow, I remonstrated. Was it named that for nothing? Surely living on a mooring in the city's one-time harbour would be truly in the spirit of ancient Oxnaford, maintaining a tradition centuries old?

'Dunno about that,' the lock-keeper shrugged. 'What with a Labour council an' all.'

We agreed it was best for our conversation to have never taken place. Promising to keep my lawless intent to himself, the lock-keeper opened the head gates and I pressed on. So did the rain. The torrents of it falling on the river again seemed to unify the horizon. As punishment perhaps for attempting the trip in such weather, the downpour seemed to single me out, driving straight into the windscreen whichever way I tacked. However, the rainwater did show usefully where the cabin leaked.

The weather improved on the third day. Or was it the fourth? Puttering against the current from dawn till dusk, opening and closing lock-gates all day, I was losing track of time. The river guide proved an invaluable reminder – marine marching orders, travelogue and vade mecum combined. It also contained some disconcerting information. With the vital statistics of every lock it gave the number and height of the arches of each bridge. That at Osney, just before Port Meadow, has a clearance of seven foot six. With its non-stoop cabins my boat sat over twelve feet off the water. This gave me much to ponder as I edged on past Sonning and Reading.

By Goring the problem was keeping me from sleeping. Various solutions and scenarios came to mind, some so surrealistic that by the light of the following day I thought I must have drifted into them dreaming. They might however be worth a try. Or not, according to the lock-keeper at Osney. I had shaved for Oxford; made quite stately progress along the Isis; been waved at by walkers on the banks, cursed by a few coxes and looked down on by tourists atop Folly Bridge; then had opened the gates and entered his lock quite cockily after twenty-seven attempts. He emerged from his cottage and came across shaking his head.

'Yes I know,' I said. 'I was wondering if we could have a word about that.' He listened very patiently as I explained my first proposal. If you load a boat it floats lower – we all know about Plimsoles – so with enough ballast might we just get the superstructure under? He looked thoughtful, asked my boat's length, beam and tonnage, and went away to fetch a pocket calculator.

'Now,' he said, returning. 'I've worked it out roughly. The ballast you'd need to lower this five feet would be about – and this is only approximate – would be about sixty tons.'

'Wouldn't that sink it?' I asked naively.

'Sink it? You'd need a mine-sweeper to even tow it along the bottom.'

So I played my second card. Perhaps the Oxford Ist XV, plus the coach to make it eight a side, could all bounce up and down together and, pushing hard on the arch above, ease it under the bridge? The lock-keeper shook his head again.

I'd saved my ace for last. 'These locks,' I said. 'I've noticed they all have, like water-level measures, up to twelve feet or so.' He nodded: 'Headwater gauges and tailwater gauges they're called'.

'Right. So if we spoke nicely to your colleague upstream – at Godstow, is it? – and he held back an extra few feet just long enough to get me under the bridge . . . It's worth a bob or two to me.'

He was visibly impressed. 'Sounds all right to me, Sir. But we'll need authority to keep that much back. I'll go and talk to Thames Water.'

He soon returned, still unsmiling. 'Well, I've spoken to my supervisor in Reading, Sir, and he agrees, technically you're quite right.' I brightened. 'But he's asked me to point out that letting that much go again would risk widespread flooding throughout the lower Thames Valley.'

So, not wishing to inconvenience anyone, I backed down and out of the lock.

My return along the Isis was more deflated than stately. Whether tourists gaped, walkers waved or coxes cussed I failed to notice. I threw myself on the mercy of the next marina down stream. They could, they said, crane me out and back in again if a trailer could be arranged. A haulier had one and could deliver to Port Meadow if a Wide Load escort was arranged. Readers requiring a Wide Load escort might like to know that Thames Valley Constabulary can provide one free of charge if given three days' notice.

One week plus three days from Staines, my ideal if illicit floating home was moored at Port Meadow. A few floating home-improvements, then the Aleutian was ready for not so much a maiden as a second-marriage voyage. We planned this to be up stream to Lechlade. I had checked the depth all the way there – ample for our three-foot draught. *Idem* the height of every bridge en route – all well clear of the Aleutian's super-structure. We proceeded happily the length of Port Meadow; the weather was clement, the current considerate: had there been trees or buildings on the bank they would have sailed out of sight in no time.

Coming into sight before long was Godstow Bridge. It was soon sufficiently so for the party to fall silent. Everyone looked at me. I looked at the river guide. Its authors, publishers, distributors, wholesalers, retailers and holders of subsidiary rights should be jointly and severally sued. They had omitted to mention the width of the largest arch. It was rather narrower than the boat.

I served a muted lunch then sailed back the length of Port Meadow. Which for the remainder of my Oxford boating days constituted the Aleutian's full cruising range.

And yet a case could now be made for *force majeure*. The boat was my home: we had nowhere to be forcibly removed or safely repatriated to. I sought riverine asylum. And not unlike the Home Office with a tricky refugee, the Council kept my dossier pending for so long that some law of limitations might have applied. The Aleutian and I and the birds on our bow became the only residents (officially connived-at) of Port Meadow.

MICHAEL TOMKINSON

True Romance

The most romantic thing I ever did happened quite spontaneously, hurt no one and still leaves a warm glow. I had persuaded a company which manufactured hot-air balloons that I might buy one and they sent one down to Maidenwell for a week, with a pilot to teach me to fly it. Very early in the morning and in the evenings, when the wind was light, we made a series of flights over much of Cornwall, which taught me a lot about the topography of the countryside, as well as allowing me unusually intimate views into friends' gardens.

One morning we set off at six o'clock from Port Eliot on the eastern edge of the county and drifted slowly west, just inland from the English Channel. We passed over a series of deep valleys running down to the sea, descended into each and so caught secluded hidden treasures unaware in the dawn sunlight. In one wooded coomb we were able to descend until we almost touched the floor of a sunny glade where tall foxgloves grew thickly.

Leaning out of the basket, I was able to gather a large armful of the flowers. Across the valley there was a wooden chalet perched on the hillside. As we started to ascend, drifting silently towards it, a pretty girl in a white nightie came out onto the balcony and stretched her arms ecstatically above her head. She was looking away from us, gazing out to sea. I looked at the pilot and he nodded. We passed a bare arm's length from her and, as she turned in surprise, I leaned out again and passed the bouquet to her. For a moment our eyes met, and then there was the roar of the burner and we shot up into the sky. I will never know if there was a disbelieving someone still in bed indoors, to whom she tried to explain the flowers, but I do know that we shared a rare moment of true romance.

ROBIN HANBURY-TENISON

One of the Best

To celebrate the centenary of motor car manufacture a year or so ago, *The Times* ran a series in praise of 'the best twenty cars ever made in Britain', chosen by a poll of readers of *Classic & Sportscar* magazine. Each was to be commemorated by a full-page article with a specially commissioned drawing by a leading industrial artist. Framed copies of the drawings signed by Lord Montagu of Beaulieu could be obtained by subscription. The roll of honour ranged from the Rolls Royce Silver Ghost of 1907 and the Jaguar XK120 to the more mundane Morris Minor and Mini. I was surprised to find in the list the Ford Y Model of 1932. I had once owned just such a car, but it had not occurred to me that it was one of the best.

The Y Model was designed in an emergency by Henry Ford and his team with the aim of saving his colossal investment in the factory complex at Dagenham. Finished at the time of the Slump in the early Thirties, it desperately needed a mass-production car to sell in sufficient quantity to keep the company going. Ford designed a simple four-seater saloon that could be made and sold at a profit for £120, later reduced to £100. It saved the Ford UK company and was manufactured continuously for over twenty-five years.

On my salary in 1958 of sixteen pounds per week I could not afford a new car, so my wife and I were delighted when a colleague offered to sell us his twenty-year-old Ford Y Model for what he had paid for it: fifteen pounds. It gave us six months of motoring without any need for expensive luxuries such as servicing. It was a good runner but did have some shortcomings. When applied, the rod brakes made little difference to the car's speed: as the absolute maximum was barely forty mph this did not bother us unduly. The windscreen wipers, powered – or supposed to be – by a rubber tube from the engine manifold, rarely moved when needed. I should perhaps have bought a new tube but in the fine, dry summer of 1958 it slipped my mind. Only once or twice did I have to drive through a downpour with my head out of the window.

The bodywork had a respectable appearance when viewed from a reasonable distance – say ten yards – and it was held together by coats of house-paint applied by a previous owner. The nearside rear wheel-arch had come adrift but had been secured by self-tapping screws through the bodywork above. Unfortunately, the screws were a couple of inches too long and projected close to the tyres' surface. One had to take left-hand corners slowly because otherwise the car would lean over so sharply as to puncture its own tyre. A certain amount of abrasion was desirable, as there was little tread left anyway.

There was a leak in the roof where the original sliding panel had been replaced by plywood which had subsequently rotted. I solved that by filling the holes with Polyfilla and covering the whole roof with black Fablon.

Our summer holiday was spent motoring in the West Country. Driving home through Taunton we rattled over some cobble-stones and part of the exhaust-pipe fell off. Embarrassed by the stares of passing shoppers, I jumped out and retrieved it. This turned out to be a fortunate move as later in the journey the driver's seat came away completely from its rusty bolts when I stamped hard on the brakes. In consequence the seat and I fell smartly backwards. I looked around for something with which to prop up the seat and found that the pipe was exactly the right length.

The Y Model had other technical features rather different from those of cars today. One was that the doors were hinged to the rear. This was somewhat dangerous were they to swing open whilst driving. And swing open my door did increasingly often because the catch was worn. However, serendipity came to my aid again in the form of a yellow duster. It was just the right length for us to tie the inside door handle to the steering-column. We got used to tying and untying it each time we got in and out.

Later in the summer a more serious problem emerged: the clutch was so worn that we had to change gear without it. Switching on the engine needed special ingenuity: the secret was to start the car in gear so that it hopped forward like a sparrow.

When autumn came we began to wonder how much longer we could keep the thing going. One evening the door-bell rang and two men politely enquired if the old Ford outside was ours. They were renovating a van and needed just such an engine. Did ours run well and were we interested in selling? I assured them that it was a good runner and that I would

FROM A LETTER TO MY MOTHER, 1940

consider any serious offer. They proposed four pounds, which I immediately rejected as unrealistic. Vigorous negotiations resulted in a price satisfactory to both parties, viz. four pounds ten, or £4·50 in modern money. Off they went to raise the cash. Before they returned the next morning I thought I had better tidy up the car, in case its dilapidated appearance put them off in broad daylight. I gave it a good dusting, cleaned the windows and removed the yellow duster from the steering-wheel and the broken exhaust-pipe from behind the driver's seat.

Next day they returned with the four pounds and ten shillings in exchange for the key and the log-book. I threw in a cautious explanation of the starting procedure. We watched nervously from behind the curtain as they got into the car. It started first time as usual and, as it hopped forward smartly, the driver's door swung open and the driver's seat collapsed backwards.

We hid behind the sofa and listened for angry footsteps. None came; we peeped out; they and the car had gone. It was after all a good runner, and a good jumper too.

MICHAEL ALLEN

From a Letter to my Mother, 1940

All the excitement started at 4.57 p.m. last Saturday, 7 September. A friend and I were at the Gaumont Cinema in Chelsea and, apart from the fact that the police refused to let us leave owing to 'their' being overhead, we knew nothing of this raid, which was in fact the commencement of the Blitz. We left for tea just before the All Clear sounded and, other than a few people staring eastward from the Albert Bridge, nothing seemed to be amiss. I then left Oakley Street just as the siren was going at about 8.30 p.m., saying airily that I had someone to meet at Trafalgar Square at 9.15 and had, so I thought, plenty of time to walk along the Embankment. By that time the rumour had got round that the docks were on fire and when I saw the glare in the sky I knew that this raid was really one to be worried about.

I had not got very far along Cheyne Walk when I heard a 'plane overhead and a second or two later was petrified to hear a screaming bomb falling – it seemed – on me. I dived across the road to take cover under a wall and then to my relief heard two explosions on the other side of the river. By this time I was thoroughly frightened – my left hand had become temporarily paralysed – and I felt there was only one thing to be done, and that was to find a public shelter. I saw the welcome 'S' sign in the distance and was haring off in its direction when I heard someone from one of the flats in Royal Hospital Road asking me if I would care to go in for shelter; needless to say, I loped in gratefully. I was made very welcome by this family; we had cigarettes, beer and chatter and in no time I had recovered myself. The fire could be seen very plainly in the distance now that it was dark and there seemed to be a lot doing.

I finally decided to leave for my 9.15 rendezvous at Trafalgar Square at 9.20 – which was the earliest lull there seemed to be. I found it impossible to get a bus and had to walk all the way to Charing Cross, where I arrived at 10.15, by which time my friend had gone. I hung about for twenty minutes or so, then decided I should make an effort to find him and get back to Lewisham as quickly as possible. The two places he might be were the Strand Palace Hotel, where he had put up the previous night, and a public shelter under Charing Cross station where we had been on a previous occasion. I plumped for the Strand Palace first; I was unsuccessful but left a note; the second alternative I did not try as it was getting late and bombs could be heard falling in the vicinity. I went to the station and found a train for Ladywell due to leave any minute.

Having found a seat, I was hoping to get home adequately early, but to my dismay the train did not move for nearly half an hour, and in that time we heard four high-explosive bombs drop quite close – in fact it seemed that the station or Hungerford Bridge must be hit. Imagine my relief when a train was heard coming over the bridge and into the next platform. We left Charing Cross at about 11.15.

The fire in the east could now be seen quite plainly and, as we ran (very slowly) along to London Bridge, we saw four other small ones. At intervals we had to flatten out on the seats as the whistle of bombs sounded too close. From London Bridge to New Cross we passed close to the western edge of the conflagration, which seemed to stretch for miles – it was in fact reported to extend for seven miles. At times there was a blaze on either side of the track and for the whole journey it seemed as if we were illuminated by some giant demoniac neon light. With so many enemy aircraft overhead we felt rather excited and impressed by the sight. The silhouette of the ships in the docks could be seen, and the roofless, flaming warehouses made the whole scene seem unreal, like some fantastic film.

Lewisham station was at length achieved, and here I faced the dilemma of getting out and walking the rest of the way to Ladywell (the next station) or being taken by train. I decided to go by train and so sat tight – with bombs and bombers cruising round. After sitting there for half an hour, I gave up and started to walk.

I had not gone more than a hundred yards when things became hotter and I took shelter under the railway arch – over which my train proceeded to pass. Two or three fairly heavy explosions shook me – they seemed unconscionably close – but after a few minutes the activities passed on to another quarter and I made my way home as quickly as I could. On this very short journey I encountered a middle-aged man, very tired and worn: he was a 'gasman' and had just left Greenwich where they were keeping watch on the gasworks, fearing an explosion. This fortunately never came.

When I arrived home I found everyone at our next-door neighbours' – in their cellar taking shelter. These people were the kindest and sincerest I have ever known. I was given whisky and ginger beer, biscuits and smokes. There we all sat, half sleeping and half waking, all night long. The glare in the sky changed slightly every time we went out, but its intensity hardly changed at all, only its position. One or two bombs came perilously close; in fact one caused us all to hold our breaths and press in against the wall. At last things died down and, after a cup of tea (the most welcome I have ever known), I went to bed at about 5.30 a.m., thoroughly exhausted. Apart from being disturbed by the All Clear, I slept until 7.30 then got up and went to church.

During the service we could hear explosions in the distance – delayed-action bombs, we learned afterwards. I walked back and saw some of the first air-raid damage: there were craters here and there and the showrooms of the Electric Light Company had had a direct hit. This was a new building constructed on a steel frame, and it lurched over the main road, seeming to leer at the civilisation that had constructed and destroyed it.

I had arranged to go to Kew for lunch, but as we were worried about relatives who lived at Surrey Docks, I promised to go via Rotherhithe and see how they were faring. I left home at 10.15 and made my way to Lewisham station. This I found closed because the bridge had been damaged, apparently by the explosion I had sheltered from beneath it the previous night.

I was lucky to catch a bus, the one that usually went right to the area I wanted, but found before long that there was no means of transport into south-east London north of Deptford Broadway, east of the Old Kent Road and south of the river. At New Cross station I decided to start walking. All along the roads broken glass was piled in heaps. One large pub full of sailors was almost completely open to the street, and shop windows had their wares crazily poking out onto the pavement. I had my first sight of London refugees: true to type, wheeling prams or hand-carts piled high with personal belongings, including the inevitable mattress and in many cases domestic pets.

When I found the relatives – not in their own home – they told me wearily that they had had to evacuate their house on account of delayed-action bombs in the back garden. They were leaving London for a day or two and would have to walk to London Bridge to get transport. I was by this time thoroughly nervous and tired. It was getting late and the general chaos and cinematic atmosphere were wearing me down. I hurried back the way I had come but had not gone very far when I heard the sickening sound of the sirens. Everyone started running and in seconds the whole area seemed deserted of people except wardens and police. I found myself in a shelter with a batch of tired and worried but friendly Cockneys. One young woman had mislaid her husband and was trying to keep her two young children quiet as best she could; they were wide-eyed from exhaustion from the previous night's horror. An old lady was weeping silently: she could not stand the strain of being shut in underground, and eventually persuaded her son and daughter-in-law to take her home to their Anderson shelter. I had a long chat with a not very communicative stevedore: he had been one of the last to leave a block of flats that had been split in two by an explosion and then burned.

At long last I got back to New Cross but by then it was too late for lunch in Kew. So I tried to call but found the telephone out of order. I returned to Lewisham as quickly as possible to get some lunch and 'phone from there, but this exchange too was out of order.

Travelling to work at the hospital in Whitechapel on Monday morning took untold effort and ingenuity, but finally I got there. Buildings in the Aldgate area had been badly knocked about and fires were burning all around. One rather relevant sight was that of a small, dirty, curly-haired boy peering through a completely glassless window-frame at a street crowded with gaping sightseers and firemen. Smoke and dust filled the air and we seemed to be encircled by smouldering buildings.

The hospital had been hit in five different places: the nurses' home twice, the road in front, the laundry (which was completely gutted) and almost on the door-step of the Students' Hostel. The nurses were behaving wonderfully but were naturally rather shaken – Sister Dental had had a narrow escape. She had been in one of the rooms involved, had thrown herself on the floor away from where the wall was collapsing and then crawled out. She had rounded up a few frightened 'pros' and endeavoured to get back to her room to change into uniform: there was some doubt as to whether the foot-bridge connecting the two homes had been hit, and Sister volunteered to test it. The darkness and dust made the task doubly perilous but she achieved it and all the staff had been got into the shelter safely. There was not a single casualty in the London Hospital the whole of that first week – though work soon became impossible owing to there being no gas, light or water. Incidentally, no patients either!

Each day presented more transport problems, which were now becoming part of one's everyday life. When I finally reached the hospital on Wednesday, I found the whole of the Out-Patient Department closed because of a time-bomb just outside the new Massage Department. Toing and froing was repeatedly interrupted by raids. We would hurry for shelter and, when the All Clear sounded, set off again in search of a bus that was running or a station that was open. On one occasion I counted fifteen fires. Fountains of earth and buildings rose at intervals into the sky as the time-bombs exploded. I made my way through hose-water, smoke, dust and broken glass – a tram had been hit and overturned by an incendiary bomb. These little pleasures lay at intervals of about one hundred yards, covered by their little mounds of earth. Two furniture depositories near Lewisham station were on fire and being very obstinate to treatment; this

143

and delayed-action bombs caused the railway to be closed. There seemed no way out of this awful inferno. I felt panicky for the first time, and then I made up my mind that if necessary I would walk to London.

Thursday came and after managing to reach hospital I found that all trains to south-east London had stopped. So I looked up a colleague at Westminster Hospital that afternoon and found he was safe and sound though slightly harassed: all the responsibility was falling on his shoulders, with St Thomas's having been hit, just over the river. I also looked up Sister Pauline at the Italian Hospital. Both she and Ma Sœur were tired and worn – they had not removed their habits for six nights – but the light of battle glittered in their eyes. This was the sort of situation that the Sisters of Charity, the Sisters of St Vincent-de-Paul, had dealt with ever since the fifteenth century. The Great Ormond Street Hospital for Sick Children, which is only about twenty yards away, had been hit twice, but apart from shock the Italians had suffered only six smashed panes of glass! The little Catholic church of St Cecilia in Holborn, which housed many relics from the chapel of the Sardinian embassy, had been destroyed. That really upset them, but their one thought was for the living and the sick – they with many others of their kind were fulfilling a really holy mission.

Friday was quite aborted – a four-hour raid in the morning cramps anyone's style – and I ended by not going to hospital at all. Instead I shared lunch in a public shelter with a young Jewish refugee boy who was really charming and who told me sadly that he had fled from Berlin to Amsterdam and from there to London and was now going on to America to try to find sanctuary there.

So my dear, that is my impressions of the first week of the Blitz. I shall not write any more now: the days are so much like one another really – warnings and All Clears – we lose track of them sometimes. If anything really exciting crops up I will write you about it but I think you will find this quite enough to stomach for the time. The amazing thing is that in spite of the terrific bombardment we are getting, there is still quite a lot of London left and the casualties are very small.

PETER MACKENZIE YOUNG

D-Day Plus One

The most significant and exciting journey I ever made was very short: no more than a Channel crossing from the south coast of England. But it was made under very exceptional circumstances.

In 1944 there was never any doubt that the Allies were going to launch an invasion of the Continent of Europe, a Second Front as it was termed. Strategic bombing was weakening the German home front, but unless the Allies could put armies onto the mainland of Europe to advance on Germany from the west and link up with the Russians who were making such progress in the east, the Nazi clique would never capitulate. The only question was when and where that invasion was to take place.

The Americans had contemplated such an attack in 1943, perhaps even in 1942, but had been rightly steered off it by the British Chiefs of Staff in favour of a North African landing and a Mediterranean strategy. An assault across the Channel in those earlier years would have been disastrous. So it was looking more and more like an invasion in the spring or summer of 1944, when the weather was favourable.

In early May 1944, as a twenty-year-old lieutenant, I was sent to join the 2nd Battalion of my regiment, the King's Royal Rifle Corps (or 60th Rifles) at Worthing. The battalion had been fighting in North Africa, then Italy, since before El-Alamein, and was full of battle-wise veterans who, unlike this newly-joined subaltern, thought they knew everything there was to know about fighting battles (although many of them also felt that it was time that others rather than themselves stuck their necks out).

We were billeted in the genteel little houses and villas clustered round the bowling green in West Worthing, and did our final preparations up on the Downs behind the town in the cloudless days of that exceptionally hot May. On 2 June however (the invasion date having by then been selected as 5 June) we were moved to an assembly area around the village of Botley, north-east of Southampton. Surrounded by barbed wire, we were incarcerated and allowed no contact with the outside world. It was here – and I remember it so well – that we were given a child's attaché case full of maps and found out that our destination was to be Normandy.

In the early hours of 6 June – D-Day having in the meantime been postponed because of bad weather – we moved out of our camp on a slightly circuitous route via the Winchester bypass to what is now the Isle of Wight ferry terminal. On the bypass we had stopped to have a quick brew overlooking the Winchester College cricket ground where I had played two years earlier. There we heard the first reports that at dawn that day and even earlier, Anglo-American forces had landed under the land command of General Montgomery and the Supreme Command of General Eisenhower, that progress was being made from the beaches inland, but that the Germans were counter-attacking (this thankfully not yet strictly true).

In Southampton that afternoon, just as the first casualties were coming back from the beaches, we boarded a United States flat-bottomed tank-landing ship – we were motorised infantry in International half-tracks and tracked carriers – and set sail across a pretty rough Channel, arriving off Juno Beach at a place called Courseulles-sur-Mer the next day, D+1. After a certain amount of jockeying for position we landed there later that evening – in six feet of water and in the middle of a desultory air raid.

We were clearly taking part in the biggest combined operation the world had ever seen, or thankfully, was ever likely to see. The armada of ships, as far as the eye could see, was fantastic, with the heavier warships using their guns to engage targets inland. Despite the weather, which was to turn even worse, and thanks to the wonderful efforts of the Allied navies who put us ashore and the air forces who gave us air superiority, over 150,000 men had been landed on the beaches or by airborne operations on D-Day alone.

All the beaches had their problems and had to be fought hard for. Indeed, there were many signs of battle as we landed: landing craft destroyed or damaged by underwater obstacles or mines, burned-out tanks and charred pill-boxes. Only with the Americans on Omaha Beach, however, had there been anything approaching a disaster, which took a whole day to rectify and as a result incurred a disproportionate number of the overall casualties.

Had the whole operation failed, and at times it was a close-run thing, the end of the war in Europe could have been postponed almost indefinitely. Hitler could have devoted all his energies to stabilising the Eastern

Front; the V-bomb attacks on London and the south-east of England, soon to cause terrible casualties, could have continued with far greater impunity, and Hitler might have discovered the secret of the atomic bomb, with unthinkable consequences. This was therefore undoubtedly one of the most decisive battles in history.

When we went over, however, despite an inspiring pep-talk from Monty (and not so memorable ones from others), we had no idea what we were in for. I suppose our feelings were a mixture of excitement at being part of such a great enterprise and apprehension – not so much of being killed or wounded (after all we were young and mostly unattached) but of somehow not coming up to expectations and doing what was expected of us. I remember, when bobbing about on that sick-making crossing on our flat-bottomed ship, an old sweat coming up to me and saying: 'Don't you worry, Sir, we'll look after you'. But you knew that in fact many of them had already had too much of the War, and it was up to you to look after them. How could you possibly fail with thirty pairs of eyes boring into the back of your neck, watching every move you made?

Two things in particular have since struck me most about this great undertaking. Firstly what we all owed to the leadership of General Montgomery, as he was then. I think he contributed enormously to the success of this ambitious enterprise, by his clarity of thought in the planning stage, his professional competence in controlling a battle and his overwhelming confidence that everything was going to be all right. This communicated itself right through the ranks and was typified by his going ashore himself on D+2 and putting his headquarters right forward under artillery fire, in front of many of his subordinate commanders. Churchill, Eisenhower and the Chiefs of Staff all had doubts, but he had none, and exercised leadership of the highest quality.

I was lucky enough to meet him two or three times later on. Once I remember, before being ushered into his presence, being told by his Staff Officer that the Field Marshall (as he was by then) would ask if one had met him before.

'He doesn't mind you saying Yes or saying No, but he doesn't like you saying you can't remember.'

The second thing that particularly struck me was the enormous contribution made by the Allied air force, both tactical and strategic, in winning the battle over Germany. They not only kept the Luftwaffe 'off our backs' but ensured that reinforcing formations, many of them SS and very fanatical, were severely damaged before they entered battle. It might otherwise have been a different story.

By the time we reached Juno Beach the 3rd Canadian Division, who had landed ahead of us, had not only cleared the beach defences and the town of Courseulles but had also advanced some miles inland. So, urged on by the splendid beach masters shouting instructions, we were able to negotiate our way through the clutter, move inland some two miles or so and harbour up for the night in a small orchard. The very next day, D+2, we were in action a few miles north-west of Caen. Beautiful Normandy became a brutal battle-field, increasingly ravaged by the destruction of every town and village, the appalling din, the stench of dead cattle and horses, and with casualties, for a time, on a par with the First World War's.

The immediate task of our 4th Armoured Brigade (one of the Desert Rats – consisting of Sherman tanks and ourselves, the motorised infantry) was to plug a dangerous gap between the hard-pressed Canadians and the 3rd British Division to the east, where the Germans were now starting to counter-attack fiercely. We reached our battle-positions at a place called Villons-les-Buissons by crossing open, rolling farmland and, at Douvres, having to circumnavigate a formidable German strongpoint which was still holding out. We dug in around a small château on the outskirts of the village. It had good observation over the key road from Luc-sur-Mer to Caen (the towers and spurs of which we could clearly see in the distance) and was an obvious approach for the Germans wanting to push the landing Allies into the sea.

It was here that we experienced our first shelling and sustained our first casualties, one member of my company being nearly decapitated by a shell which landed at least fifty yards away. We also got the impression – having had a furious row with a French farmer who objected to our commandeering some of his corrugated iron to provide overhead cover for our trenches – that the locals were not as pleased at being 'liberated' as we might have expected.

We could see tracked vehicles, probably from 21st Panzer Division, milling around in woods some three thousand yards in front of us and were able, through our communications, to bring formidable fire to bear on them before they could mount a major attack. The Canadians, however, in the next village to our right, were not so lucky: they were brutally assaulted by the fanatical 12th SS Hitler Youth Division. Casualties were heavy on both sides and there were some nasty episodes of prisoners being shot.

As the Allied line gradually edged forward, around the western side of Caen, and the country became more wooded with high hedgerows and deep ditches, we met increasing resistance: from the formidable Tiger tanks, SP guns, Panzerfaust anti-tank weapons, Spandau machine-guns and not least from the fearsome, multi-barrelled *Nebelwerfer*, the 'Moaning Minnie' as we called it. This gave warning of its imminent arrival with an alarming scream before landing multiple heavy-mortar bombs over an area about the size of a football field. Quite an experience!

The journey from the assembly area at Botley to this intense front-line action north-west of Caen lasted little over seventy-two hours. But it had been the most memorable, stimulating and exciting experience I could possibly have asked for. It was of course the prelude to many more weeks of very hard pounding before victory in Normandy was finally won.

'DWIN BRAMALL

Post-War Whitehall

Post-War austerity still prevailed in the London of 1950. There were stirrings of fashion and luxury here and there, but they were attempts to revive pre-War standards rather than to create new ones. When I started work in the Foreign Office, on four hundred pounds a year, I rented an unfurnished room in Upper Berkeley Street, with a separate bathroom downstairs, for three guineas a week. The room was small and I could only fit in a 2'6" bed. I had no kitchen or refrigerator. My butter was kept in a pottery cooler on the window-sill. Once a week I fried my meat ration on a gas ring; some evenings I scrambled eggs on it; at other times I ate out, inexpensively. Of course I had some social life; but most of my energy went into the office.

Attlee's Labour government was still in control. Abroad, the Iron Curtain seemed impenetrable, while the Korean War menaced any hopes of greater international harmony. Yet we had emerged quite recently from an exhausting struggle. Although we did not expect too much, I think we took it for granted that things must in time get better rather than worse. The instinctive, limited hope was of 'getting back to normal', though without the unemployment and social deprivation of the 1930s.

At the Foreign Office too the prevailing wish – at least subconsciously – was the preservation, or restoration, of as much 'normality' as possible. This was natural enough in a country that, though fully aware of relative decline, still had many of the attributes and responsibilities of a great power. The Foreign Service had been reformed and democratized. But the Foreign Office itself still kept remarkably to what I suppose were its pre-War methods and atmosphere.

The actual building, then approached freely from Downing Street, evoked mid-Victorian splendour and authority. The offices occupied by ministers and the permanent under-secretary were and still are imposing. Other senior officials could boast portraits and high ceilings. The rest of us were more economically housed, but we walked down the same impressive corridors. At the top of the grand staircase the famous frescoes (forgiveable, because painted by a foreigner) showed Britannia teaching her sons the arts of war and peace. Over the private office a smaller fresco enjoined Silence on a profession of communicators.

The Locarno Rooms, which have since been refurbished, were particularly splendid because they were originally used for receptions. During the War, with the need for more office space, they had been divided by partitions. Sir Roger Makins (later Lord Sherfield) occupied the largest room as deputy under-secretary for economic affairs. Shortly before I joined the service, he was kind enough to ask me to lunch at the Travellers Club, because he knew my father.

The Northern Department was on the second floor. Its offices, though built to last, were not architecturally distinguished. The head of the department had a not very large room, alongside a smaller one occupied by his personal assistant and a typist. The assistant head and another First Secretary also had small rooms of their own. The lesser fry (known collectively as 'the Third Room') were divided between two medium-sized offices, each with three desks. On the floor above, the registry clerks shared larger and more crowded quarters with the files. We all shared the windows with the pigeons.

The Northern Department covered the Soviet Union, its five satellite countries and Scandinavia. More properly it should have been called the East and North European Department. But I believe its title was a survival from Tudor and Stuart days, when two secretaries of state – for the Northern and Southern Departments – divided home affairs and international relations (then largely confined to Europe) between them. Similarly, when I joined the Foreign Office, the Southern Department still survived, though its province had shrunk to the Mediterranean countries.

We needed to wear thick clothes in winter because we had to work in temperatures lower than is now usual. Some people kept old jackets to work in, to prevent their best suits getting too shiny. A few wore the traditional Civil Service garb of striped trousers and short black coats. The young and the smart sported bowler hats and tightly furled umbrellas. The bowler hat was making a brief come-back as part of the nostalgia that, at a different social level, inspired the Teddy Boys.

The young men of the mid-Victorian Foreign Office had been likened to the fountains of Trafalgar Square because they played from twelve to three. We had to put in longer hours and there was not much playing. We started later than nowadays: I think I used to arrive between half past nine and ten. This was supposed to allow time for the telegrams to circulate; perhaps it also reflected the social life of pre-War senior officials. At lunchtime we regularly took an hour off, to eat in the clubs and pubs of the neighbourhood, and did not feel guilty about taking a bit more, if we had time and were shopping or meeting friends. On the other hand, we worked later in the evenings. I believe I seldom left the office before eight o'clock, sometimes not till half past eight or nine. At least once a week I took work home and, after a meal, continued with it till midnight. We worked on Saturdays too, though rather less formally and not always after lunch. However, we were allowed to take every third Saturday off completely, so it was possible to enjoy some long weekends. I can still remember the glorious feeling of liberation when, late one Friday evening, I was at a dance in a country house and realized that I could look forward to two whole days away from the office.

Most of the work consisted of reading and writing. There were elaborate rules, and more or less archaic formulæ, for corresponding with the public and other government departments. We were 'directed by Mr Secretary Bevin' (in fact we directed ourselves) to acknowledge or reply to communications. We invited Admiralty or Treasury officials to lay our observations 'before their Lordships' and so on. This Trollopian style was later relaxed. Once mastered, it had its advantages but it was clearly not in accord with the spirit of the age.

Most of my drafting was done in pen and ink: during this first spell in the Foreign Office I never really learned to dictate. In any case there was nobody for me to dictate to, unless there was time to summon an unknown typist from the pool. By what must even then have been an anomaly, the personal assistant, a dignified elderly lady, could not, or at any rate did not, type. She protected the head of department and coped with his boxes and papers. (Once a year, at Christmas-time, she asked the young men of the department to sherry in her Kensington flat.) This meant that the departmental typist had no time for the Third Room. However, an efficient dictaphone service was available, though I preferred to read into it what I had already written by hand.

Until the merging of the Foreign and Commonwealth Relations Offices, every incoming document was enclosed in a stiff paper 'jacket', with the registry clerk's brief summary of its contents. (Curzon was reported to have spent part of his diligent days correcting these summaries.) Then it was up to the desk officer concerned to minute his recommendations for action on the jacket and, where necessary, attach draft replies. If he simply initialled the jacket, it would be returned to the registry and might never see the light of day again. If he thought somebody in another department should read the document, he would write the name of this official (or officials) under his own initials. If he wished the document to be returned to him, or to submit it to his superiors, he would write his name in full, under whatever comments or recommendations he thought fit. On the relatively rare occasions when a document seemed likely to rise higher than the department and its under-secretary, an 'ideal minute' might be prepared for the head of department's signature. Sometimes, even when there was no incoming document, the department might need higher authority for a course of action.

At an entirely different level, ministers and senior officials might reach decisions on the basis of incoming telegrams without awaiting departmental submissions. When there were crises with political overtones, meetings might be summoned hastily and there might be little time (or wish) to delegate to the Third Room. But relations with most of the countries covered by the Northern Department tended to be frozen rather than fiery.

The whole system was of course extremely hierarchical – and no doubt, to a considerable extent, still is. My minutes or drafts reached the head of department (when he needed to see them) through two officials, one of whom felt in honour bound to correct them quite heavily. Between the head of department and the Private Office there were an assistant under-secretary, a deputy under-secretary and a permanent under-secretary. Like the Third Room, any of these officials could initial papers off so that they would proceed no further. They would then return to the department, where the initials of a minister or the permanent under-secretary always aroused some excitement.

Bevin was then Foreign Secretary, much respected and loved by those close to him. I met him only once, when a colleague introduced me in Downing Street. I was deeply impressed when another colleague, who had attended a meeting with him in his official flat, told me how Bevin had personally decided how to handle the matter under discussion after thinking about it in his bath.

The permanent under-secretary was Sir William (later Lord) Strang. Edifying advice from two of his predecessors was displayed in framed minutes on his mantelpiece. One, by Sir Alexander Cadogan, seemed to strike exactly the right note of gentlemanly petulance: 'To send a piece of tape like this to the Secretary of State is really quite wrong'. Another, by Sir Orme Sargent, was undated: 'Always put a date on your minutes'.

I was disappointed to find that the tape used to bundle jackets together was pink rather than red. One had to learn the correct way of tying it. There was also a correct way of using pins to attach 'flags' to supporting papers so as to reduce the risk of drawing senior officials' blood. It took time to feel at home with the different methods of circulating more or less urgent papers round the office – pouches, boxes and tubes. Tubes, used for telegrams, were rapid and alarmingly technological, as they emerged from a fearsome network of pipes. Often we achieved still greater rapidity by taking papers to other parts of the office by hand. From the outset the importance of co-ordination in the work of government was drummed in on us. We had to learn what papers needed to be seen by what other departments in the office and what other departments in Whitehall.

Another routine skill that had to be learned was security classification. The use of 'top secret' was exceptional; 'secret' was quite sparingly used, but there was a temptation to err on the safe side and grade everything else as 'confidential'. Periodically we were told to downgrade papers to 'restricted' or even declassify them.

A lot of attention is paid in the Foreign Office and posts abroad to good, clear drafting. Perhaps there is, or used to be, rather too much correction of drafts. But the general aim was to avoid obscurity and pedantry, to keep things simple and to prevent clichés taking the place of thought. Sometimes it was not easy to eschew impersonal language when writing anonymously or in somebody else's name. But bureaucratic evasions like 'It is considered that . . .' were not encouraged. Even secretaries of state took an occasional interest in the way their officials wrote. Eden had a particular horror of 'It is appreciated', and once had a circular put out telling us never to use 'appreciate' in the sense of 'realize'.

It would be misleading to suggest that we wasted much time on the pleasantly archaic forms still in use in the early post-War period. Similarly, it would be a mistake to conclude from anything I have written that the pace was leisurely or that business was conducted inefficiently. On the contrary, we were usually fully stretched, working at the double and trying – perhaps just managing – to catch up.

I did not realize when I was in the Northern Department that the challenges would expand with seniority. I thought that we did the real work in the Third Room: above us was a dignified area of unruffled decision-making and judicious delegation. To my surprise and disappointment I found that, as I climbed the ladder, I took 'the real work' with me. I do not quite know what conclusions to draw from this, except that we are all blinkered by our current experience.

RICHARD FABER

Trollope in the Taklamakan

It had long been a dream – a fancy of successions of Chinese governments, all the mandarins and warlords and commissars alike – that one day a railway line might be built to link Shanghai with Amsterdam, a line that would give China the same kind of access to the Western world that Russia has had since the tsars built the Trans-Siberian Railway. But the difficulty and the costs involved were prodigious: to make the link would require engineers to pierce China's great western mountains, to blast a railway cutting through where the Silk Road ran, to have express trains roaring through the mighty western entrance to China they still call the Dzungarian Gate. Such a wonder as this, said a century's worth of dreamers, might make all the difference in the world but would be well-nigh impossible to create.

Then a decade ago, after years of scheming and planning and dithering and wondering, they finally stopped talking and did it. Engineers from China National Railways (an organization so immense some say it has more employees than the current total population of England), working with their counterparts from what was then the Soviet Railway Authority, jack-hammered and pinioned and smelted a three hundred mile-long connecting line that did indeed make all the difference. It ran from an ugly western Chinese city called Urumqi to a smaller but equally ugly city called Aktogay across the frontier in what was then the Soviet Union but today is Kazakhstan.

And crucially, since Aktogay lies on the main north-south railway line to Novosibirsk, a Chinese train starting at Urumqi could henceforth and quite easily make a journey all the way to Moscow. And since Urumqi is linked by rail to Shanghai, and Moscow is similarly connected to Amsterdam – well, the rest is obvious. Thanks to these three hundred miles of new track built ten years ago across the remote and inhospitable wastes of Dzungaria, China became finally fully connected, and properly harnessed, to the rest of the outside world.

I was living in Hong Kong at the time the line was opened and I decided, as soon as the various permits had been granted by the Chinese and (more trickily) the Soviet authorities, to make the journey. An old friend of mine named George, who like me seemed to have much time on his hands, came along. We flew one autumn weekend from Canton to Urumqi in a Russian 'plane with a Russian crew – this latter oddity being the even odder result of a barter deal that had involved two hundred railway wagonfuls of Chinese-reared pigs. We found the railway station and, in due course, its newly opened International Travel Office. Here, for a small sum in folding money, we bought ourselves two one-way, first-class soft-car tickets to the Kazakh capital of Alma Ata.

The train ran only twice a week, the next departure being the following morning at ten. We arrived at nine to be on the safe side (Chinese railway stations being notoriously trying places) and found the express with unanticipated ease. Unlike all the others drawn up in the station, which were painted in an unlovely olive drab, ours was hauled by a grey-blue and scarlet-trimmed diesel monster, and had its dozen carriages adorned with a livery of exotic patterns picked out in umber and ochre. Our compartment was similarly exotic, a soufflé of white lace cushions and small beaded chandeliers. There was a restaurant car, serving Kazakh curries. There was beer available, and sweet Georgian sparkling wine.

We left, on schedule, at ten precisely. At first we went slowly, rattling west through the factories and suburbs of Urumqi – past a scattering of yurts in the meadows, home to migrant Uighurs who had come to the city to trade. Within the hour, though, we had picked up speed, and soon we were scything noisily through the mountains and across a hundred bridges in that rarely visited, rarely seen range known as the Tian Shan. To our north, limitless and white, were the sands of the Dzungarian Basin; to the south, when the lines of hills parted, we caught glimpses of the immense expanse of dunes of the Taklamakan Desert – the trackless and blinding yellow fastness where, as the name in translation so starkly warns, You May Go In But You'll Never Make It Out.

After a while the hills flattened and the train began to beat tediously steadily across a wide, sandy plain. A cold and pitiless sun threw such scenery as there was into sharp relief. And then there was really nothing to see – no cities, no nomad camps, no livestock, no people. Just sand, scrub, the occasional outcrop of grey rock and, livid in the distance, the horizon, razor-sharp.

An hour or so of this and suddenly, without warning, the brakes caught hold; there was a screeching from beneath the carriages; the train slowed, then slid and squealed to a stop. All was immediately silent. I looked outside, to see just a tiny, ramshackle halt – a small platform, a siding, a water-tower, an oily road with a single dun-coloured truck, a camel-cart with a ragged-looking Bactrian, and a pair of bicycles. The name 'Kuytun' written in Chinese, Uighur and English was the only indication of any reason for our stop; and my map did indeed show a settlement of that name, though some miles north of the railway. There was no other sign of habitation: no house, no tent, no campfire. Only the name Kuytun, which didn't seem to mean anything at all.

George was dozing on his lace cushion, and it seemed best to let him be. I clambered down from the train, breathing in the cold, still air – just a hint of cooking fire and the unmistakable smell of a camel, which grunted disagreeably in its harness fifty yards away. The guard was the only other person on the platform. The train would stop here for thirty minutes, he said. He didn't explain why. I mooched over to the engine and tried to have a conversation with the driver – a friendly enough man but with a Sichuan accent so thick I could only make out one word in five.

And then from behind me, and so unexpectedly that I jumped, came a woman's voice.

'Excuse me please,' she said. 'Do you by any chance speak English?'

I turned around to see a young Chinese woman of the most astonishing loveliness smiling at me. She was thirty or so, tall, with a long mane of black hair; she was wearing a brilliant red sweater and a long tartan skirt. She had a scarf, black I think it was, to keep off the cold. She looked radiant, dignified, intelligent.

I spluttered something about how yes, why of course, naturally, yes I speak English, and how could I help her?

Her smile broadened for a moment – then she looked down at her wristwatch. She frowned a little, then spoke again.

'This train stops here for another, let me see, for another twenty-four minutes. We have little time, so let me ask you this right away: do you know anything about the writer Anthony Trollope?'

This wasn't happening, I said to myself. It can't be. I'm deep in China, far from everywhere. I'm at a miserable little halt on the edge of one of the world's most notoriously dangerous deserts. And here is a beautiful Chinese woman asking me in English if I know anything about Trollope?

She smiled up at me and asked once more: 'Do you know of him? Please.' I realised that this was all too real. So I replied that yes, of course I know, and that he is a writer I read whenever I can, one whose books and stories (I was spluttering now) are part of my own assembly of joy, always there to offer comforting pleasure. Yes indeed I know of Anthony Trollope. And how.

She smiled again, then put on a more serious face.

'Good,' she said, now rather matter-of-fact. 'I would like to discuss' – she looked at her wrist again – 'the plot of *The Eustace Diamonds*, and in particular the character of Lady Glencora. Is this fine with you?'

We had by now gone way too far for me to challenge or disbelieve. One day yet I might awaken, but for now I might as well go along with whatever this strange phenomenon truly was. And so for the following twenty-four or twenty-three minutes I spoke as best I could to this vision of loveliness about Plantaganet Palliser's wife, and such of this good lady's views as I could recall, and I spoke about Lizzie Eustace and Lord Fawn and Mr Emilius and all the other figures in the book, and if I stumbled vainly through a thicket of distant reminiscences, I could surely be forgiven, since all the while I would have had to be wondering if there would soon be a tap on my arm, and the ordeal would come to a sudden and embarrassing end.

But it was the train guard who eventually brought it to a stop. He strode imperiously out of his office, blew a shrill blast on his whistle and began to wave frantically with a green flag. The young woman, smiling broadly, suddenly said: 'Quick! Back onto the train. You're leaving. You have to go!'

There was a roar of diesel machinery; the locomotive and its gaggle of carriages jerked forward. And I did indeed climb back into the carriage, if somewhat under protest and somehow somnambulant, re-embarking as if in a dream – and all the while I found myself saying to this mysterious woman words like 'Yes of course, but who are you, what are you, why are you here? I think I could love you, I don't want to leave you'.

'Don't be so silly,' she said. 'Get into the train. But give me your card if you like. I'll write.'

I tore into the compartment, woke George, found a card, hurriedly tossed it out of the window. The train was moving now, and the last vision I had was of the Chinese woman scrabbling on her knees in the sand, searching for the tiny, white oblong of board with my name and Hong Kong address. Then the train rounded a bend and wherever she had been vanished clear away. I gazed back out of the window for the next ten or twenty minutes – but there was nothing behind me now but sand. Even the oily road had disappeared, and the view on all sides was merely flatness, and the horizon, and nothing more at all.

George was astonished by what he had seen. She was adorable, he kept muttering. Adorable. And when I told him about the conversation, which I could see he didn't want to believe at all, he kept shaking his head. 'Unbelievable,' he would say every few minutes, and gaze out at the darkening sand. 'This country never ceases to amaze me.'

We travelled in Kazakhstan and Kyrgyzstan and Mongolia and Siberia for the next six weeks or so, and in time contrived almost to forget that strange half-hour on Kuytun station. When I came back to Hong Kong, to my little flat on Macdonnell Road, there on the door-mat, among the bills from China Light & Power and The Sincere Company and Wing On Limited, was an envelope in an unfamiliar, feminine hand, with a smudged postmark from a Chinese town. It was her. And this, in paraphrase, is what she wrote:

'My dear Mr Winchester,

'Please permit me to introduce myself. My name is Xing Yong Zhen; I am thirty-four years old. I was born in Xi'an and went to university there. I have been married for the last nine years to a Mr Lu, who is a senior cadre in the Party. We have a five-year-old son named Henry.

'We lived in Xi'an until two years ago when my husband was abruptly transferred to Kuytun. They never said why. It was probably a punishment for some error about which he was never told. He was made to be in charge of an experimental hydroponics factory. A serious demotion for him, and a bad business for us all.

'Kuytun is a horrid place. A desert fortress-town, that's all. It is dirty and broken-down. It is miles and miles from anywhere. No one interesting lives here. My husband and I do not get on well with one another. We are very miserable. I am, at least.

'My only love, for the last ten years, has been the English language, and the literature of the nineteenth century. I studied it at university and I fell in love with the works of Anthony Trollope. I have read all the novels, all in English. My favourite of all is *The Way We Live Now*. And yes, I love *Phineas Finn* – the man and the books.

'But here in Kuytun no one knows Trollope. It is a joke to imagine that anyone might. No one knows English. I believe I am the only person in the entire town who speaks English. And because of this I have a terrible feeling of sadness – that if I never speak English any more, if I never talk to anyone about English literature, then I will lose it all one day. I worry about this, very much.

'Some months ago the international train service was started. When I heard the news I thought to myself: perhaps someone who speaks English will ride on this train. And so I have begun a routine. The new train comes through two times a week, on Tuesdays and Thursdays. The station is about twenty kilometres from where I live. So each Tuesday and Thursday morning I bicycle to the station and wait for the train – and (I have no pride!) I tap on the windows asking the people inside if perhaps they speak English.

'Sometimes there is a foreign worker who speaks a few words. Sometimes there is a Chinese man who knows a little. But usually I have little luck. For all of these last six months I have heard maybe fifty words in total – and I tell you frankly I have been thinking of abandoning this quest.

'But then today I bicycled down and saw this tall man speaking to the train driver – and I asked if he spoke English.

'And you turned around, and not only did you speak English but you were English, and when I asked about Trollope and you knew him, and we spoke of him, it was just unbelievable, just wonderful, just unimaginably wonderful. Today I think has been one of the best days of my life – and all I ask now is that you and I will write to one another, and that you can help keep me from losing my grasp of English here, and telling me things about Trollope and other writers who the two of us enjoy so much.'

Of course I wrote back; she replied to me; I sent her some books; we kept in touch, regularly; and a year later I flew to Xi'an, she came by train, and I met her and Henry – who speaks English too – and for whom his mother had asked me to bring a book of Kipling's verses.

We wrote to one another for several years following. I gave her an English name, Laura, and as Laura Xing she eventually managed to defend, entirely successfully, a PhD thesis at the University of Xi'an – not on Trollope as it happens but on Victorian cookery: she turned out also to have been fascinated by Mrs Beeton. So now she is Dr Xing, Dr Laura Xing.

In the autumn of 1997, a few months after Hong Kong had reverted to Chinese rule, as I was preparing to leave the territory for a new life in America, she stopped writing. There was neither warning nor explanation. Letters sent to her address were returned without remark. When I telephoned, a recording in both English and Chinese came on, saying simply and brusquely: 'The number you are calling does not exist'.

I have no idea what happened. I sometimes wonder if she was officially reprimanded – as a Party official's wife – for having dealings with a foreigner. I wonder too whether she and her husband – for whom she had precious few kind words – separated, or if they remained together. I have no way of knowing now whether or not she stayed in Kuytun and if she continued to cycle to and from the Alma Ata Express twice a week to find out if there were any passengers who spoke English and who might know a little of nineteenth-century writings.

In fact all that I know for certain these days came from a single telephone message that she left on my answering machine. She was very excited, she said. She had never been abroad before but now she had permission, and a passport, and was telephoning from the airport in Beijing – on her way to a conference in Paris. The Kuytun Hydroponics Plant made a special kind of tomato sauce, her message said: she was going to exhibit a sample at an international food fair.

And then my tape and the message ran out. She never called me again. She never called from France, nor were any of my further letters or telephone calls returned. That was three years ago. Whatever had happened to Xing Yong Zhen, Anthony Trollope's greatest admirer in the Taklamakan Desert, is now, sad to say, no more than an enduring mystery.

SIMON WINCHESTER

161

Blind Date

The rendezvous was at the town clock, a tall, slim construction that resembled a Soviet architect's attempt to synthesize the exoticism of a minaret with the scaled-down grandeur of Big Ben. It stood in a concrete square reached by several steps up from the main street. My taxi stopped at the foot of the steps. As the driver counted out my change in worn and dirty notes, I looked up at the clock. Ten past eleven. I was late.

What did my date look like? The Russian interpreter had described her as being in her thirties, good-looking, from a respected family and intelligent. Perhaps not in that order. She was Kyrgyz, not Russian, and had recently separated from her husband. He had not met her himself but his wife knew her mother well. Had his wife met my date? He thought so. When the latter telephoned me to arrange this meeting her voice, while soft and charming with its broken English, gave no clue as to her appearance. I wondered how we would recognize each other.

Small groups of people sat on the steps, huddled together talking. The glare of the sun warmed them but they seemed clothed for a colder season. Children were shouting, in some game. Their faces had that Mongol-Asiatic look that triggered images of ancestors riding across the steppes, sweeping down on frightened city dwellers. Their clothes, like those of the adults in the square, had none of the boisterous colours that those horsemen would have worn: only the grey, anonymous style designed by a Soviet tailor for mass-production in the state factories. Some had Caucasian faces, but their clothes had the same bulky, faded look. A foreigner would not blend into this scene. I was all too recognizable. She had not forgotten to ask.

'Excuse me.' I turned at the sound of the voice. The first thing I noticed was the large sunglasses that hid the upper part of her face. The second was the small mouth beneath the high cheek-bones that the glasses emphasised. Her hair was dark and fell almost straight to just above her shoulders. She was taller than I had expected, only a few inches shorter than myself. I wanted to speak but found myself staring at her. She seemed amused. 'I am Aigula,' she announced, removing the sunglasses. My hand reached out to touch hers. Her eyes were large, slightly narrow and very Asiatic. The look they gave me was bold. If some Mongol war-lord had been her ancestor – and it was possible – he would have been proud of her. I introduced myself and suggested we go for a stroll in the Panfilov Park.

Bishkek was, like many cities in Central Asia, a creation of Stalin and his security-obsessed imagination. He designed new republics to combine local traditions with the Soviet policies of resettling populations and imposing the Russian language. Cities were established on a grid system, villages and nomadic settlements swept aside. But while the modernization agenda was clear, there was difficulty in defining the traditions to be 'preserved'. No matter. Like Victorians inventing Scottish tartans and giving them a history linked to the clans, Moscow breathed cultural life into the Kyrgyz, as into the Kazakhs, the Uzbeks and other peoples of the steppes. Their heroes were celebrated in the names of municipal buildings and streets. (In Kyrgyzstan the national hero was Manas, a legendary warrior-khan in the style of Tamburlaine.) The peoples' contributions to the war against the Nazis were also commemorated by large, centrally placed monuments in the heroic style. Everywhere there were concrete squares and statues dedicated to the enthusiastic Central Asian support for the Bolshevik Revolution and its heroes, especially Lenin.

Reinventing the past selectively was not the only challenge the Kremlin set itself. Art, like sport, could be organised and stimulated with the help of central direction. The Kyrgyz had a long tradition of artistic creativity unmatched in the region, except perhaps by carpet-weaving. So opera, theatre and painting became the focus of subsidies for cultural promotion. And it worked, for a time. Bishkek became a centre of artistic excellence in the Union of Soviet Socialist Republics.

Aigula's father and mother, she told me, had been well-known actors, popular with the media and able to perform in both Russian and Kyrgyz. They encouraged their two daughters to act, play instruments and sing. It was a family troupe, like a music-hall act but without the financial pressures. The theatres were always packed with young people and often their parents.

But the family fell on hard times even before the collapse of 1991. After a severe heart attack Aigula's father stopped working and her mother stayed at home to look after him. She had a pension and some savings. The rent was low and fixed by the state. She was sometimes asked to give newspaper interviews on her career in the theatre. Then came the news that the Soviet Union was to be dissolved and replaced by a new federal entity called the Commonwealth of Independent States. No one knew what this meant, but everyone assumed that life would go on much as normal.

Aigula talked a lot, using her hands and interrupting herself from time to time with excuses for her English. I listened like a keen student. Her name in Kyrgyz meant Flower of the Moon. As we walked and talked I studied her. She was elegant, dressed in a dark suit and carrying a black handbag with a French designer logo. She was studying me too.

In the following weeks we met several times, usually in the evening. Something clicked between us. She knew the better arts and craft shops, and bargained for me in Kyrgyz and Russian. I found myself beside her at the theatre, watching a costume drama and understanding nothing, but enjoying the experience.

An invitation to her home followed. It was a spacious Soviet apartment, with sad wallpaper and sombre furniture. Her mother lived with her and seemed to be in charge: she hovered between the living room and kitchen, checking that I was eating the abundant cakes and drinking tea. Her English was even more limited than my Russian. Eventually she left us alone and I took the opportunity to look around. Opposite me there was a dark wooden cabinet and on the shelves a number of framed photographs. Aigula followed my gaze and smiled. She reached over and picked one up. 'My daughter. And my sister.' She paused. 'And my husband. Before. Not husband now.' She fumbled for the right words but the meaning was clear enough.

'You can see my story.' She took a bundle of black-and-white photographs from a drawer and spread them over the table. The girl in the pictures was very young and strikingly beautiful. I looked up and recognised that beauty even now. She had told me she was thirty-four but I guessed that was an under-estimate. The athletes in several photos caught my attention.

'Beauty contest,' she grinned. 'My friends persuaded me. A joke. But I won! I was the most beautiful woman in Kyrgyzstan!' She laughed. 'Then

I went to Moscow and came second in another contest. Miss Soviet Union contest. Here, I present medal to sportsman. Uuum, Olympic. International sport competition. In Moscow. You see – national dress.' Her long dress was elegant, and the high, traditional head-dress looked exotic, almost baroque. Perhaps Marco Polo had met women dressed like this.

Later her fame earned her parts in two films. 'They both lost money. Maybe because of me!' I wondered what had happened to this one-time golden girl, why she was sitting in this gloomy room talking to a foreigner about her past.

Before long, the new republic was in turmoil. The currency was decorated with Manas warriors and wise-looking old men but each month it bought less. Western goods arrived in the shops but their prices, and all prices, reached ever higher levels. More and more Russians left to join relatives in the Russian Federation, or simply to find employment. Not only the Russians were looking for a way out.

One evening Aigula told me she would make a decision. I had asked her back to my apartment several times and each time she had said No. Why?

'I do not like you one hundred per cent.'

'How many percentage points then?' She paused: 'About ninety'.

There were other candidates apart from me, it seemed. An Italian businessman wanted to take her back to Milan. He was very charming, telling her of the beautiful cities he would take her to. The one she liked most of all was Florence, since she loved painting and sculpture. He had shown her photographs of art in a place with a name she could not pronounce. We concluded it was the Uffizi. I continued to press my case. Ten points to go.

The day after this conversation we met as usual for dinner. She announced very formally that she had decided. She produced a piece of paper and read some words in English. It was a positive assessment of my character, and concluded: 'I hope to have with you a good correlation and I expect to have from you mutuality'. The caviar suddenly tasted better, the champagne more exhilarating than ever before. The seven flights of stairs back to the apartment did not seem wearisome at all.

As our relationship deepened, she told me more about her country and her past. I listened intently, entering into a world entirely new to me, the

Soviet Central Asian world that had already passed into history. Through her I felt I was being taken back in time. The missing pieces of the puzzle fell into place.

Her rôle in the Moscow Olympics and her films had given her celebrity status. Her photo appeared in newspapers and magazines. She was often on television. This fame was to bring with it a terrible price that changed her life.

One day she was leaving her local store clutching a large bag of groceries. She turned towards her parents' home near by. After a few steps she was aware of a man on her left. Then another on her right. The first grabbed her arm while the other seized the bag. She was pushed into a black car. It was already driving away when she began to strike out, kick and shout at the men. Too late. They took her to a house somewhere in the city.

One of them told her he wanted her as his wife. He had seen her photograph many times and found her beautiful. He wished to marry her in the traditional Kyrgyz way: she would have sex with him and then he would reach agreement with her parents on arrangements for the marriage. Telling the story, she showed no emotion. He kept her prisoner for three days, and took the first step in his marriage proposal. Then he casually asked for her parents' telephone number.

'He told them his name and said to my father: "Your daughter is in my house. I want to marry her". He gave address. Three days. They did not know where I was. Very worried.' She showed the first sign of emotion.

When her parents arrived, the young man's parents were already there to discuss the formalities. Aigula walked to the front door and stepped outside to freedom. She did not turn round and her parents took her away. 'I never saw the man again.' And the police? They questioned the man, she replied, and filed a report. The custom had been outlawed but she did not press charges. I wondered why.

Later she continued her story. She went to university and worked hard. Her degree almost completed, she realised that she liked a fellow-student very much. She had refused sex for four years. He seemed likeable and good company. She married him and they had a daughter. Then the story darkened again. Her marriage stumbled on a rock well known in this society. His work did not go well and he took to drinking, in larger and larger quantities and at all times of day and night. He became jealous of her friends and any men she was with. She left him after he started to hit her. Afterwards he would cry and cry, begging forgiveness. Even on his knees. Then the drinking would begin again. Her main concern was for her daughter, growing up in this household. Aigula and her husband agreed to separate and he now worked in Kazakhstan.

All of this story was punctuated with questions about Europe, the weather, the shops, my house and my life at home. When would I return home and what arrangements would I make for her to join me? There would be difficulties for her with the language perhaps. 'I have interpreter,' she smiled at me.

The date for completion of my work in Bishkek was set. The imminent return to Europe focussed my thoughts on Aigula. It was clear what she wanted. Or was it? Was it me or my passport? She had nothing to gain by staying here. She had often remarked on how foreigners married local women. They were attractive enough, rather like Japanese but taller. In her case, how much calculation was there? Without a doubt the relationship worked, but would it work in a different setting?

Postponing a decision seemed the easiest option. Besides, I expected to be back here in a couple of months. Perhaps some time to think would help clarify things. I promised to contact her with her travel arrangements.

The last time we met I walked her home through the dimly lit streets. Once off the main avenue, we walked in the road to avoid the pot-holes in the pavements. There was little traffic. She was silent but I knew she had been crying. At her house we kissed and said goodbye. At the door she turned to me: 'Call me tomorrow before you leave'.

My long absence in Bishkek meant that there was much to do back home. The weeks passed quickly. My birthday came. After a celebratory dinner I came home and played back the answering machine. One of the messages was from Aigula. She wished me a happy birthday and added: 'I wish you a symphony of harmony and much fun and frolic in the next year'. That dictionary of hers!

The next day, my decision made, I applied for her visa. It was not easy. Sending the money for her ticket was not enough by a long way. It took some weeks more to complete the immigration procedure. I decided to call and surprise her with the news that everything was almost ready.

She had given me several telephone numbers, including a mobile. The first call failed to connect. The second also failed although a recording replied in Russian. Which I did not understand. The mobile did not work outside Kyrgyzstan. Frantic, I started to work out how to contact her. Some days later the Kyrgyz embassy told me that the international dialling code for the country had just been changed. When I tried with the correct code, the operator told me the first number had been discontinued and refused to give a reason. The second connected to an unfamiliar voice that spoke only Russian. I understood enough: no Aigula was known there; there was no one of that name in the house. Had she rented her apartment, I wondered? In any event I had lost her.

The follow-up work did not materialise and I never returned to Kyrgyzstan. Aigula had my address, but soon afterwards I moved back to the UK. Sometimes I flick through my mail for a letter that might have been forwarded. If it ever arrives, I am sure it will have an Italian stamp on it.

PETER DUNCANSON CAMERON

An Easter Holiday in China

In 1957 when I was serving in Peking, I made a trip to Kaifeng. This had been the capital of China during the Sung Dynasty. It had many exotic monuments, including a stele commemorating the Jewish community which had survived until the eighteenth century.

I was in a rickshaw, and had just changed my film after taking what I thought was a rather picturesque photograph of women washing clothes in a stream. I was suddenly surrounded by security police, who said that I had photographed an army barracks, and I was arrested. I was taken to police headquarters and it was demanded that I surrender my film. As it happened, the film that I had taken was in my pocket, while the new film in the camera was blank.

I asked to be allowed to collect my luggage from the state guest house. They agreed and in packing my case I managed to conceal the used film in my sponge-bag.

Back at police headquarters I was charged with spying. I showed them my identity card that said I had diplomatic immunity. This was clearly a concept new to them: they said they would need to refer the matter to Peking. They insisted on my giving up the film – which was, of course, blank. I explained to them that the film used a process unknown in China and, if they developed it, it might appear as a total blank. I was seriously worried whether this bluff would prove disastrous.

So I was thrown into prison. This turned out to be a beautiful, former Buddhist monastery. I was understandably put with the political prisoners. They turned out to be a charming group of intellectuals. We wrote poems in the dust of the courtyard. Dreadful food was thrust through the gate. But the scholars had grown a considerable range of herbs between the stones in the yard and succeeded in flavouring the mess we were given to make it verging on the delicious.

My aching fear was that when the authorities consulted Peking they would be told that they were in error to detain a diplomat. I thought that the only way for them to save face would be for me to have an unfortunate fatal accident. 'Poor Mr Morgan fell under a train. He was clearly drunk.'

I had been imprisoned on Good Friday, and the days stretched to Easter Monday. At dawn that day I knew that my worst fears had been realised. A group of security police ran into the yard and rapidly tied me up like a chicken with my arms and legs securely bound behind my back. I was then carried away to the cheers of my new friends, and thrown into a cart. I was sure that my body would later be found on a railway line. Sure enough, I was taken to Kaifeng railway station, where I was dumped in a line with other prisoners similarly trussed.

My hold-all was beside me and, as I was a great deal larger and furthermore a foreigner, I became the centre of attention. A large crowd surrounded me. By then, the constriction of my arms and legs had become excruciatingly painful. I lay on my side and waited to be thrown on the railway line.

After what seemed an age, the train arrived. The other prisoners were thrown into what looked like a cattle-truck. I was picked up and thrown into a corridor with, to my surprise, my hold-all beside me. The train set off. For hours my limbs became increasingly numb.

169

After an eternity a sweet young lady – a sort of train stewardess – appeared. She had a knife in her hand and deftly cut my bonds. 'Oh,' she said. 'You are clearly a guest in our country and should rightly be in "soft class"' – the Chinese equivalent of first. I stumbled to the luxurious berth I had been allocated and was given a delicious meal. I arrived back in Peking a day and a half later. The British chargé d'affaires decided that there were no grounds for an official complaint. The photographs were not spectacular.

JOHN MORGAN

The Advantage of Plain Language

I was in the middle of a three-month spell as British chargé d'affaires in Seoul, enjoying sitting at the ambassador's desk, when one morning his secretary rang through to say that Hwasub Chang was in the embassy and anxious to see me urgently. If a Korean can look ashen-faced then that would certainly have applied to the Cathay Pacific representative. He was in a very nervous state indeed as he told me of his most recent experience with the South Korean Central Intelligence Agency.

In the 1970s the government of South Korea had good reason to be security-conscious. It had been discovered that the North Koreans had for some time been digging tunnels under the demilitarized zone, tunnels large enough to disgorge quickly hundreds of North Korean soldiers some distance behind the first South Korean lines. Anything that might suggest a South Korean was acting in a way that could prejudice the country's security could be counted upon to raise the immediate interest of its very heavy-handed CIA. Hwasub Chang told me that he had been taken in by them the day before and given a very bad time before being released. He had had an earlier experience of their methods and style of interrogation. After his latest experience he was convinced that he was going to be arrested again shortly and that he would not survive the next 'interview'.

As Cathay Pacific's representative he had apparently provided the airline with information that would normally have been considered routine in the airline industry. It may have been details of Kimpo Airport facilities or something related to passenger traffic. To the paranoid security service this smelled of treason. Hwasub Chang had come to ask if there was anything I could do to help.

There would be little point in trying to work through the usual diplomatic channels. Time was clearly of the essence if he was to be saved from a further knock on the door in the middle of the night. I was not at all sure that the Korean Foreign Ministry carried much weight with the Korean CIA, and it would certainly take some days to go through the procedures. If I sent a message through the usual embassy channels to Cathay Pacific in Hong Kong it would be electronically encoded even without a security classification. The Korean CIA would not be able to read it.

They had to be given prompt reason to pause before again attempting to persuade Hwasub Chang to confess to something he had not done. So I sent a telex message in plain language from the embassy's Commercial Department to the British Trade Commissioner in Hong Kong, reporting the problem that Cathay Pacific's Seoul representative was experiencing and requesting confirmation from the company's head office that he had been following normal airline practice. What they replied was immaterial: the objective was to convey to the Korean CIA – who almost certainly read every uncoded message that entered and left the country, and no doubt listened to all telephone calls as well – that the embassy was involved and concerned that Hwasub Chang's actions were being misconstrued.

It worked like a charm. Two days later he came back smiling to tell me he had heard that he was no longer suspect. I sometimes wonder what would have happened now, when telex is not used and fax not that often, when all embassy communications and even private emails whether classified or not are all apparently sent using high-tech methods which require sophisticated encryption. Perhaps there would nowadays have been no way of saving Hwasub Chang. Plain language sometimes helps.

RICHARD TALLBOYS

171

Country Style

On various visits to Japan in the 1970s and '80s I had developed a great liking for Japanese traditions, arts and crafts. Whenever I could, I visited historic temples, especially those in Kyoto. When I was allowed to, I liked to patronise traditional restaurants: over the years my Japanese hosts showed an increasing and deplorable tendency to frequent hamburger bars, pizza parlours and other imported fast-food joints.

In the 1980s my friend Peter was appointed EMI's resident director in Tokyo and in him I found the ideal companion in cultural exploration. He introduced me to an izakaya restaurant in the Rappongi district. The word, I think, means Country Style, and there is a pleasing rusticity in its arrangements. Some twenty or more diners, all of them men of course, sit at counters on three sides of a square. On the fourth side kneel two cooks with, in front of them, neat piles of fresh-prepared raw fish, meat and vegetables and a fiery grill – originally wood, one imagines, but now electric. The diners toss down glasses of sake and order their food by shouting to the cooks, who acknowledge by shouting the order back as they reach for the portions and put them on the grill. The cooking is accompanied by more sake and more shouting until the food is ready when, to yet more jovial shouts, it is passed across on a long wooden paddle. The atmosphere is convivial and boisterous to the point of comicality. An evening there always put one in a glow of high spirits.

One free weekend we decided to visit Nara, the ancient capital of Japan before Kyoto, and an easy, three-hour journey by bullet-train from Tokyo. A happy day was spent exploring the temples, shrines and monasteries disposed around the deer-park, which forms the centre of this little city. We goggled at the Todaiji Temple, which houses the largest statue of the Buddha in the world (dating from AD 743) and is itself the largest wooden building in the world.

Culturally replete, we walked back through the deer-park and looked out for the sacred deer about whose courtesy the guide-book spoke eloquently: if one stood before them and bowed, it said, the would bow back.

We duly came upon a group of them. We stopped and bowed, slowly and ceremoniously: the largest of them stepped forward solemnly and bit Peter's arm.

This rather impaired the magic of the afternoon. We speculated whether the deer knew that we were foreigners, who in those days were rarely seen in Nara.

Back at our Western-style hotel, we looked with some horror at the rough imitation of Louis XV furniture in the dining-room and the fake French menu to match. However, on enquiry to the hotel porter, we were delighted to learn that an izakaya restaurant could be found in a different part of Nara. A map and a half-mile walk soon took us there and, as we shouldered our way through the swing doors, our spirits rose at the sight and sound of the boisterous rustic scene so similar to our favourite spot in Tokyo. There were the happy diners, shouting, eating and sipping sake at the counters – and we were in luck, there were just two empty seats.

We advanced towards them smiling and bowing, but as we did so a nasty silence fell. First one, then all of the diners began waving their arms and shouting forbiddingly at us. We broadened our smiles and deepened our bows and continued to advance. They looked increasingly alarmed. Several made unsuccessful attempts to put their meaning in English. At last one of them recollected the right word, as he thought, and yelled 'Empty! Empty!' Immediately all the rest of them took up the cry and, with shouts of 'Empty! Empty!' ringing in our ears, we retreated to the street.

Whether the two seats were already bespoken I rather doubt. Most probably it was the presence of foreigners in their snug little eatery which aroused the other guests' anxiety. We trudged disconsolately back to the dubieties of our hotel menu.

MICHAEL ALLEN

Avoiding Arrest

Foreign correspondents are not encouraged to court arrest while on their travels. But neither should they strive to avoid incarceration, for spending a night or two in the cells does spice up a story and add to the row of medal ribbons on a journalist's chest. After over thirty-five years' travelling throughout South Asia I have still to win one. I was once sentenced to be flogged, but the sentence was not carried out and I have never got nearer the cells than the desk in a police station.

That police station was in Dhaka, which at the time was capital of the eastern part of Pakistan. In 1971 I was among the first party of journalists to be allowed into East Pakistan after the army's brutal crackdown on the liberation movement led by the Bengali nationalist Shaikh Mujibur Rahman. We had been told we could go anywhere and film or photograph whatever we wanted. As I was focusing on what remained of shops in the Shakahari Bazaar, a Hindu stronghold pulverised by Pakistan Army mortars, the camera was snatched from my hands. Two burly Punjabi policemen half lifted, half dragged me away and, when well beyond range of the shops they didn't want me to see, let alone photograph, began an impromptu interrogation. They addressed me as *Sala*, not a very polite word in Punjabi, followed by one rather ruder. When I explained in Hindustani, a mixture of Hindi and Urdu, that I was a journalist, the havildar or sergeant said: 'He speaks Hindi, he must be an Indian spy'. And marched me off to the nearest police station.

There the two tall Punjabis, transferred from West Pakistan because the authorities in the East could no longer rely on the local Bengali police, were not warmly greeted by a small, pot-bellied Bengali officer. In heavily accented Hindustani he asked wearily: 'What have you dragged in now?'

When they explained that they'd caught a spy he sighed and asked me in English: 'What have you got to say for yourself?'

I produced my accreditation card and explained that I'd been told I was free to go where I liked and photograph what I wanted. The Bengali officer thumbed through the latest government orders and to his delight found confirmation of my claim. Rounding on the Punjabis he said: 'You people have been sent here because the government doesn't trust us to do our job. You can't speak our language. Apparently you can't even speak your own. And you can't read orders in English. All you can do is harass gentlemen like this and waste my time with arresting innocent people. Get out of my police station'.

The Punjabis, to my surprise, slunk out without remonstrating. The delighted Bengali officer offered me a cup of tea. While we were enjoying that ceremony, essential to any contact with sub-continental bureaucracy, he sounded off about the Punjabi police, the Punjabi army and the Punjabi government, which was what he called the rulers of Pakistan. He summed it up by saying: 'The sooner we Bengalis get rid of them all, the better', then added hurriedly: 'But you won't quote me, will you, or the Punjabis will get me'.

I promised I wouldn't and left the police station with my camera un-opened, my film intact and not so much as a sight of the cells.

It was four years later, in 1975, that I was sentenced to be flogged. The sentence was passed in Delhi by Mohammed Yunus, a long-standing friend of the Nehru family. Although bereft of any official position, he was an influential member of what had come to be known as Indira Gandhi's kitchen cabinet. On the day that the Iron Lady declared a state of emergency, Yunus rang the Minister of Information and told him the BBC had claimed that two cabinet members had resigned in protest. He went on to order the minister, Inder Gujral:

'You send for Mark Tully, pull down his trousers, give him a few lash-es and send him to jail'.

The Information Minister replied: 'Look, Yunus, this is not my job. This is a job for the Home Minister so you talk to him'.

Gujral was perhaps the only minister who did not jump to obey orders any member of the kitchen cabinet issued on the day that dictatorship replaced democracy in India. Instead he hurriedly rang All India Radio who monitored every word broadcast by the BBC: Yunus had picked up one of the many unfounded rumours clogging the government's informa-tion sources. Neither I nor anyone else in the BBC had reported ministe-rial resignations because there had been none.

When Gujral informed the Prime Minister she excused Yunus saying: 'Maybe he heard some other radio station'.

But Gujral still lost his job to a more compliant minister who saw to it that I and most other correspondents left the country.

I didn't know how near I had come to a far worse fate until Gujral told me when I was allowed to return to India eighteen months later.

The second time I fell foul of the Pakistani police, they were not Punjabis but Pathans. It was after the Soviet invasion of Afghanistan and I was on my way to win my campaign ribbon by doing the obligatory walk-around of that mountainous country for a week. I had been taken to a safe house in a small town in Pakistan's North-West Frontier Province from where I and a colleague from Agence France Presse were to be escorted into Afghanistan by the Mujahidin. They said the mission was so secret that we couldn't be told the name of the town. But we found the house anything but secret or safe. Half the town passed through, had a good look at us and went on their way. When a police officer accompanied by a constable walked through the door I thought: 'We've had it, no foreigners are allowed in the tribal areas of the North-West Frontier Province'.

Sure enough, the officer immediately saw through my disguise – a long brown shirt worn outside baggy trousers, and a flat hat not unlike a Beef-eater's sitting at an awkward angle on my head.

He came up to me and said: 'You are no Afghan, you are a foreigner called Mark Tully and you speak Urdu'.

I denied both charges, pretending not to understand a word he was saying. He went on to insist that he had stamped my passport when I crossed the border legitimately a few weeks earlier and so recognized me. After several minutes of futile questioning, during which I continued to play the daft willy, the exasperated officer said:

'I know you are Mark Tully even if you don't admit it. I also know I should arrest you but I can't be bothered. Just make sure you get lost in Afghanistan and don't come back'.

The following morning we set out early on the climb to the pass which was the entrance to Afghanistan. After some hours I sat down to avoid falling down. My head was spinning from the altitude, the unusual exertion and an empty stomach. I was quite unable to climb on without a rest. Our far from sympathetic Afghan escorts ruled that out and continued the climb, saying I would have to find my own way down the mountain after I recovered. I stared down at the plains of Pakistan, wondering how I could face the humiliation of not even reaching Afghanistan. And meeting the policeman again who this time would surely arrest me.

But then I heard magical music – the tinkling bells of a mule train. I persuaded a mule-driver, for a consideration, to off-load his cargo and load me instead. And so entered Afghanistan mounted on a mule.

The greatest danger I faced, once there, was navigating the Kunar River on an inflated buffalo-skin. Nevertheless, after a footsore week being driven up and down mountains by hissing Mujahidin, I felt entitled to award myself the Afghan campaign medal. That was some compensation for failing a third time to win the higher honour of occupying the cells of an Asian police station. Now that I am no longer a foreign correspondent, and my travels are of a more light-hearted nature, I don't expect I will ever achieve that honour. But you can never be sure in India where, philosophers say, nothing is certain.

MARK TULLY

Climbing Iceland's Vatnajøkull

I first met Robert Geoffrey Tunstall St Leger, Bob to his friends, in our first year at Aberdeen University. We had both joined a climbing club named after the famous Lairig Ghru Pass which runs through the Highlands from Braemar to Aviemore. Most Sundays in winter the Lairig Club ran a bus to Braemar, dropping off climbers who then had all day to attempt one of the nearer Cairngorms. One Sunday Bob and I got off to climb Beinn a'Bhuird, not far from the road and, at just under four thousand feet, a respectable day's expedition. To reach the foot of the mountain we had to walk through pine forest where at every step we sank several inches into the soft snow. This was hard work but cured our hangovers from the previous night.

Beinn a'Bhuird is an impressive mountain with one big precipice but little else of real difficulty. It was a strenuous but relatively straightforward approach until we reached the slope beneath the summit: the wind had scoured its cone bare of snow, leaving only a sheet of solid, extremely slippery ice. Taking it in turns, we cut steps with our ice-axes right to the top, which was both slow and tiring, but the last few steps onto the flat summit were immensely satisfying. The panorama of the Cairngorms spread out around us was superb.

The cold, dry air; the crisp whiteness of the surrounding mountains; the deep blue of the sky made me feel I could run all the way back to the road. Light-headedness may have also made me careless. As we descended the ice-steps we had cut on the way up, I slipped and found myself sliding remarkably fast down the icy slope. I tried to dig in my ice-axe without success, and had slid perhaps fifteen or twenty feet when I felt a sudden jerk. Bob had caught me on the rope. I dug in my ice-axe and disentangled myself, realising that but for him and the rope belayed round his ice-axe, the outcome might have been very different.

A keen naturalist, Bob suggested we spend the summer of our third year in Iceland. Apart from seeing the thousands of sea-birds and duck on Lake Myvatn, we would try to cross the huge glacier of Vatnajøkull, which occupies most of south-east Iceland. This turned out to be impractical because of the melting of the ice-cap in summer, so we opted instead to climb the highest mountain in Iceland, which rejoices in the name of Hvannadalshnúkur. At 6952 feet, it is much higher than anything in Britain. In August we sailed from Glasgow aboard the MV *Hekla* to Reykjavik, where we did some sightseeing and visited a local newspaper editor. When we told him our plans he looked surprised.

'No one, as far as I know,' he said in careful English, 'has ever climbed Vatnajøkull in summer.'

'Why not?'

'Because it is too hot,' he replied, adding: 'If you do succeed, you must write an article for my paper.' We shook hands on that and left the next day on an Icelandic Airways DC3 for a tiny hamlet called Fagurholsmyri, on the edge of the ocean, landing on a black, volcanic gravel strip in the shadow of Vatnajøkull.

Shortly after arriving we met a local farmer whose hospitable nature and excellent grasp of English impressed us greatly. That night he asked us to dinner, producing an Icelandic speciality which consisted of mutton which had been buried in the ground for a couple of months. The ground is so cold, even in summer, that the effect is somewhere between a deep freeze and a game larder. In this instance the game larder won and, delicious though it may have been to the Icelandic palate, the two-month-old mutton was so high as to be barely edible. We chewed and swallowed dutifully. Revived by strong black coffee, the conversation resumed. Tomorrow, our host said, a German vet residing in Iceland was arriving to make his bi-annual tour of inspection and would take us with him to the last farm below Vatnajøkull. It was uninhabited, so we could use it as a base.

The next morning we set off on horseback with the jovial vet, named Hans, and a local guide. We trotted through the tall green summer pastures, bright with Arctic flowers between the mountain and the sea. Icelandic ponies, although small, are strong and sure-footed, and carried us with ease, a remarkable feat considering Hans must have weighed fifteen stone or so, plus saddle-bags.

We arrived in the afternoon at Sandfell, a white-washed, two-storied farm-house only two hundred yards from the snout of a huge moraine. Perhaps that was why it was deserted. Hans and the guide showed us in and then rode off, promising to return in two days' time. Our base consisted of two main rooms downstairs and two bedrooms upstairs, both fitted with old-fashioned wooden box beds such as you still see in the remoter parts of Scotland. Apart from the beds there was no furniture.

Anxious to see what the next day held, we were out of the house before eight, striding towards the scree a few hundred yards away. This was worse than we expected, almost the whole mountainside consisting of small, round lava stones which skittered away beneath our feet; for every step upwards, we slid back half a step. Still, we must have been reasonably fit because I was able to smoke my pipe and not be out of breath by the snow-line. Looming above us, the peak did not look particularly difficult except for one thing: the whole slope ahead was defended by crevasses, criss-crossing the mountain in deep, black-shadowed gashes, some of them big enough to swallow a house. We would have to zigzag round them as best we could.

It was already hot and we climbed in shirt-sleeves, winding our way round and between the crevasses. They were often beautiful in a sinister way, their sides shading from dazzling white to green, dark blue and then black. Peering down into a crevasse was a chilling experience. We crossed one or two snow-bridges, a nervy business when the sun begins to melt the ice, as was happening now all round us. However carefully you test the bridge with the tip of your ice-axe, you are never sure until you put your whole weight on it, and then it may be too late. As we moved steadily higher, the sun became hotter and the melting increased apace, the water spattering down the sides of the crevasses like a leaky gutter after heavy rain. At midday we reached the foot of Hvannadalshnúkur, a steep-sided cone of rock and frozen snow, and sat down to lunch on bully beef, biscuits, chocolate and water. The slope ahead was steep but not impossibly so. What was worrying was the amount of melting and one or two ugly crevasses. I suddenly understood what the editor in Reykjavik had meant.

Determined to reach the peak and be down before dark, we started off again at a good pace, reinvigorated by the rest. It was now my turn to lead. We were already well up the face and going strongly when suddenly right in front of me was a narrow, deep crevasse. Unseen from below, it blocked our way completely. We scouted left and right, trying to find a way round, but it appeared to link up with other crevasses which encircled the peak like a grotesque necklace. We came back to our starting-point where one slender chance remained: a narrow, arched snow-bridge. Making sure Bob had me securely belayed on the rope, I edged up to the lip and studied the rather alarming prospect. Below, the walls darkened to bottle green, submarine blue and then black. It would be a long drop, with little hope of one of us being able to pull the other out. The ice-bridge was melting visibly. About five feet wide and ten feet long, it arched away from me and up to a solid slope on the far side. I tried it with one foot. It held, but I could not reach out far enough to test it properly. I prodded it with my ice-axe. The steel-tipped point hit hard ice, but I hesitated to put my whole weight on it. I could feel myself sweating, not entirely from exertion.

I was conscious that Bob was waiting below for me to make up my mind. If we decided against the ice-bridge, we would have to find an alternative route, which would take time, and if we failed, we would have to abandon our attempt altogether. My mind seemed to make itself up of its own volition.

'No,' I shouted down. 'It's too risky. I don't think it will hold our weight and it's a hell of a long way down. I'm coming back.'

180

As I climbed down a new thought formed in my mind. 'We're on the south face,' I said, panting. 'So there's bound to be a lot of melting here. But if we can get round to the north face, the snow should be harder.'

'I'm game to give it a try,' Bob agreed.

For the next half-hour we climbed in silence in a semicircle to the west and north, the snow gradually getting harder and the crevasses fewer. I stopped and looked up. The slope rose smoothly, showing only a few crevasses right to the triangular summit.

We were so excited we almost charged the slope. The packed snow squeaked under our nails as we went up in a fast-breathing rush. Then, just short of the top, a huge crevasse opened at our feet. It was very deep but only about four feet across. I went right to the edge: it was as hard as concrete. Without hesitation I jumped right across it.

We sprinted the last few yards, hardly noticing the steepness of that final slope of smooth, hard, windswept snow that led up to the small pyramid which was the peak. We stood panting for a few minutes, grinning at each other in sheer delight. To the north and east, the huge mass of Vatnajøkull lay before us, an ocean of ice, combed with crevasses. Ranges of mountains receded into the haze to the north and west; and below us, to the south, the grey Atlantic looked from this altitude like another frozen sea.

Blue shadows were creeping over the snow-fields as we began our descent, zigzagging between the crevasses. Occasionally the roar of falling ice broke the silence. Then, skirting the end of a crevasse, I felt one foot go through the snow. Luckily my weight was already on the other foot, which held. Looking down, all I could see was a black hole. The snow-bridge was on the point of collapse and I stepped off it smartly. We reached the snow-line in less than an hour and turned for a last look at the mountain, the peak serene in the evening sunshine.

We ran down the scree in a third of the time it had taken us to climb, the slip of the stones carrying us like slow-motion skiers. Sandfell was already in shadow, unmoved by our triumphant return. That night I had a nightmare in which I kept falling, falling off a mountain. Bob was made of sterner stuff. He slept like a baby.

SANDY GALL

Under Close Arrest

On a break from an Arabic course in Beirut, I was taking a constitutional through the port of Lattakia. Post-prandial, about the time for evening prayers. Trails of fairy-lights hung draped across the darkness, and naked light-bulbs mustered bugs. The call to prayer soon sounded across the city from a dozen different mosques. Out of sync and in a dozen different keys, its effect, on me at least, was not entirely devotional. Unseen waves slapped heavily, a *continuo* counterpoint, against the harbour wall below.

They put me in mind of Earnshaw. He and I had gone neck and neck through the Fifth and Lower Sixth, keeping upper school abuzz with our contests of useless knowledge. I personally had been most impressed with his reciting the then forty-eight States in alphabetical order. This had however been disallowed by the self-appointed Upper Sixth umpires as being conceivably useful for wowing American friends. My present-tense paradigm of *avoir* in Old French then held him off beautifully until someone noticed this very fatuity as a question in an Oxbridge entrance paper with a fifty-pound scholarship on offer. Its uselessness evanesced.

Earnshaw came back with the fact that, contrary to popular belief, the Mediterranean is not completely tideless. Objections: that could be useful to yachtsmen. And what about harbourmasters? Deep-sea divers? Clam diggers? 'All right then,' smirked Earnshaw, trumping himself, 'but the tide is measurable only in La Skhira and Lattakia.'

La Skhira? It had taken me a drive from Cairo to Muswell Hill to locate that, years later, low on the Tunisian coast. Lattakia was where I now was: could he have been right? There would be tide-marks on the harbour wall, and I had a pocket torch. So, finding a gap in the balustrade where worn stone blocks descended to the water's edge, I turned on the torch and stepped cautiously down. '*Shu ta'amal?* What are you doing?'

Surely it was easy to see what I was doing, looking for tide-marks by torch-light at night. Explaining this to the voice at the top of the steps was not so easy – the Arabic for Harbour Wall eluded me momentarily – so I climbed back up and confronted a swarthy man scowling in plimsoles and a dirty polo-neck.

'*Salaamu 'alaikum*,' I said.

In lieu of the usual *Wa'alaikum as-salaam* came another question. Where was I going? That at least let me off the Arabic for Contests of Useless Knowledge, and I had read the guide-book over dinner.

'To the Latin Church,' I replied.

'I'll show you the way.' And motioning me to move, he set off at a brisk pace it seemed discourteous not to keep up with.

We padded – plimsoles and Bata brothel-creepers – noiselessly through the city. My attempts at polite conversation failed. My silent escort's only response to comments and questions on the fine Ottoman double-doors to either side was to step up the pace. The back of my brain was still working on the word-lists – Wall was no problem but was that Harbour as in Grudge? – when my companion stopped, stooped, then flung himself at me in a full, 1st XV shoulder-charge. Barged sidelong through a double-doorway – Ottoman I knew not but fortunately half-open – I found myself sprawled on the flagstones inside.

'*Jaasuus!* Spy!' my no longer silent guide shouted. '*Jaasuus ajnabi!*'

A semi-uniformed policeman lounging beside a hubble-bubble blinked at us.

'*Jaasuus ajnabi!*' my captor cried again, 'a foreign spy!'

'*Jaasuus ingleezi*,' I corrected him, parodying Poirot. Being barged at was bad enough but all this *ajnabi* was adding insult to what could have been injury.

I got up and greeted the policeman. Tucking in his shirt, he buckled his belt and heaved himself bulkily to his feet. He smiled, shook my hand and asked after my health, family and general well-being. I reciprocated and, when the ritual pleasantries were ended, he said: 'Now how can I be of service to you?'

'Well it's not so much me, it's this gentleman who seems to think . . .'

'He's a spy!' cried my captor, visibly incensed by our cordiality. 'Arrest him!'

'I can't arrest him without a charge,' said the constable, the 'charge' made to sound like an unconscionable breach of hospitality.

'The charge is espionage, spying! I caught him snooping in the port.'

Torn between his friendliness to foreigners and a sleepy sense of duty, the policeman apologized. Would I mind waiting a moment while he checked? Spies were something he didn't get a lot of. I made sympathetic noises and, pushing aside his hubble-bubble, he opened a steel cabinet behind him and brought out from beneath packs of tambagh a weighty-looking tome.

He blew off the dust, plus some of the tobacco, and found his place. The contents, which he began reading aloud, were apparently in alphabetical Arabic. '*Jaani*' – Felon, '*Jariima*' – Crime, '*Juththa*' – Corpse. The English equivalent would have been Sodomy, Soliciting, 'No, Spying isn't here. There's no *jaasuusiya* so no *jaasuus*.'

He shut and returned the Offence Book to its place with palpable relief.

'Where's the inspector?' demanded my captor. He was clearly not settling for what, had the expression been coined then, looked like being a cop-out.

'Gone for prayers. Him and the sergeant.' Two cops out. I made moves to leave. The policeman, uncertain, offered tea. Or would I like to try the *biss*, the nipple of his hubble-bubble? My captor rather less uncertainly reached for a chair and, setting it squarely in the half-open doorway, sat down and dared me.

He soon had to move. Footsteps approaching *crescendo* through the otherwise silent streets materialized into what I assumed to be the sergeant and his chief. Over regulation shirt, socks and shoes both wore double-breasted grey jackets and matching skirts.

'*Salaamu ʿalaikum.*' '*Waʿalaikum as-salaam.*' We shook hands heartily and asked how each other was. Then the inspector asked the constable what all this was.

'This man,' the latter replied, 'says he caught this gentleman spying.'

'In here?' The inspector looked incredulous. 'We haven't got any work, let alone secrets.'

'No, in the port,' my captor intervened.

The inspector ignored him. 'Anyway spying's not a police matter, it's military,' he said decisively. 'It's for the colonel, not us.'

Everyone looked relieved. Except me.

'*Tafaddal.*' The inspector ushered me through to his office at the back, where papers fluttered under an overhead fan.

'I'm so sorry we couldn't help you here,' he apologized. 'If I'd been on duty alone I'd have soon seen off that *Abu Khafafi*, that Father of

Plimsoles, 'and not kept your honour waiting. But with them all here, and me being in charge, and the colonel tight on security . . . ' I could see his problem.

'You're sure you don't mind having a word with the colonel?' He was too charming for me to be churlish.

'That's most kind of your honour. His office is in the barracks, straight on uphill. I'll give you someone to show you the way. He won't need a lift back.'

A moment of incomprehension that was not linguistic.

'You have got your own transport?' he asked.

'No, haven't you?'

'Er no,' said the inspector. After some silent and presumably unproductive thought, he excused himself and returned to the outer room. The words I caught most frequently through the open office door were Taxi and *Fuluus*, the latter meaning Money, followed by silence.

The inspector returned, excusing himself again.

'*Tayyib*, you should be all right in a taxi, but they charge extra at this time of night' – embarrassment once more – 'so would your honour happen to have . . .?'

'No,' I cut in firmly. Paying to be taken into custody indeed!

Another awkward silence was interrupted by the appearance of a youth in the doorway.

'Would the company like coffee?'

The coffee-boy was nodded in and proceeded to pour a long, curving arc into each of the tiny cups he deftly handed round. We each reached the cup back twice for the customary second and third serving before shaking it in time-honoured fashion to show we couldn't stomach any more. As he poured, the coffee-boy chattered inconsequentially until, conscious of the lack of response, he asked what was wrong. The sergeant vouchsafed him a word of explanation.

'I've got my mobilette,' he piped up.

'Can it take two?' the sergeant asked.

'Takes my little sister to school. She loves it. Although . . . ' The coffee-boy sized me up.

'Could we try?' The inspector turned to me. 'Would your honour mind?'

Outside, the coffee-boy's vehicle proved to be some sort of motorized bicycle, vintage unknown. Its seat, coming apart at the seams, was a mock-leather pad not eighteen inches long. He sat on it and motioned me to mount pillion. There was nothing to hold on to so, making this close arrest, I clasped his waist.

The inspector came out, still looking apologetic.

'This really is very good of your honour, a great help.' I tutted deprecatingly. 'Please come back and be my guest for dinner if, er, when the colonel lets you go.'

The others all came out to see us off. Amidst thanks for the visit and wellwishing for the trip, we shook hands. The coffee-boy slipped into gear and revved the motor.

Alas, the motor was willing but the frame was weak. With so much weight aft, the front wheel wobbled uncontrollably. Beneath me some underparts must have pressed on the back wheel. It blocked. We fell off. I was sprawled on the ground for the second time that night, this time outside the fine double-doorway. It *was* Ottoman, I decided.

'*La ba'as? La ba'as?*' Cries of concern from the policemen. No, we weren't harmed, thank you, just embarrassed. Lights had come on in upper windows and the gallery of heads that had appeared at them, indignant, was now settled there, intrigued.

'You need more weight in front,' observed the sergeant. 'Can your honour ride one of these?'

'No problem,' I replied, never having tried.

We remounted. To renewed thanks and wellwishing, this time from the gallery too, we set off. Now I was under even closer arrest: my escort's arms were round me.

We had a very pleasant ride. The coffee-boy directed me up out of the city, pointing out the more significant sights. His elder brother's puncture repair-shop, the kindergarten where his sister worked. The night was balmy; other road-users overtook us wide to get a better stare, and the view back as we climbed was of fairy-lights and bare bulbs in a twinkling chiaroscuro. We shook off the city and chugged on across a *cordon insanitaire* of abandoned vehicles and haphazard barbed wire to the barracks.

The barrier was down. Two guards with sub-machine guns blocked our way.

'This gentleman is to see the colonel,' the coffee-boy announced.

'Does he have an appointment?'

'D'you have an appointment?' the coffee-boy asked me.

'Er, not exactly.' I tried to smile disarmingly. 'You see . . . '

'The colonel's gone home. You'll have to come back in the morning.'

'That's a bit awkward,' said the coffee-boy. 'I've got to get my sister to school.'

At that moment the 'phone rang in the guard-house. One sentry went in to take the call, talked for a while then returned.

'Are you the foreign spy?'

'Well, yes and no . . . '

'*Tafaddal.*' He took me firmly by the arm. Without time even to take proper leave of the coffee-boy I was unmounted and marched across a sandy parade ground to a long, bleak building. The sentry banged on its iron door.

This prompted responses from within. Such as '*Imshi!* Get lost! *Skut! Diin ummak!* Bloody shut up!'

'Prisoner for the night. Open up!' The sentry pounded the door again.

'Sorry, no vacancies!' The author of this last belied his own wisecracking by opening the door and ushering me in. I was the object of some curiosity. To those, that is, whose sleep had been curtailed by the commotion.

The door of the guard-house clanged shut behind me. I was lucky one sergeant's aunt had died, said the joker: he had leave for the funeral, leaving me his bed. I was shown to it and lay down fully clothed. In the next bed a heavily hirsute soldier was reading by the light of a pocket torch. I offered him mine; it was light-years better. On the other side a soldier was humming softly.

'So you like Oum Kalthoum?' I asked as he paused to scratch.

'Prefer Fairouz really,' and he switched to humming one of hers.

I hummed along. Somewhere in the darkness someone tapped out the rhythm. It was not an unmusical moment.

'Like a cigarette?' somebody asked.

'I'd prefer a *biss.*'

Despite the Islamic precept that Prayer is Better than Sleep, those who were by now giving up on the latter seemed to find ribaldry a more attractive alternative. From the hubble-bubble's nipple we joked on to other manly subjects. Arabic, with its rich vocabulary derived for the most part from surprisingly few roots, lends itself to puns and *double entendres*. Risqué small talk took us through the small hours.

Daybreak caught us dozing. The dawn call to prayer ensured that all save me were up by the time reveille sounded. I rose dutifully, excused myself from the cold communal shower, and was wondering whether to borrow a razor and try shaving in the coffee that was offered when a sentry banged on the door. It was open but he banged again. It clearly gave him pleasure.

'Which one's the foreign spy?' he bawled.

Most of the soldiers in the guard-house raised their hands.

'Mad buggers' was, roughly translated, what he muttered as he walked me out and up some stairs. We stopped at an impressive door panelled in padded red leather. While the sentry was wondering how to knock there was ample time to read the name-plate.

The colonel's name-plate may have been Arabic, he was for the rest pukka Sandhurst. Short, in his thirties and impeccably turned out, he waved me in with one hand and the sentry away with the other.

'Do have a seat, old chap,' he said. 'Can I get my man to shave you? No? Well, apologies for all this anyway. Slim – that's the inspector – he's put me in the picture.' The colonel's blue eyes twinkled. 'And I suppose it's too late now to shoot you at dawn.'

'Though I must admit neither of us could figure out what you were doing with that torch.' I explained about Earnshaw.

'Useless knowledge, eh?' he smiled. 'You could have had the contingency plans for this place and won hands down.' Had life not obliged him to put away childish things, the colonel would have made a promising contestant. Returning to the matter in hand, he asked: 'But why didn't you make a break for it? Right at the start. That shower at the station would never have caught you.'

'Or tickled the coffee-boy and hopped off the mobilette?'

'That's right, alight at the lights.' His English was a delight.

'That could have been resisting arrest,' I suggested. 'And the chap who turned me in, he of the plimsoles, he looked pretty mean. And fleet of foot.'

'But not so fair of face? Talking of which, I hear you like Fairouz. I do too. What's your favourite piece?'

'Oh there's so many,' I replied. 'But *At-tahuuna*'s pretty amazing.'

'Yes, the way she takes it from a diminished seventh on the tonic to another diminished seventh on the supertonic and then again on the major mediant . . . ' I was glad we were speaking English; I couldn't have managed that with undergrad. Arabic. Nor, I imagined, could most of the locals without it.

We chatted on, about the lute he played; the Kurdish problem; the plans to dam the Euphrates; Devon cream teas. The telephone rang and cut it all short. The colonel apologized; duty called. I left him with genuine regret – one of the most impressive officers I have ever had the privilege to be arrested by.

'You may as well have a cushier ride back,' were his parting words. 'Afraid we haven't got a mobilette, you'll have to take my staff car.' He rang for his driver.

'Just tell him wherever you want to go. And Mustapha, unfurl the pennant.'

It would thus have been in some style that I returned to the hotel. Had the driver not cut down across town, past the police station – I waved majestically – and back through the port. Where I noticed that gap in the balustrade with worn stone steps descending to the water's edge. I bid the driver goodbye. I had lost out on sleep and the evening's prescribed dose of vocab: I owed it to Earnshaw to salvage something from the night.

MICHAEL TOMKINSON

Let's Get Outa Here

We were greeted with profuse apologies by our hosts on arrival in Buenos Aires because the Union Jack was not to be seen amongst all the other conference flags. It was only five years after the Falklands War and diplomatic relations had not yet been resumed. Argentina was not perhaps top of the list for a visit at that time, but the International Bar Association had chosen Buenos Aires some time before as the venue for its conference; as I had just been responsible for setting up a new specialist committee and was its first chairman, there was never any question of my not attending.

The conference followed the usual pattern with each committee allotted a day and a half for its meetings, the rest of the time being free. Law enthusiasts could attend plenary sessions or meetings of other committees; social events and excursions were available for the rest. My wife and I toured the city and saw amongst other sights the artists' quarter and Eva Peron's mausoleum. We were entertained by gauchos and fed with vast barbecues as part of the conference's 'social programme'.

But we wanted also to see something of the country, so we opted for a full-day trip to Aconcagua, the highest mountain in the Andes and indeed the Americas. This entailed a one-hour flight to Mendoza, which lies at the foot of the Andes, then a long coach drive through the Sierra de los Semillos, and finally up the pass which leads to Chile and Santiago.

It was only on the way to the airport that we were told by our guide that our destination, the viewpoint for Aconcagua, was in a no-man's-land between the Argentinian and Chilean frontier-posts. We were not carrying our passports as another young and rather nervous guide had told us on arrival that they should be deposited in the hotel safe and left there for the duration of our visit.

The guide on the coach thought there should be no problem and indeed we sailed through the frontier-post on the way up to the top of the pass. There we climbed out of the coach and, looking up a V-shaped cleft, saw the snow-fields and summit of a very high mountain. It was not exactly a panorama, just enough to say we had seen it. After a brief rest we started on the return journey, back to the Argentinian frontier-post.

Here there was trouble. The guide went into the office and was away for a long time. When she emerged she was accompanied by an Argentinian army sergeant armed with an automatic rifle. They were arguing fiercely. We could imagine what was being said.

'But you saw our bus go through just half an hour ago.'

'How do I know it was the same bus? Why haven't your passengers got passports?'

'They weren't told they would be crossing the frontier.'

'That's no excuse. For all I know they might be a lot of Chileans.'

Finally the guide, looking very upset, boarded the bus followed by the sergeant. He told the driver to drive a short way down the road and stopped him at a lay-by. Then he turned to us and shouted:

'Any British, OUT!'

I suppose that my wife and I could have tried to conceal our nationality but that might have made things worse for the others. So we rather meekly left our seats at the back and walked the full length of the coach to the door. A Zimbabwean lawyer offered to lend us his passport. A German with whom we had made friends said to my wife: 'Don't worry, we'll wait for you'. But an excitable American, seeing us being marched off up the road, was heard to exclaim:

'They're gonna be shot. Let's get outa here!'

One other Brit accompanied us on our scary walk back to the frontier-post with the Argentinian sergeant on our heels. Our companion did have his passport but by this time we had stopped worrying whether that would be a factor in our fate. We had discovered before landing at Mendoza Airport that it was one of the main bases of the Argentine Air Force and home to many of the pilots who had flown in the Falklands War.

So it was with considerable apprehension that we entered the office, to be lined up by the sergeant in front of a counter behind which stood an immigration officer. A very small man in a dark blue suit, with only a few words of English, he was obviously under the sergeant's thumb completely and in great doubt as to what to do. After some hesitation he handed us a form and a pencil and told us to write down our passport details. I was just about to launch into a tirade about not knowing my passport number and the stupidity of being told to lock our passports in the hotel safe when a great weight landed on my toe.

It was my wife's foot. It served to remind me how exemplary she is in dealing with a crisis. So I stayed silent and she took the form. Our companion whispered: 'One letter and eight digits'.

My wife conjured up two suitable numbers for us and handed him the form for his. The immigration officer took the form. There was a pause. Without a word the officer motioned that we were free to go.

Our escort back to the coach was a mere private. As we climbed aboard the coach our fellow-passengers greeted us with a chorus of Rule Britannia. With a real sense of relief we set off. Initially the tension collapsed in animated talk, but slowly built up again as people began to realise that the hold-up had made us seriously late. We might not reach Mendoza in time for the return flight. The driver took the coach down the mountain road as fast as he could, but it seemed to be taking ages.

Then – roadworks! The silence in the bus was electric. It was bad enough for the others but my wife and I had the added dread of the false passport numbers being checked on a computer at the very moment we were stuck here on the road. If we were delayed in Mendoza and forced to spend the night there, we could be in real trouble. We finally cleared the roadworks, however, and the driver forged on brilliantly – who cared at that stage how many times he risked our lives? We got to the airport and scrambled into our seats on the 'plane, its engines already running.

That should have been it. But whereas the flight out had been non-stop, there was an intermediate touch-down on the way back. As we taxied to a halt at this small airport, a mass of uniformed officers swarmed aboard. I cowered in my seat. So they had discovered our deception! The officers crowded into the cockpit, surely to examine the passenger list before coming back for us. But what was going on? They were all laughing and joking. And weren't those airline uniforms, not police? . . . One of the flight crew was getting married; the ground staff had all come to wish him well!

We were glad to get back to Buenos Aires. The news of our 'arrest' had spread around the conference. Some colleagues none the less took the same excursion the day after our return. I hope they had a more experienced guide. And remembered to take their passports.

RICHARD CREWDSON

The Falklands and Grenada

The Falklands Campaign was the highlight of my military career. I was Chief of the General Staff, professional head of the Army. Most would agree that the campaign was most remarkable, conducted as it was eight thousand miles from home against numerical odds and without the air superiority which normally would have been essential for this type of operation. Our Task Force had to win the air battle as it went along, flying Harriers off of flat tops bobbing around in the rough South Atlantic. As a result, risks had to be taken, particularly by our surface ships during the landing and build-up. Once the troops were ashore, they were to meet resistance in places but, as the air risks against them declined, they proved more than a match for the now mostly conscripts opposing them.

There are many good stories about Margaret Thatcher, who was such an effective and inspiring war leader. This was perhaps her finest hour. One story concerns her intervention over the Gurkhas. The Foreign & Commonwealth Office was not keen for the Gurkhas to go down to the South Atlantic, and wanted to remove them from the Task Force because of the so-called susceptibilities of the Third World. This was entirely fallacious: to remove Gurkhas from their own brigade just when it might have to fight a war would have been a crowning insult.

I managed to win this battle with the help of the Secretary of State for Defence, John Nott, who had himself been a Gurkha. One day when we were all at Chequers and I saw the Prime Minister approaching, I said in front of the Foreign Secretary and his Permanent Secretary:

'Prime Minister, you do know, don't you, that we are sending a Gurkha battalion with the Task Force?'

There was a momentary pause. Then looking at the two gentlemen she said: 'What, only one?'

Collapse of stout party!

It was also about this time, at Chequers, that Dennis Thatcher, who was warming his bottom in front of the fire, was suddenly heard to say at the top of his voice:

'Well, thank God we have a Prime Minister with some guts at last.'

I was Chief of the Defence Staff when the US invaded Grenada. The island was, of course, part of the British Commonwealth. At a Defence Committee meeting a few days earlier I gave as my opinion to Margaret Thatcher that, although I had no concrete evidence, I felt in my water that President Reagan was going to invade.

'What on earth would make him do a stupid thing like that?' she said. So I reminded her that the United States had just had 250 men killed in the Lebanon, that the relief force going to Beirut was just by coincidence about eighty miles north of Grenada, and that I believed President Reagan, whose citizens had experienced some 'aggro' from Grenada, wanted a success to balance the losses the Marines had sustained.

The Foreign Secretary, however, did not agree and said that he was in touch with the Secretary of State: the President was going to play it very low key and there was no chance of military action.

'There you are,' said Mrs Thatcher.

Much later that night, at around 1.30 a.m., my wife and I were fast asleep when my Naval Personal Staff Officer burst into the room – we had obviously not heard the telephone – and said:

'The Prime Minister wants to see you in Downing Street right away'.

Well, there was no transport, my own car being locked inside the underground garage which closed at midnight, so the staff officer and I sprinted up into the Park where at last we found a taxi. It was by now about ten to two. I found myself saying to the driver: 'Number Ten Downing Street' – he thought we were a couple of drunks!

At Number Ten there was absolute pandemonium: President Reagan had just signalled to say that he was invading that very morning, and Mrs Thatcher had told him he shouldn't, it wasn't any of his business. She never once said anything to me like 'Well, you did warn me' and I was too polite to say 'I told you so'. Instead I asked her if she wanted to be associated with the operation in any way, because if not I'd have to get some orders out to ships in the vicinity.

'Certainly not,' she said very firmly – a decision which I can say made no difference to our NATO relationship or to the remarkably close Reagan/Thatcher bond.

'DWIN BRAMALL

194

Dinner with Mrs Thatcher

The old city of Salzburg lies below the towering rock of the Hohensalzburg and above the rushing waters of the Salzach River, in an exquisite setting between the Austrian lake district and the Bavarian Alps. Once an independent city-state of the Holy Roman Empire, it was for generations governed by the fun-loving prince-archbishops who adorned their fiefdom with the most magnificent palaces, churches, squares, fountains and gardens. To this most beautiful of cities have been added in the last century the opera houses cut into the rock behind the seventeenth-century façade of the archiepiscopal mews. They house the celebrated Salzburg Festival, by far the most glamorous of all music festivals.

For thirty years my work in the international management of what is now called EMI Classics took me to Salzburg. The festival has immense prestige for leading artists and it is to support them that their record companies undertake advertising and promotion during the festival period.

This is why I first attended but, as my responsibilities changed and grew, I always found compelling reasons to come back every year. More of my colleagues came too, as did our contemporaries from rival companies. On the principle that anyone who has ever been to the Salzburg Festival at the company's expense will find a convincing reason to return, it has gradually come about that the senior managers of all the major classical music companies find it essential to be there. The artists expect to see them there too, both as a sign of personal support and for repertoire discussions and contract negotiations. This in turn attracts the artists' agents and managers, and the beautiful old city became in the 1980s akin to a classical record convention. Leading companies vied with each other with elegant offices, lavish parties and generously catered press conferences.

In parallel, the festival-goers, who in my early years were mostly rich Austrians and Germans, became more cosmopolitan and as likely to be from France, Japan or the USA. Film stars, politicians and multi-millionaires were to be seen at Karajan concerts and the principal opera performances. Outside the *Festspielhaus*, the concert hall, the crowds lining the pavements to admire and applaud the arriving celebrities became so thick that the crash barriers had to be extended further and further down the street. In due course even British luminaries began to be seen.

EMI's star young conductor Riccardo Muti had been successfully launched into the festival, particularly in 1982 with a striking production of Mozart's *Cosi fan Tutte*. As Muti's birthday fell in the first week of the festival, it became an EMI custom to celebrate with a dinner party. Sometimes this was generously hosted by Lord Weinstock, the boss of GEC and a keen opera-goer who was a particular admirer of Muti: for *Desert Island Discs* all eight of his choices had been of Muti recordings. Apart from race-going, Muti performances seemed to be Arnold Weinstock's favourite relaxation, and I met him and his friends (including Isaiah Berlin) on many such occasions.

In 1983 when *Cosi fan Tutte* was revived, it became known that Mr and Mrs Thatcher were near by, taking a holiday in Austria for the first time. So shortly after the Falklands Campaign Mrs Thatcher was of course at the height of her fame and power. Though not known publicly as a supporter of hers, Lord Weinstock immediately arranged that this year's dinner party should be in honour jointly of Mrs Thatcher and Maestro Muti – implying a flattering parallel between conducting orchestras and conducting government, both needing a strong lead as it were.

After the performance my wife and I made our way to the Schloss Hotel some five miles from Salzburg where the dinner was to be held in a private room. The lobby was crowded with opera-goers in evening dress returning to dine in the restaurant.

'Come this way please.' Two large Englishmen in dinner jackets had singled us out.

'But we're guests of Lord Weinstock.'

'Yes, we know,' they replied somewhat smugly, ushering us into the private room. Evidently they were from the Secret Service. We were impressed and mildly alarmed that they recognized us without our ever having seen them before.

We were about twenty for dinner: friends of Lord Weinstock, a few of us from EMI, the Mutis and Mr & Mrs Thatcher's party including the British ambassador and his wife. We found ourselves immediately talking to Mr Thatcher, who was as affable and down to earth as the *Dear Bill* letters had led one to expect.

'Has Maestro Muti arrived yet?' asked the ambassador's wife.

Glancing round, I pointed out the darkly handsome conductor in the doorway, already deep in conversation with Mrs Thatcher.

'Oh God, the Boss has got him,' said Mr Thatcher. Tacitly welcoming this confirmation of Mrs T's family sobriquet, I assumed this was an apprehension that Muti would not now be able to circulate and meet the other guests. He was right: neither Muti nor Mrs T circulated. Heads together, they conversed closely and at length until and after we sat down to dinner – about problems of leadership, one supposes.

In due course the time for speeches arrived. Lord Weinstock rose and revealed a side of his talents hitherto unknown to me. In his long and monumentally successful career he was revered as one of the greatest British industrialists, but on this particular evening one realized why he had arranged that the chairmanship of GEC should always be held by a leading politician. Weinstock was no public speaker.

After he had shifted uncomfortably from compliments to Muti to compliments to Mrs Thatcher, he gave ominous signs of being about to attempt an after-dinner joke and unfortunately so it proved. He confided that he had only recently learned that Stalin's name meant Man of Steel and therefore that when the Soviet government designated Mrs Thatcher the Iron Lady they were perhaps, um, suggesting a flattering comparison with their former, um, formidable leader. Brief laughter was followed by an ominous silence as we all turned to see what her reaction might be.

'I fail to see the connection,' she pronounced in that chest voice rivalled in dramatic intensity only by the late Maria Callas.

'You've put your foot in it there, Arnold,' called out the British ambassador gaily.

Rapidly Weinstock concluded his remarks and looked to Mrs Thatcher to reply. She rose, clutching some notes, and looked keenly around the expectant table. As she opened her mouth to begin, a stout gentleman rose at the end of the table and began himself to make a speech.

'Were you asked to speak?' said Mrs T in that majestic voice. The stout gentleman waved a genial hand and continued to speak.

'Were you asked?' said Mrs T, still on her feet and even more majestically. He waved another genial arm and said that as an Austrian and a dedicated admirer he insisted on making a speech in her honour.

Mrs Thatcher repeated 'Were you asked?' once or twice more before subsiding back in her chair, to await the end of this unwanted and lengthy encomium, defeated perhaps for the only time in that glorious decade. We concluded that the jovial speaker was either uninstructed in protocol, or drunk, or both. At last he finished and the Prime Minister was able to deliver her gracious remarks elegantly but a trifle tensely, with occasional anxious glances to where her unwanted admirer now slumbered.

The hour being far advanced, the party broke up soon after. We all departed into the night without further conversation. We had had dinner with Mrs Thatcher. But not actually met her.

MICHAEL ALLEN

Commando Snowcraft

I was coming to the end of my second year on an Antarctic sledging base. It was midsummer and the sea-ice had gone, alas: ships were beginning to sail self-importantly in and out of Hope Bay again. They held to the curious myth that we were pleased to see them and all that they brought. We were not. We had been very busy and perfectly happy in our own world of dogs and sledging, and news of the outside world held little appeal.

The *Shackleton* had already visited and taken a survey team off; the *John Biscoe* was due shortly; then HMS *Protector* announced its imminent arrival. We had the bathroom and its plumbing dismantled and, when weather permitted, were busy painting and black-varnishing the hut. All this naval activity was extremely inconvenient. I was base leader and, as the *Protector* rounded into the bay, I was summoned aboard to confer with the captain.

A quick change from the black-varnishing scruff order into a stiff white collar and suit which had been in the loft for a year. As I left the hut with a helicopter hovering to pick us up, I could see a deterioration in the weather and grabbed a particularly manky sealing anorak which we wore to feed the dogs. There was some consternation among the welcoming officers on board, but they relaxed visibly when I discarded the garment.

After an excellent dinner a surveyor and I joined the captain to discuss the logistics of a survey round Paulet and Joinville Islands – not far from the Elephant Island of Shackleton fame. The captain said that he was also sending thirty Royal Marines ashore for snowcraft and rock-climbing experience. Where would we suggest? The Mondor Glacier about six miles from base seemed ideal. It was not far away and its surrounding mountains had been tempting the frustrated climbers amongst us for the last two years.

As we left, the captain asked if he could come ashore in the morning to see the base and get some letters stamped – one of our more irksome and time-consuming chores when ships were in. So back to base, out of the suit and into scruff order again. We finished scrubbing the hut at 1 a.m.

The captain's visit went very well except when we saw the captain from a neighbouring Argentinian base approaching. We made a prompt, un-scheduled detour to a penguin rookery. Not surprisingly, the Argentines were getting anxious as helicopters started flying overhead with sledges slung beneath them, and thirty Marines could be seen assembling on the slopes of Nobby Nunatack a few hundred feet above the base. The captain of the *Protector* and the survey team set off leaving five of us behind. I had asked if there was anything we could do to help, but had been assured that the Marines had maps, sledges, skis and considerable experience.

An hour or so later there still seemed to be some confusion on the hill-side and no progress. So the base's dog man and I harnessed up the two teams remaining on base and drove them up to see for ourselves. Our offer to give the Marines a lift round to the Mondor was accepted gratefully. We had only the emergency tent and stores which we always took when more than a couple of miles from base, and so had plenty of room on our two sledges with seven dogs each. But each Marine had a fifty-pound pack as well as his skis. We put as many packs as we could on the sledges and set off, towing the Marines. The temperature was a comfortable freezing, the surfaces were excellent and we all thoroughly enjoyed ourselves.

It was too late to return to base by the time we reached the head of the Mondor Glacier so we pitched our tent and fed the dogs. We had done all our routine chores and made our first brew-up and were surprised to hear a lot of activity still going on outside. We looked out to find that we were right marker for a row of nine tents. The sledges had been similarly aligned. It looked very military but never would we have pitched in such an orderly manner. It would not take much of a blizzard to drift the whole outfit up. But who were we to criticize? The Royal Marines surely knew best.

The Marine captain joined us in our tent and we spent four or five happy hours exchanging views on equipment and techniques until the early hours. The following day the wind veered south-west and blew a continuous blizzard up the valley: there was no question of Marines climbing mountains or of us returning to base. I recorded 'a deliciously idle day catching up on some sleep, dreaming, smoking cigars and dabbling in *Pickwick*'.

It was still snowing, drifting and manky the next day but we had left the base very lightly manned and felt duty-bound to return. We left the Marines and travelled back on a compass course. For the next two days a dense blizzard continued with winds of up to eighty-eight knots. Ideal weather to replumb the bathroom. It was totally dismantled when the *Protector* sailed into the bay and asked after the Marine party. So far as I knew they were still on the glacier. At that moment, out of the blizzard and very lightly equipped, the Marines reappeared.

Their camp had become completely uninhabitable. They had, apparently, had to cut themselves free through the peaks of the tents, so snowed up had they become. Equipment, radios and sledges had all been abandoned; the Marines had travelled back on ski. We issued them with rum, beer, bread and cheese and sleeping bags. Thirty-five men in a hut with fifteen bunks made for a very convivial evening.

The blizzard continued all the next day. The Marines were wonderfully helpful with the plumbing and the joinery. The *Protector* managed to send in a helicopter in the afternoon to take off the main party. The captain and three Marines remained behind to salvage equipment once the weather settled. One Marine offered to stay and finish off our plumbing.

It was another couple of days before a team could return to the Mondor Glacier. There was no sign of the camp whatsoever. Two tents and the sledges were salvaged. The rest – radios, equipment, the lot – was lost. I suppose there was an inquiry.

NEIL ORR

Journey to the Centre of the Centre

We are in a long-wheel-base Land Rover with reinforced suspension, heavy-duty shock absorbers, reinforced front-axle casing, reinforced steering dampers and heavy-duty, cross-country tyres, one of which is now flat, punctured by a sliver of ironwood as sharp as a nail and as hard as its name implies. There are two sixteen-gallon fuel tanks and more petrol in jerricans; a lot of ice-cold water and ice-cold beer and ice-cold food in a huge polystyrene chest, and all the impedimenta of camp life except for tents, which are a waste of time and energy down here in the middle.

The driver is a girl called Diane Byrnes and she is a partner in Annaburroo Tours and Safaris, who specialize in journeys to the bush. They also run more prosaic excursions from Alice Springs to Ayers Rock in the season. She is wearing the outback uniform – bush-shirt, shorts, knee-length stockings and suede ankle-boots. So is her friend Marge, ostensibly brought along to cook but really to light Diane's cigarettes – this girl is the greatest compulsive chain smoker I have ever seen – and perhaps to prevent her from being bored or what the *News of the World* used to refer to as 'interfered with', or both. They are immaculate. All the members of Annaburroo Tours and Safaris are girls and can handle any known form of vehicle or human being.

We are in the Northern Territory at 23½° south and 132° west, in an alluvial plain between the James Range and the Macdonnell ranges, 150 miles west of the Trans-Continental Telegraph line, the Stuart Highway from Adelaide to Darwin and the railway line. All of these converge at Alice Springs. And we are about fifty miles west of the Hermannsburg Mission, where the last buildings are, in this direction, until you get to the other side of the Gibson Desert. The mission was founded by German Lutherans in 1877 to save and succour the Aboriginals, many of whom up to that time had never seen a white man and had no need of being saved by Christians or otherwise succoured. Now having been given the civilization treatment, they need all the help they can get.

201

We are near the centre of what the Australians actually call the Centre, about 220 miles, peanuts here, west-south-west of central Mount Stuart, a point which, except to mad pedants, is about as near centre as you can get in this weird, eroded continent.

It is, in fact, a pretty lonely place by English standards and, as an Englishman, I feel it. From here (if only you were allowed to make it which you're not and if you could survive it) you could make the journey overland to the Great Australian Bight, six hundred miles to the south, or to Eighty Mile Beach, seven hundred miles west-north-west, without crossing more than one real road and probably without seeing another living soul. You are not allowed to because this is the threshold of the great Aboriginal Reserve which stretches away north and south, east and west, 100,000 square miles of it, and there is only one way through it to Western Australia and you have to stick to it. Beyond it are the deserts – the Great Victoria, the Gibson and the Great Sandy deserts. There are still semi-nomadic Aboriginals in the Musgrave Ranges in the South Australia part of the reserve and, who knows, perhaps there are still men and women living in the dreamtime out in the deserts. The Central Reserve Committee think there may be about fifty living a nomadic existence in the central desert. Altogether there are about two thousand Aboriginals and part-Aboriginals in the reserves, living mostly round the missions. I met a truck driver in a pub in Alice Springs who said he'd seen some real nomads a few days before. He had just come up from the south.

'I'd been up to Mulgathing Rocks on the south of the Victoria Desert and I was just short of Tarcoola; that's a station on the Trans-Continental Railway. It was blowing a real bedourie (sand-storm) and I couldn't see more than twenty yards in front of me, so I nearly ran 'em down. They were crossing the road. There were two families of them, a fair few, and apart from G-strings they were as naked as they were born. The men were carrying spears, the women had the kids across their shoulders. They looked like a lot of bleeding stone-agers. This was no walk-about. You could see they were on bush tucker, they were that thin, and I'll swear they'd never even seen the outside of a mission. You think I'm telling you a Johnnie Warby (tall story) . . .'

Where we are now, at the centre and to the north and south, was the region in which the great Victorian explorers, those to us unbelievably intrepid and courageous men, became imbrangled while trying to force their way westwards across the continent through the great sandy deserts to the sea; through the spinifex plains and sand-hills, the gibber stone plains, the endless ranges that are like tidal waves, thirty, forty, fifty and a hundred miles long; through dense stands of desert-oak among which the traveller can see nothing at all – suffering from scurvy, their camels dying, poisoned by strange vegetation, all the time forced to tack miles off course, as if they were in a sailing ship, by the one consuming need – to find water; so that a modern map of their combined explorations looks as if it has been made by centipedes whose feet have been dipped in ink.

Even today the only way through the Centre to Western Australia is by a very rough track through the Petermann and Warburton ranges and across the top of the Great Victoria Desert to Laverton about two hundred miles north of Kalgoorlie, much of the way completely waterless.

Snatched from death often by what seems nothing short of a miracle, they would return again and again to the quest until they either succeeded in doing what they had set out to do or died. The names that one reads today on the big-scale maps are those they themselves bestowed on their discoveries. They are never their own. They are invariably the names of other explorers or of dim, minor royalty, German cartographers, colonial governors, their own patrons, members of learned societies and those of their own companions who perished on the way (quite often the leader perished too and his companions survived), in which case the former got a posthumous by-line on his own expedition), so that if you know the circumstances in which these rocks and ranges and peaks and deserts and other natural phenomena received their rather banal names it endows them with a positively sinister quality.

We are just about to jack the wheel up when some wild horses (the Australians call them brumbies) see us and come bounding out from the shade of the ghost-gums on the banks of a creek in which, somewhere, according to Diane, there must be a soak of water or they wouldn't be there, although it looks as dry as a bone.

Brumbies are the descendants of horses that escaped from outback cattle- and sheep-stations and bred in the bush. These are all chestnuts. For a moment they stand looking at us; then they go tearing off under the noonday sun with their manes streaming in a wind as hot as that produced by the hottest hair-dryer ever made, the elders in line ahead, the colts straining to keep abreast of them. They run out between the shrubs of mulga, a sort of acacia, and the desert-oaks into the plain of pale yellow spinifex, with the 'whirlies' – moving whirlpools of sand – syphoning up on either side of them, out towards the Macdonnell Ranges.

The Macdonnell Ranges are said to be the shape of an elongated boomerang, if you can imagine one two hundred miles long made of sandstone and quartzite and granite and gneiss and schists. They have peaks between four and five thousand feet high and the effect is impressive.

At this moment the mountains are purple, as if covered with heather, although the guide-book threatens even more improbable effects, according to the time of day and the season; but this is quite enough for one day. They look very close but it is doubtful if the brumbies will go to them, for in fact they are all of thirty miles away and few men except perhaps nomadic Aboriginals even at this time of year, early autumn, could reach them alive in daylight travelling on foot. Here, without water, in five or six hours you would be dead.

In this country, even if you stay in the shade and do not move, the longest time that you can survive without water is forty-four hours. The brumbies will probably double back into one of the gullies in the James Range where there is enough water for their needs.

We left Alice Springs late yesterday morning – all the best expeditions I have ever been on started late. It is currently fashionable for writers who have flown out for the day from one or other of the four conveniently situated principal cities (the nearest is Adelaide, 857 miles) to take the mickey out of Alice Springs, especially in the holiday season. But the Australian holiday season in Alice Springs is not necessarily when British explorers foregather there, and I think that any of us who returned to it after days, weeks or months in the Petermann Ranges or fresh from admiring that out-of-the-way wonder, the Schwerin Mural Crescent, would regard the place as the lap of luxury. I do, after one day away from it. Those mickey-takers can jump in the lake. (The nearest convenient one is Lake Amadeus not three hundred miles away, which is almost solid salt so they will probably break their necks.) So much for Alice Springs. Goodbye, I've done my best for you.

We have come a long way since then. Diane, Marge and I in my new bush-suit from Woolworth's, which is looking even less good since I helped change the wheel, have been thundering down the red dirt-road between the long, red ridges of the Macdonnell Ranges, among the mulga-trees and the ironwood and the pallid ghost-gums, which look as if they have had their bark ripped off by vandals, seeing the Aboriginals at the settlement at Jay Creek sitting under the trees in Western clothes waving to us to come over for a boomerang lesson, or riding out of the bush with strings of camels.

We drive along the foot of the Waterhouse Range. It is as if an enormous whale had been stranded here when the tide went out and left the continent high and dry. It looks endless but is only thirty miles long. We enter a country in which blue grass grows and there are cattle almost invisible in the dark pools of shadow under the trees, and along the roadside there are broken bottles and beat-up motor cars abandoned even by the Aboriginals, who are brilliant at making old motor cars, which have given up the ghost to the white, go.

This was, and is, the country of the Aranda people and a sign 'Boggy Hole 18 miles' points the way to one of their sacred places, where there is perennial water. They were a people whose curvilinear and circular motifs were at their most complex in the decoration of the sacred *tjurumba*s, pieces of wood or stone coated with ochre, to house the owner's spirit.

Looking at photographs of the Central Tribes made soon after the Great War, one is impressed by their powerful physique. Seeing their descendants, men and women, at the Hermannsburg Mission, one is startled by their obesity. They have been destroyed by middle-class morality and carbo-hydrates and there is nothing anyone can do about it, except kindly refrain from photography. The symbol of the failure of the so-called policy of assimilation is Albert Namatjira, the remarkable Aboriginal artist who became world-famous and was discriminated against to the last. He was refused permission to build a house in Alice Springs and, at the end of a life in which every conceivable humiliation was heaped upon him, built himself a stone house near Hermannsburg with his own hands. Even this, shamefully, has been allowed to fall into ruin.

We enter the gorges of the Finke River and grind through deep, dry sand in four-wheel drive. 'Oldest river in the world,' Diane says. That is as

may be, but this part of it scarcely qualifies as a river at all, having currently only one small pool of water twenty yards long. The Aboriginals call the
Finke the Larapinta, Snake, and with reason. Typical of the rivers of
Australia that so bewildered the explorers, it goes nowhere, finally expir-
ing, after perhaps a thousand miles of absolutely pointless meandering,
in a vast uncharted area of flood-flats at the bottom end of the Simpson
Desert in South Australia.

We stop to eat in a small puddle of shadow under a solitary desert-
willow and are instantly smothered by flies. They are so abundant that,
looking through the view-finder of an eye-level reflex hoping to record
the occasion, I can see nothing at all. We spray one another with a preparation called Scram which they detest and get down to lunch from the
miracle ice-chest before the effects wear off: cold meats, crisp salad and
ice-cold beer, followed by hot, smoky, orange-coloured tea brewed in a
billy.

Overhead the sky is peppered with little white clouds, and a pair of
huge, wedge-tailed eagles are going round and round in it on the look-
out for rabbits. Until recently the government paid a bounty for every
wedge-tailed eagle shot, because they allegedly attack sheep (they do kill
dying animals), but so many thousands were destroyed that now they
will have to be protected, otherwise they will become extinct. Later we see
one of their nests, a large, crazy-looking construction of sticks high in a
tree.

We turn into a wide, deep canyon which enters the river from the west
and is a tributary of it. The Finke itself continues its madly involved course
through the James and Krichauff ranges for a hundred miles by way of
Boggy Hole. From the floor of it, now in the afternoon partly in blessed
shadow, enormous palm-trees soar upwards into the blinding sun. They
are *Livistoma mariæ* and this is the only place on the entire continent
where they grow. Relics of the prehistoric, some of them are 1800 years
old. They were discovered in 1872 by Ernest Giles in the Glen of Palms
near Boggy Hole, when he and a party of four were attempting to cross
a thousand miles of unexplored territory on horseback to the Western
Australian coast. And there is a strange, seed-bearing plant called a cycad
(*Macrozamia*) which has its origins in the Mesozoic period two million
years ago.

There is an eerie feeling about this place below the blood-red cliffs under a sky of indigo blue, and the bright blue Port Lincoln parrots squawking among the gums do nothing to dispel it. Here in Palm Valley I half-expect to see the saw-tooth grin on the face of a pterodactyl and hear the clashing of its wings. Only the detritus deposited by generations of Australians anxious to make their country as hideous as possible reminds me that I am indeed in the present and that the tins and non-returnable bottles will remain forever because down here in the Centre there is no one to take them away. Fortunately, this is a national reserve of 113,000 acres of which up to now only a minute part is ever visited by the public. It is a pity that Palm Valley is one of the places that is.

The sun departs from the valley in a blaze of glory at seven p.m. So do the flies and the cat-bird whose cry (it can scarcely be said to be a call) makes one's blood run cold and glad that one is not alone here in the wilderness.

We retire to our alloy beds. The dingoes, wild dogs, move in close enough to eat the remains of our dinner and they do this to the accompaniment of blood-curdling howls.

Dawn is at six and at 6.20 the flies begin. With the ironwood already embedded in the tyre we set off for our puncture and our meeting with the brumbies.

All through the afternoon we drive through what the itinerary describes as 'the gas-fields' in the Mereenie Anticline. Natural gas and oil have been discovered here but not in exciting quantities and there is little to show it; no rigs tower against the sky. The road is rust-red gravel, the sand-hills are the same colour and so are the ant-hills which look like rotten teeth sprouting from the ground. It is an utterly lonely place with the long, straight tracks of the prospectors running through it and soon we are lost, not because we are disorientated – the compass and the sun between them are enough to reassure us where north and south lie – but because Diane has never been this way before and the place is a maze of tracks with gibberish signposts on them and which no map except an oil company's would show.

Finally we see the George Gill Range, forty miles away. As we drive towards it with the sun sinking on our right and the beautiful dingoes watching us curiously from all around, it looms up redder and redder as the sun sinks lower and lower until we are close and it is blood-red under an apple-green sky and lapped by hard, wind-furrowed sand in which a few tussocks of grass grow. In this terrain a Land Rover is as incongruous as the melting watch in that Dali landscape.

After some days in the stony red centre of the continent where, from early morning until late afternoon in the warm weather, nothing is worth looking at or even visible except liquescent or upside down in mirage, Diane becomes obsessed, because she has been entrusted with the job of ensuring that I witness them, with getting me to the dawns and sunsets on time. It is in this spirit of urgency that she whirls me down a vast avenue fifty miles long into the nothingness in which Ayers Rock resides, seeing on the way only two red kangaroos, the first to appear so far, not surprising considering that 200,000 a year are slaughtered for soup or fun.

We have more beer at Curtin Springs – in this weather you do about twenty miles to the can in high summer – and rush on past Mount Conner, a large, flat-topped mountain fantastic enough to make the majority of visitors think it is 'Ther Rock' and rush off towards it in their motor cars, where they lose themselves in the bush.

By driving past the ticket office at the real Ayers Rock without stopping – shouts of 'Oi!' – and roaring out westwards along the southern side of it, Diane succeeds in getting me to the sunset at the precise moment when it is passing away and the colour is a rather depressing sang-de-boeuf. I photograph away gloomily, sure that I have failed in my mission (although why should I care – there are enough pictures of Ayers Rock in circulation to paper the Albert Hall) but months later I am surprised to find that the effects which I have recorded on Ektachrome are as improbable as those of 'real' photographers, nothing like those I saw with my own eyes.

The first European to set eyes on the Rock was Giles in the course of the same expedition in which he discovered the Glen of Palms; but he did not name it. At the time he was more than fifty miles away from it on the north side of Lake Amadeus and could find no way to cross the lake. He also sighted and named Mount Olga, a fantastic conglomeration twenty miles away to the west of the Rock which, to my mind, is even more memorable than the Rock itself; but he did not finally reach it until 1874 in the course of his next expedition.

This was the expedition on which his friend and companion, Gibson, after whom Giles named the desert, died and on one stage of which, alone in the wilderness, he carried a twenty-kilo keg of water on his shoulders for sixty miles and, at the end of the stage, finding a small wallaby weighing not more than two ounces, in his own terrible words 'like an eagle I pounced upon it and ate it, living, raw, dying – fur, skin, bones, skull and all'.

It was William Gosse, a young man in the Surveyor General's Department, who finally reached and named the Rock in 1873, the year after Giles first sighted it. Travelling with a party of eight which included three Afghan camel-drivers and the indispensable Aboriginal boy – this one was called Moses – Gosse said of the Rock: 'The most wonderful natural feature I have ever seen . . . a sight worth riding over eighty-five miles of spinifex sand-hills to see' – a camel-ride that makes one's arrival in a Land Rover rather shaming.

Then apart from a party of savants who visited it in 1894, for almost sixty years no one went near it until a constable of the Northern Territory Police rode to it on a camel and climbed it in 1931.

That Ayers Rock is geologically a rock there is no denying – geologists say that it is arkose sandstone (sandstone with felspar and quartz additives) from the Tertiary Period only about seventy million years ago, and that it stood in the middle of a lake.

There, so far as I am concerned, its resemblance to a rock ends. Seen from its foot on any side, its awful, smooth, mostly unclimbable but never vertical slopes loom eleven hundred feet over the wretched, insignificant visitor, a tidal wave in a nightmare that never breaks. No wonder the Ulu-titdja, the Aboriginals who lived by it until they were tempted to abandon it for the missions and cattle-stations some time before 1910, believed that it contained within it the essence of life.

ERIC NEWBY

Excavating with K.

I had recently graduated from the Royal College of Art and, not knowing quite what to do next, was still living at home in suburban Surrey, to the exasperation of my father. A kindly next-door neighbour asked me what was my immediate aspiration. To travel, I replied, desperate to escape from the post-War depression which still hung like a grey shroud over England.

To my surprise, he passed over the garden fence the next evening the names and addresses of a dozen British archæologists; he had read archæology at university, and retained an amateur interest in the subject. He said if my ambition was to travel, then maybe I should consider becoming an archæological draughtsman. I composed twelve identical letters, to eleven of which I received almost identical replies of regret, but promising to forward my request to the Institute of Archæology.

As the twelfth letter had already been sent there, the Institute had the lot. Which collectively generated from the Secretary one negative reply. As luck would have it, however, the eminent archæologist Kathleen Kenyon was shortly thereafter fuming over morning coffee at the Institute about the defection of her draughtsman for her forthcoming dig. Somewhat facetiously the Secretary mentioned my enthusiasm and, to everyone's surprise, she asked for my address.

Thus I came to meet her for an interview. I nervously climbed the stairs, the peeling walls decorated in sub-Pompeian style. Though only three in the afternoon, it was almost dark. I knocked on her door and a gruff voice barked 'Come in!' I was immediately confronted with the back of a roll-top desk (inherited from her father, Sir Frederick Kenyon, Director of the British Museum) and grumpily told to sit down. Had I done any archæological drawing before? No, I weakly replied.

At this point what appeared to be a shaggy carpet levitated and advanced towards me. It was her sheep-dog. I have been petrified of dogs since being bitten in childhood, and in my horror tried to pat it back down on the floor. This was mistaken as a sign of affection by K. (the diminutive by which she was universally known). The next thing she said was: 'Want to come to Jericho?' I was so taken aback that I unthinkingly said Yes!

'Good,' she said. 'Be in the Grand Hotel in Marseille on December 26 at 7.30 a.m.' And that was that.

When I arrived in Marseille on the appointed day, I found I was not the only traveller bound for Jericho. There was a collection of cheerful ladies, all roughly dressed in tweeds, who introduced themselves as Ron, Cecil and other chaps' names, and told me that K. had flown on ahead to Jericho. Were we to have coffee? No, apparently we only used the Grand Hotel for its 'facilities'. We boarded the *Corinthia* for Beirut, a decrepit Greek vessel which had recently sunk in Piræus, and set off across the Mediterranean. Both the weather and the food were terrible and I was sick most of the time. But I vividly remember drifting through the Corinth Canal on the way to Athens and my first sight of the Parthenon.

Arriving in Beirut, we booked seats in a *service* taxi all the way to Jericho. We sped over the mountains of the Lebanon; I had my first taste of Lebanese food at lunch in the Bekaa Valley; I saw my first camel, and then promptly fell sound asleep. We sped through the Syrian night down into the Jordan Valley, crossed the river and arrived in Jericho long after midnight. At the Winter Palace Hotel – a long, low, mudbrick shack – we were met by K. and other tweedy figures by torch-light, but I was so tired I barely registered and tumbled into a camp-bed.

Next morning I was woken by what I thought was a searchlight in my face. It was the sun streaming in. In amazement I looked out of the window at the brilliant blue sky, the palm-trees and the vegetation with flowers such as I had never seen before. It was as if someone had turned on the light for the first time in my life.

The archæologists were camped at Jericho on the edge of the oasis near Elisha's Spring, where a thousand gallons of fresh water burst out every minute from the foot of an ancient mound. Our tents were arranged around a ramshackle farm-house, the upper storey reserved for the surveyor and a dining-room, with the photographer and the kitchen below. The work was exhausting but fascinating; for me the tedium of drawing thousands of unglazed earthenware sherds was relieved by the excitement of the dig. In the first season K. quickly discovered that the so-called collapsed walls of Jericho, visible from an earlier excavation, were much too early. Joshua's period (the late Bronze Age) was represented only by a tiny area on the very top of the *tell*, the mound.

Besides working on the tell, I also drew plans of underground Bronze-Age tombs and their contents a short distance from the ancient mound. To locate them we had to ask a large Palestinian refugee population to move their tents to left or right, which they generously did. I was at first puzzled by this enormous tent city and naively thought it was some kind of jamboree. But the Palestinians quickly enlightened me. They had fled from Bethlehem, Hebron, Ramallah and their villages in the hills over-looking the Jordan Valley to escape the savage battles of 1948. They told me they thought they were in Jericho only until the fighting subsided, but they had now been there for over two years and still hadn't been allowed to go back home. There were over 60,000 refugees in Jericho alone. When I next got back to England, would I please tell someone about their fate? I did, but no one in London seemed particularly interested. That was fifty-odd years ago. In fact, the Jericho refugee population was in 1967 dispersed, not to return home but to be chased across the Jordan by the Israelis and resettled in new camps outside Amman. There they remain to this day.

The excitement of the dig increased as the days and indeed six seasons of excavation passed. The trenches went down and down until the walls of a great Neolithic city were uncovered, the first evidence of urban civilization long predating that of ancient Egypt. Abutting these walls was a massive stone tower, and I was put down its internal staircase to draw the skeletons of its last defenders. When elsewhere on the mound and almost ninety feet below the surface the earliest levels were reached, K. bellowed 'Get Dot!' This was Dorothy Garrod, the distinguished prehistorian, who was immediately flown out to Jericho and sent down the trench for two whole days. She finally emerged and pronounced: 'You've got it'.

What was 'it'? 'It' was the moment, just after the last Ice Age, when mankind left its comfortable caves and a hunting/gathering existence to settle beside the spring at Jericho and build a village based on agriculture and the domestication of animals – the first definite evidence of a link between the historical past and prehistory.

JOHN CARSWELL

Here Comes the Madman

My wife Fiona and I were riding slowly down the Siq at Petra on donkeys provided by Hani, the young son of the shaikh of Wadi Musa, when there was a loud shout from high above our heads.

'What is he saying, Hani?'

'Here comes the madman,' was the reply.

In 1964, the previous year, I had made a day-trip by taxi from Jerusalem to Petra with Martin Kenyon and some other friends. We were determined to get to Ad-Dair, the magnificent carved temple hundreds of feet up narrow, slippery, rocky steps at the far end of Petra. I have paralyzed legs and was on crutches, so the only hope of success within the time was to hire a donkey. Hani had one and we enlisted them both. The perilous ascent was accomplished by the exertions of all, with the final stretch along a sloping ledge clinging to a precipice. No one before had been foolhardy enough to attempt it on a donkey. My local reputation for eccentricity was to prove a boon.

In those days there was no hotel anywhere near Petra. A small encampment of tents near the Qasr al-Bint was accommodation for visitors. One day we were invited by Hani's father to a midday *mansaf* in our honour. We set off from our tent on our donkeys through the Siq and when we reached Wadi Musa we noticed the local youths peeing into Moses' famous well. Apart from Fiona, into whose mouth the shaikh put what he thought were the choicest tit-bits, all those at the meal were men. The shaikh's two wives presided in the kitchen and his sons brought in a splendid Benares tray mounded with lamb, rice and strange spices. Drink was essential to help the food down but, having seen the much-vaunted source of the local water, our manners failed and we refused it. Instead, arak aided every mouthful. It had a powerful effect. Luckily our donkeys, onto which we were hoisted, knew their way home to our tent, where we awoke the next morning.

Some years later we decided to take our children to Petra. Tancred was thirteen and Sophie eleven, with long blond hair. We had written to Hani for advice. He arranged with Salaman, the shaikh of Petra itself, for us to stay in his cave, which was fifty feet up the rocky ascent to Ad-Dair. We reached Wadi Musa just after sunset and found Hani waiting with several donkeys. In pitch darkness we set off down the narrow Siq, hemmed in by towering cliffs. We could see nothing. After half an hour, the defile turned to the left and there, just in front of us, brilliant in the light of a full moon, was Al-Khazna, the Treasury, one of the largest and most perfectly preserved of the rose-red Nabatæan façades. Astonished, we rode on towards Salaman's cave.

Like our hosts at the embassy for three days previously, Salaman and his family were very hospitable. Their cave consisted of two spacious rooms. They had moved out of the better one and we moved in. There were no beds, but there were rugs, mattresses and blankets. We were surprised to find electric light and a television set on an elaborate cupboard. Salaman turned on *Upstairs Downstairs*, which had Hebrew sub-titles. He and his family joined us to watch it. We asked no searching questions, but later learned that Salaman was the foreman on the building site for a restaurant in the valley and that work had been suspended because the generator had mysteriously disappeared.

It was a privilege to live in Salaman's cave. Between evening and mid-morning we had Petra almost to ourselves. Our children rode on their donkeys to collect water from the wadi and we heard some Americans take them for albino Beduin. We saw locals with large pieces of delicate Nabatæan pottery break them into fragments for selling to groups of tourists. We entertained a New Zealand girl who had been so smitten by Petra that she had married a Beduin and was living with him in a nearby cave, where she expected shortly to give birth. We made long excursions to Aaron's Tomb and to the ruins of Sabra, where we scattered and my camel suddenly decided to roll before I could dismount. Fortunately there was a patch of sand deep enough to receive a complete impression of my body before the camel rose up and wandered off with my crutches.

Fiona and I and our children were invited to Hani's father's house for another *mansaf*. We met Hani's charming elder brother, Muhammad, who had a First in English Literature from Amman University and was clearly the family scholar. Sophie was invited into the kitchen to watch the preparation of the feast and soon reappeared with ashen face. She whispered that there had been an accident. The Benares tray had been dropped and the entire meal had fallen into a muddy hole in the kitchen floor. It was scooped up again and reassembled. We ate it with courage.

Two days later we had to move on to Aqaba. Hani's father insisted on driving us in his elderly Mercedes. I sat in the front beside him, Fiona and the children behind. Halfway to Aqaba the shaikh said: 'Muhammad has seen Sophie'. This seemed to be stating the obvious, but it was the prelude to asking for her hand in marriage to Muhammad. I was temporarily struck dumb. We had all met Muhammad for only a few minutes before the meal, and Sophie had been surprised to receive an agate necklace from him the following day. Our driver then said: 'They could live half the year with us in Wadi Musa and the other half with you in London. Because of your English customs, Muhammad would wait for two years before the marriage and Sophie would always be his senior wife'. The proposition was becoming ever more unusual. I thought of discussing dowries and camels, but resorted to saying 'You must ask Sophie'. He did: Sophie dropped silently to the floor of the car. Hardly another word was said until we got to our hotel in Aqaba. We invited the shaikh to have coffee with us. Very reluctantly he came in but refused to drink the customary three cups.

It was ten years before we were again in touch with that family. We tactfully avoided asking but Muhammad, I'm sure, would have acquired at least one wife during that time; he seemed such a nice chap.

ALICK BARRATT

Tattooing in Colours

Whilst working with Kathleen Kenyon on the famous excavations at Jericho, the archæologists went off at weekends to visit other sites, and I was left alone to my own devices. At that time I was paid one pound a week with all expenses found, which was sufficient in those days except that I smoked and had learned (from K.) to drink. This meant that there was little left by Sunday, but at least enough for my bus fare to Jerusalem.

I got to know the Old City well, and one day I saw there an intriguing sign on a coffin-maker's shop: 'Joseph Razzouk Tattooing In Colours'.

Joseph was a Copt and, as a sideline to being an undertaker, tattooed Egyptian Copts at Easter with designs to commemorate their pilgrimage. He showed me his family collection of carved wooden blocks which he used both to help pilgrims choose their design and also, when their turn came to stamp it on the flesh, to trace around with his needle. I asked him if I could borrow the blocks, and printed off ten sets at the Greek Orthodox Press round the corner. I then went one stage further and composed a single page of text and had them all bound and numbered. The sets were acquired by various friends: K. bought one, and Gerald Lankester Harding, the Director of Antiquities, took two, one for the museum in Amman and the other for the Palestine Archæological Museum in Jerusalem. I covered my costs and kept for myself the first set, which I still possess.

One day I was twenty feet underground planning a tomb when a visitor came down on a rope. She was American, and asked me what I was doing. I told her I was an artist, but this was what I did for a living. She said she was an artist too, and invited me to lunch. She was engaged to be married and was just about to give up her job teaching art at the American University of Beirut. Would I be interested in the post? Again I said Yes and, improbable though this may seem, I got the job. There is no doubt that I was the only member of the AUB faculty ever hired out of a Middle Bronze-Age tomb.

Shortly after I arrived in Beirut to teach in 1956, I discovered that the university had a publication fund. My suggestion for an expanded edition of *Coptic Tattoo Designs* was accepted, so I wrote a lengthy introduction and catalogued each design. Of this two hundred copies were printed. They were bound in the summer of 1958 during the Lebanon's first civil war, the sheets being carried from the Christian printer over the barricades to the Muslim binder on the other side.

Again thanks to my new interest in tattooing and Coptic art, I was introduced in London to Dr Margaret Murray, an Egyptologist and well-known Coptic scholar, who generously agreed to contribute a foreword to my youthful work. She was then ninety-four; I was twenty-five and we hit it off immediately. She had not only been the favourite pupil of the famous Egyptologist Sir Flinders Petrie (much to Lady Petrie's chagrin) but was also the world authority on witchcraft. By the time I met her she had shrunk to about four feet tall. She had a flat in Endsleigh Gardens next to University College, of which she was proud to be a Fellow. She lived to be a centenarian, and her last work was her autobiography *My First Hundred Years* which she wrote when she was ninety-nine.

She taught me a lot: how to learn Arabic easily (visiting-cards), how to proof-read accurately (again, visiting-cards) and much more. There are many stories about Margaret Murray but my favourite is how she dealt with the problem of a misguided academic appointment. In the late 1930s a new director was appointed to the Institute of Archæology whom nobody liked. No one could think what to do. Someone suggested getting in touch with MM to enquire if she could help. She agreed and asked to be taken to the Institute that night. When she arrived at the gloomy mansion in Regent's Park, she went down to the basement. Here she produced a saucepan, an old book and various oddments out of a carpet-bag. The saucepan was put on a gas-ring and she began to read aloud from the book in a matter-of-fact manner, from time to time throwing in a rat's tail and other scraps. She finally snapped the book shut, brought the contents of the saucepan to the boil and poured them down the lavatory. She said she was rather tired and wanted a taxi home.

Next morning the new director arrived at the Institute to take up his appointment. He was all right at nine, but by ten o'clock said he wasn't feeling well and by eleven came out in enormous boils and had to be taken away. His malady was never diagnosed, he was obliged to resign – and the right man got the job.

Amongst the many things that I learned from Margaret Murray one in particular sticks in my mind. When I wrote my new edition of *Coptic Tattoo Designs* I showed the manuscript to an eminent Keeper at the V&A, who dismissed it with one word: Rubbish! Mortified, I took tea with MM to seek solace. I told her what had happened and her reaction was swift. 'Nonsense,' she said. '*Never* listen to anyone who works in a museum! We have been there and we know; they haven't and they don't.' Which is, come to think of it, a point of view to which all of us Travellers subscribe.

JOHN CARSWELL

Funerals and Faux Pas in Monrovia

In his memoirs some years ago a former British minister to the Holy See commended funerals as an excellent means for a diplomat to extend his range of contacts in his host country. He may well have been right; certainly they shed some interesting light on its society and its politics as I discovered from my first visit to Monrovia as Canadian ambassador.

I had not planned on a funeral. Indeed, I had timed my visit to Liberia to take in the country's 130th independence celebrations. As Liberians attach a good deal of importance to this annual holiday – a second Christmas, as someone said – I flattered myself that my presence would be particularly welcomed and that the few days before the event and the day itself should give me an excellent chance to get around and meet a few well-placed Liberians. Unfortunately I did not fully reckon with their capacity for taking days off and with the government's practice (not that it mattered in the end) of turning the independence celebrations into a geographically moveable feast.

Canada's honorary commercial representative met me at Monrovia Airport with the news that much of the capital was closed down for most of that day because of the death of the general treasurer of the True Whig Party, while the next morning was a half-holiday to mark the end of a week of national repentance. I felt at home as just a fortnight earlier I had repented for a week in Ghana. (Some say they have repented in Ghana much longer.) Moreover, the independence celebrations would, he had just learned, take place at Greensville, ten hours over a mostly dirt road from Monrovia. In short, between death, repentance, weekends and the comings and goings to celebrations the entire government would be shut down for five of the seven days that I would be there.

My outlook brightened to some degree when I realized that Greensville could present even more advantages than Monrovia if the transportation problem could be solved. My British colleague thoughtfully offered me a seat in his Land Rover. I equally thoughtfully declined.

218

Unlike him I did not have a century of British presence in Liberia behind me nor the possible sale of a Hawker Siddeley 748 in front of me to propel me down a rutted road to Greensville. A short trip by air, however risky, seemed more consistent with the extent of Canadian interests, and I accepted a seat on one of the special flights laid on by Air Liberia for carless visitors and those in Monrovia with more clout than the resident ambassadors.

Greensville had been chosen as the site of that year's celebrations to honour vice-president James Greene, its favourite son. He had been in failing health for a year or more and, politics being what it is, he was under some pressure to resign. It was said that the president would lean a little harder on him after he had paid public homage to him in his home town – his day in the sun, as it were. He missed it, poor man. Late the next day it was announced that he had died: all celebrations were cancelled and the festivities in Greensville were to be replaced by a funeral in Monrovia.

The funeral arrangements were spread over three days. The first was to lay the vice-president in state; to this the diplomatic corps was invited. The second was for the funeral, there being some uncertainty in the corps as to whether it was invited or not. And the third was for the burial in Greensville, to which the corps was clearly and to its relief not invited.

The lying in state was held in a large hall devoted exclusively to important state occasions; its floor-plan was that of a church. The corps was asked to arrive at 4 p.m. and most diplomats did so. We took our seats in what is best described as the chancel. The required dress was dark suits and black tie with decorations. The American ambassador did not feel the need to wear a black tie – perhaps because he had a black face, as one Liberian was overheard to remark with just the right mix of jest and acidulousness.

We waited. The tedium was broken as we watched the new Chinese ambassador approach and momentarily face the choice of a seat next to the Russian chargé d'affaires or by the South Korean ambassador. With skill and some physical dexterity he sidled along to a more congenial chair beside the chargé for the Central African Empire.

We waited. There was another diversion as the Italian ambassador's medals came adrift and clattered noisily to the floor. Anxious to do something useful, we all helped to retrieve them and, with his nose buried in his lapel, he amused himself for several minutes putting them back on.

We waited. We also froze – a rare event in West Africa – for blowing on our backs was an enormous air-conditioning unit turned on at full blast. One saw the spectacle of three stalwart northerners – the Russian, the Swede and the Canadian – each clutching himself tightly. Our American colleague, who at six foot six was perhaps catching more than his share of the icy draught, finally left his seat and sought shelter out of range.

At 5 p.m. the corps was unexpectedly asked to leave the hall – of which we were still the only occupants – and to walk two or three blocks to a point opposite the headquarters of the True Whig Party. It had already been draped in black for the general treasurer; more black bunting was added to it for the vice-president. There we were to join the funeral procession which had started on foot from the Executive Mansion a mile or two away. As we awaited its arrival our attention was somewhat diverted by a large and brightly clad Liberian lady who was either determined not to be cheated out of celebrating independence or accustomed to putting a good deal of heart and herself into wakes. She lurched about the street with boundless enthusiasm, fulsomely embracing the odd black-clad official. I was transfixed as she momentarily seemed to move in the direction of the German ambassador, but alas she wove off in pursuit of less uninviting targets whilst letting out intermittent whoops of joy or sorrow – it was difficult to tell which.

At last the cortège came into sight. It was headed by a Liberian army batallion dressed in American uniforms with ascots at their throats – black for the occasion. After them came what I took to be the Ladies of the Eastern Star – female Freemasons – all in white with floppy hats and some colourful sashes. They were followed by male Masons of various rites, degrees and orders dressed in black suits and hats of differing styles – black bowlers, porkpies, stetsons and fedoras. The Masons are a big factor in Liberian life. To be successful one has to be in business, in politics and in Freemasonry all at the same time. Behind the hearse and the cars carrying the Greene family walked the president and Mrs Tolbert, then members of the cabinet, the judiciary, the senate and the House of Representatives. The president was dressed in his distinctive garb of white political suit and white furry cap.

The diplomatic corps fell in behind. Some of my colleagues seized the opportunity to transact a little business: my Dutch colleague with an eagerness I did not entirely share introduced me to one or two of those eminent Liberians who happened to be near by.

We walked on until we came abreast of the hall we had left about an hour before. The casket after appropriate honours was borne inside with some frantic grabbing at one point as one of the soldiers lost his grip. The corps followed, the more experienced abandoning the nave for the quicker route through the aisles as they sought, some unsuccessfully as it turned out, to regain their seats. The hall was now packed – but not much warmer as the air conditioning rose only too well to the new challenge of cooling off several hundred warm mourners.

The ceremonies for the lying in state began. The lid to the casket was opened and the undertaker made the necessary adjustments. He went to remove the flag. It stuck. He tugged. It stuck. He tugged again. It continued to stick until someone untied the remaining cord holding it to the coffin. The Chief of Protocol and son of the secretary of the True Whig Party, appropriately decorated and sashed, called on the various segments of Liberian political life to pay their respects to the deceased. They began of course with the president and proceeded in order of precedence. The diplomatic corps came after the Masons if I remember it right.

The president then read the 'Panegyric', to cite the fine old word used in the programme of events. The acting dean of the diplomatic corps, the ambassador of Sierra Leone, had come wreath and speech in hand ready to do the honours in what it was assumed would be a series of eulogies. At the last moment it was mercifully decided to restrict speeches to the president's. By now it was 7.30. A shudder went through the corps as the rumour circulated that we were expected to return at 9 p.m. for we knew not what. This was squelched by the announcement that the immediate family would leave and those present would sign the Book of Condolences as they left. Led by the president, we lined up in order of precedence, the diplomatic corps again coming after the Masons. And a few others who had jumped the queue. It took about half an hour before we reached what was to some of us at least the comfortable warmth of a July night in Monrovia.

My next official visit to Liberia could only go better.

ROBERT MIDDLETON

A Lesson in Bargaining

It was a hot Saturday afternoon in Ibadan. We had finished work for the week, enjoyed our gins and tonic and had a modest curry lunch. (Sunday was the day for the immodest curry lunch.) We were in the entrance hall of what – with its cool marble floor and marble staircase – was probably the best company house in Nigeria. We were sitting there quietly, my wife, three daughters and I, contemplating the small courtyard where we had once rescued two little birds from a storm – but that's another story.

Enter a Hausa trader with a load of native carpets. Well actually he had with him a small boy who was carrying the heavy load of rugs and carpets.

'Would you like to buy a rug?' he asked, displaying a slightly unusual, black woollen creation with interesting patterns.

'No thank you,' said I.

Naturally this did not deter him one bit, and out came several more items, the black one on top.

'I have just sold one like this to an American down the road for thirty-five pounds,' he said.

'In that case I suggest you find another American to sell this one to. Anyway I don't want a rug and I certainly wouldn't pay thirty-five pounds.' This was a fatal mistake on my part as he immediately said: 'Thirty then'. 'No,' I replied.

'What will you offer?'

'Nothing.'

'I will come down to thirty and you must say something.'

'Five pounds.'

'Master, you cannot be serious,' came the reply, foreshadowing Mc-Enroe by some years. 'I will come down to twenty-five.'

'Five pounds.'

'No Master, you do not understand. I come down and you must go up.' And then as an afterthought: 'May I have a cold drink, please?' The house-servant and cook as well as my family were watching the entertainment, standing by the door and sitting on the stairs. The house-servant obligingly brought a Fanta.

'Now Master, let me explain the principles of bargaining. I started at thirty-five pounds, came down to thirty and then to twenty-five. Now you must go up.'

'Five guineas,' said I. Another appeal to the gods of McEnroe, then he came down to twenty pounds. I went up to five pounds ten. By now the children were bored with Dad being difficult, while the servants were wondering whom to put their money on, metaphorically speaking that is.

Our Hausa trader was in despair with this ignorant, mean, awkward Englishman who kept smiling but not yielding. It was time for another Fanta. 'Would the boy like one?' I asked.

'If you wish to spoil him' and the bargaining lesson began all over again. He came down to fifteen, I up to five pounds fifteen shillings, he down to ten and we settled at six pounds for something I did not need but still have thirty years later.

For him it had been an enjoyable, cool hour with two drinks. Had I agreed to his first price he would have regretted not asking double. Besides, I was fairly sure the weaver was paid only three pounds. One hundred per cent – not a bad mark-up.

ROBERT ELY

A Grievous Insult

The late King Hussein of Jordan was known to Western correspondents as PLK, the Plucky Little King. He was not very tall, but his qualities made him a towering figure in every other respect. He was a man not merely of robust courage but of exquisite courtesy, combining the good manners of an Old Harrovian with the graciousness of his great-uncle, the Hashemite Emir Faisal. He also had a keen sense of humour for which I had cause to be grateful on an embarrassing occasion when I responded to his courtesy with unintended lese-majesty.

I don't know if there is in the Jordan any law under which a foreigner can be prosecuted for offending the monarch but, if there is, the Particulars of Offence would have read: 'On the 27th day of October 1980 in the Royal Cultural Centre in Amman the accused did grievously insult His Majesty by telling him to bugger off'.

The PLK treated the incident as a huge joke. True to form, he did so although in the thick of a dangerous crisis on his border with Syria, where his northern neighbour had just deployed ten thousand troops and 250 tanks and was, some feared, about to invade.

It was the last day of an Arab summit in Amman. This had taken place amid mounting tension between Syria and the Jordan over the latter's support for Saddam Hussein in the Iran-Iraq war. Divisions over the war had wrecked the summit. Backing Iran because of a long-standing feud with Iraq, and ruled by a rival faction of the Ba'ath Party, Syria had boycotted the summit after unsuccessfully requesting its postponement. Algeria, the Lebanon, Libya, South Yemen and the PLO had followed suit.

The result was a triumph for Saddam Hussein – who had been fêted in Amman as an Arab hero and applauded by the summit – but a diplomatic fiasco for King Hussein. The boycott by Syria and the other five members of the Syrian-led 'Steadfastness and Confrontation Front' had made it impossible for the summit to agree, as intended, a united Arab stand on the Arab-Israel conflict to present to the newly elected President Reagan.

The king roundly accused Syria of stabbing Iraq in the back by supporting Iran, a non-Arab state. He attacked the Damascus regime for preventing the summit from hearing the Lebanon and the PLO, both parties to the conflict, and responded to Syria's troop deployment by moving Jordanian troops and tanks to the border, where travellers reported seeing them digging in.

In Amman, a Press Room had been installed in the British-built Royal Cultural Centre with typewriters, telephones and telex machines for the large number of journalists covering the summit. We scrambled for them because, however many are provided, they are never enough. An Egyptian correspondent I knew from Cairo had taken the place at a telex machine that I was using and had momentarily vacated to collect a copy of the final communiqué. He was reluctant to give the seat back. I was under pressure, filing close on deadline for the first edition. A voice behind me said: 'I hope everything is to your satisfaction, Sir'.

'Bugger off,' I retorted, thinking it was my colleague from Cairo fooling around.

Some sixth sense told me it wasn't. I turned round and, aghast, found myself face-to-face with the king. Resplendent in army uniform, he was standing in a row of senior officers. All were grinning from ear to ear.

'Your Majesty,' I gasped, knocking over the chair as I leapt to my feet and saluted. The king and his aides laughed and moved on, leaving me to my embarrassment.

The next day I went up to Ramtha on the Syrian border. Four lines of tanks and armoured personnel carriers and a line of artillery were positioned on hills facing a Syrian armoured division. The stand-off continued for several days. Meeting reporters at his palace, the king said his relationship with the Syrian president Hafez al-Assad had been irreparably damaged by the crisis. But two days later a full-scale Syrian withdrawal was under way after Prince Abdullah of Saudi Arabia flew to Damascus and persuaded President Assad to pull back.

My exchange with King Hussein won me a small place in journalistic folklore. Introduced for the first time, correspondents would say: 'So you're the guy who told the PLK to bugger off'. I take no pride in having done so, but am pleased to think that I provided the king with something to laugh about at a stressful and dangerous moment.

R BARRY O'BRIEN

King Hussein's British solicitor and close friend was Lord Mishcon, who is perhaps best known publicly as Princess Diana's divorce lawyer. (He also acted for Jeffrey Archer, as the latter's autobiography acknowledges.)

Kept completely from the media, however, were Victor Mishcon's efforts towards an Arab-Israeli settlement. Shimon Peres was another close friend, and so secret were the meetings at the Mishcons' country home between the king and the Israeli statesman that no staff could be present. Lady Mishcon hosted them single-handed.

Over drinks with a Club member she recalled one such meeting (when the king and the statesman had arrived in disguise – 'and Peres' false beard fell off'). She left the men to after-dinner coffee and cleared the table to wash up. Busy with the dishes in the kitchen, she heard a sound behind her. She turned to find King Hussein and Shimon Peres in their shirt-sleeves, drying up.

Frustrated by Fez

Being sent directly from Beirut to Fez might seem like a glamorous assignment. In reality it represents a logistical nightmare. The first problem is getting out of Beirut on a Friday when everybody else is also trying to leave. The airport is closed. There is a choice between a long sea-trip to Cyprus; a six-hour drive to Israel (or Dixie as it is known in the trade) or, with a little luck, a three-hour drive across the mountains to Damascus.

Dixie is automatically out because you cannot fly on to Arab capitals from there. The fourteen-hour boat to Larnaca is out because the Arab summit in Fez starts on Monday and I have to be there by Sunday night.

There is a Syrian visa in my passport. There is a Lebanese visa in my other passport. (Foreign correspondents are supposed to have two passports, one for Arab countries that will not recognize an Israeli stamp.) A little gratuity, as it is known, and a lot of smiling and nodding patiently at the Sécurité Générale get me a Lebanese exit visa after a two-hour wait.

Taxi-drivers in Beirut earn approximately twice what this correspondent does and they do not pay tax. After an hour's bargaining and the handing over of a sum that would keep an average British family in food and clothes for three weeks, a driver agrees to take a colleague and myself to Damascus. He does not. He is stopped at the border. He is not a proper taxi-driver. We must take a proper taxi. There are none.

Nor does one come. Eventually, nearly in tears, we hitch a ride to Damascus. A three-hour journey has taken fourteen hours. There are no more flight departures that Friday night. Saturday, yes, there is Syrian Airlines to Casablanca, but one must pay cash. My air-travel card is totally useless. The assembled might of American Express, Diners Club, Access and Visa makes no impression on the stony-faced Syrian Airlines manager. He wants one thousand US dollars in cash. I don't have one thousand US dollars. I have spent most of my dwindling cash on taxis.

Undaunted, I rummage through my briefcase. Bingo! I have an open return ticket to Paris. From there I can connect to Casablanca.

In Paris, on Saturday, the whole population, it seems, is returning from holiday. It takes three hours to get through Immigration and Customs.

At 6.10 p.m. at the Air France desk I am informed there is a flight to Casablanca at 7.40. It leaves from Paris Orly. I am at Charles-de-Gaulle Airport. In this traffic Orly will take more than an hour.

Sunday morning I fly to Casablanca. This time I've really won. This important Arab summit, which will formulate the response to President Reagan's peace plan, does not start till Monday. I have hours to spare.

Little do I know that my troubles have only just started. I am not on the list of accredited correspondents. I can go to Rabat but under no circumstances may I proceed to Meknes, a hundred and forty kilometres farther, or to Fez, sixty kilometres beyond that. I spend more of my dollars getting to Rabat. I must pay the taxi-driver double as he has to come back empty. The drive takes two hours. I 'phone the office. I have missed the deadline.

Monday morning. The office in London has promised to send a telex. It has not arrived. Go to the British Embassy. Passport, please, and Press card. I am given four copies of a letter saying I am a *Financial Times* correspondent. There are no taxis anywhere. Walk through the blazing heat to the Ministry of Information. They keep one copy. I must go to the Foreign Ministry.

'Ah, Monsieur Dalby, we have this morning received a telex from London. Your passport, please; your Press card. Please fill in two forms. Do you have two photos? Who are you? What is your passport number? What is your father's name? What is your mother's name? Where were you born and why?

I can go to Meknes. Another two-hour drive, at vast expense. I arrive at the Transatlantic Hotel where the Press Centre is. Your passport, please. Do you have two more photographs? Can you fill in three forms this time? The forms are similar. Who are you? Why are you here? What are your father's and mother's names?

A room has been set up with telexes and telephones. No, I cannot use them because I do not have a badge. Where do I get my badge? From the police. They are at lunch. Three hours later I am photographed and given a badge. The Moroccan authorities now have more photographs of me than my family. I feel so bound up in red tape I can barely move. However, at least I can telephone. I still have not got to Fez but I can call the office. I have missed the edition. London is one hour ahead of Morocco.

I decide to take the bus to Fez. Yasser Arafat has arrived. I have missed him. No journalists are allowed to talk to any of the delegates anyway, let alone the heads of state.

Return to Meknes. There is no room at the Transatlantic. I decide to file something. I go to the Palace Hotel to which I have been accredited. There are no telephones in the rooms, no air conditioning. It is the kind of place where turning on the shower makes the entire building shriek. There is no water in the shower. There is no soap in the bathroom. Never mind, I ask for a beer . . . all hotels are dry.

Tuesday. Together with sixty other journalists I board a bus for Fez. This is the first full working day. Halfway to Fez we are stopped at a road block. There is no permission for us to proceed. We return to Meknes.

It is clear that no journalist is going to get anywhere near anybody. The best we can hope for is a communiqué some time Wednesday night. I am exhausted, uncomfortable and unhappy. So much for the glamour of being a foreign correspondent.

STEWART DALBY

A Twentieth-century Savonarola

No city looks its best to a traveller arriving late at night, tired from a long journey and with nowhere to stay. Even Florence, for all its beauty, is no exception. The midnight view from the tourist accommodation office at the central railway station is not found in any holiday brochure. It was a depressing introduction on my first visit to the city because I had been looking forward to settling into the grand luxe of the Hotel Excelsior (one of the perks of foreign travel for journalists in those days being the chance to stay in the grandest hotels at the expense of one's newspaper). It was October and I had not reserved. Hotels were never full in those days before mass tourism, especially not expensive, five-star places like the Excelsior. I had taken a taxi straight from the station and been shocked to find the hotel full. 'It's the Film Festival,' explained the receptionist. He advised me to return to the station and try the accommodation bureau.

It had been my second set-back that day, the first having been my failure to make contact in Rome with my paper's local correspondent on whom I was relying to help me get the Florence story. I had rung his number several times from Rome only to hear a recorded message in totally incomprehensible Italian.

At the accommodation bureau in Florence I found myself in the company of a pretty young woman in smart Air Canada uniform who had also arrived from Rome without a hotel reservation.

'Are you together?' asked the woman in charge.

'No we are not!' the Air Canada attendant replied sharply.

The woman leafed through a book on her desk. 'I have two rooms at a pensione in the Piazza Santissima Annunziata. That is all I can offer you.'

'A pensione!' retorted Air Canada in shocked dismay. She was obviously accustomed to staying in first-class hotels during stop-overs and, like myself, had been expecting to stay in one in Florence.

'You know what a pensione is?' she said, turning to me. 'It will be a real dump!'

The pensione turned out to be an agreeable surprise. The premises, on the colonnaded west side of the piazza, looked as if they had been there since the days of the Medicis, and might have been once a small palazzo or part of a monastery.

I never knew what the flight attendant thought of her quarters because I did not see her again after we parted in the lobby, but I was more than satisfied with mine – a spacious room with a vaulted ceiling, sparsely but tastefully furnished in a slightly monastic style. A leaded window in a carved-stone surround overlooked the piazza. Unpacking, I reflected that I had not done too badly. What I did not then know was that I had in fact had a remarkable piece of good fortune, as I discovered the next morning at breakfast.

A jolly-looking woman in black seemed to be in charge. She moved from table to table exchanging pleasantries in Italian with the residents then came to my table and, to my surprise, addressed me in a Yorkshire accent. 'You're British,' she said. 'You checked in last night.' She had seen the particulars of my passport in the guest register. She told me she was British too but had lived in Florence for many years, having married an Italian after the War. She asked if I was in Florence on business or holiday.

I said I was a *Sunday Telegraph* reporter and had been sent to Florence to interview Professor Giorgio La Pira, a former mayor who had just launched a Centre for World Political Studies here in partnership with prominent British Left-wingers.

'La Pira?' She reacted with immediate interest. The sixty-one year-old, Sicilian-born Professor of Roman Law at the University of Florence had, in his ten years as mayor of Florence, acquired a bizarre celebrity (or notoriety, depending on your viewpoint) thanks to the saintly piety and simplicity of his life, as well as the eccentricity of his policies.

Thinking and talking like a mediæval scholar and mystic, giving his clothes and money to the poor, he had become known as the 'Holy Mayor of Florence'. He lived in a monk's cell in the Dominican monastery of San Marco, where Giralamo Savonarola had been prior and had taken vows of chastity, poverty and obedience. La Pira was widely believed to see himself as a twentieth-century Savonarola, cheerfully provoking nearly as much controversy as the fifteenth-century monk had done by burning Florentine art treasures, as objects of sinful decadence, in the Bonfire of the Vanities.

The professor's disregard for material things had produced an amusing folklore. A typical story from his early days as a Christian Democrat deputy after the War was that he borrowed a raincoat from a fellow-deputy on a rainy day in Rome and gave it to a beggar. 'But that was my raincoat,' the deputy protested. 'You can buy another,' La Pira replied.

After being elected mayor of Florence in 1951, ousting a Communist predecessor, he had controversially aided strikers, requisitioned the villas of the wealthy for the homeless and made Florence the venue for a succession of international get-togethers: a world meeting of mayors, an east-west disarmament conference and a symposium on the Vietnam War.

His Leftist policies had initially brought him popular acclaim but eventually, as with Savonarola, opposition to him grew. Savonarola had been burned; La Pira lost his job in the 1965 elections. But he never gave up a long-cherished hope of making his ancient city a spiritual bridge between the Communist east and the capitalist West.

His history was at that stage unknown to me, because I had been sent to Florence at short notice and had not had time for any research. I told the lady in black that I had been relying on my colleague in Rome to help me find La Pira and brief me on his background. It was then that I discovered what a lucky break I had had in not being at the Excelsior.

'I'm sure we can help you,' she said cheerfully. 'A gentleman living here is on the staff of *La Nazione*. I will ask him to introduce you to the editor, Signor Enrico Mattei.'

The offices of the prestigious daily *La Nazione* were just a short walk from the pensione. As Signor Mattei talked about La Pira, laughing as he recounted instances of his eccentricity, I realised he was prompted not just by a kind desire to help. He had been one of the professor's severest critics and had forced his proposed Centre for World Political Studies to postpone its inaugural conference by means of an editorial blast warning that it would be exploited by Communist propaganda. 'Italy has two million Communists and a further six million Communist voters. I didn't see the need to give them any further opportunities for propaganda,' said the editor.

I asked where I might find the professor. 'We will find him for you,' he replied. He spoke on the 'phone and moments later a young man came into the room. 'This is one of my reporters, he will take you to La Pira. He speaks very good English and will be your interpreter.'

The reporter took me by taxi to a building forming part of the Monastery of San Marco. The professor had made this his headquarters as well as his home. Since losing his mayor's office in the Palazzo Vecchio, he was renting three rooms with a small, walled garden for twenty-three pounds a year.

An old woman opened his door in the Via La Marmora (since renamed Via Giorgio La Pira in his honour). In two outer rooms, staff were busy with correspondence and piles of paper. La Pira – diminutive, bespectacled and intense – emerged from the room beyond. In a theatrically enthusiastic welcome he seized me by the shoulders, then warmly by both hands and led us to his office, a monk's cell.

Perhaps because he had faded somewhat from the public gaze, he seemed pleased to be interviewed by a foreign journalist. Bubbling with good humour, he talked while the reporter translated, peppering the discourse with Latin quotations from the Saints and references to Milton, Cromwell, Copernicus, Galileo, Beveridge, Keynes, the Magna Carta, Pope John XXIII, Kennedy, Khrushchev, the Medicis, Columbus and

Savonarola. He seemed to be as much at home in the fifteenth century as in the present.

Warming to his theme of the need for a spiritual renaissance, he good-humouredly dismissed his critics as Fascists. 'They think I am a Communist. I am not. I am an anarchist. I want to check the power of the State.' He laughed when I asked who was going to fund his Centre for World Political Studies, replying with a shrug of his shoulders: 'I have no money. The Centre has no money either. Money is not important. Someone will provide'.

Leaving La Pira with the story in my note-book, I reflected on the unpredictability of luck. Had I made contact with the Rome correspondent, I would doubtless have spent the night dining with him and now perhaps still be on my way to Florence. Had the Excelsior had a room, I would not have had my story presented to me on a plate, a breakfast plate as it happened.

R Barry O'Brien

Into the Cauldron

The most memorable journey I ever made between two capitals was also one of the shortest – the two hundred-odd miles which separate those one-time twin pillars of the Hapsburg world, Vienna and Budapest. What made the trip unforgettable was the date: 25 October 1956, some thirty-six hours after Hungary had erupted into a spontaneous, nation-wide revolt against Russian occupation and the Communist tyranny it sustained.

Now, at 11.40 a.m. on that murky Thursday morning, all removable contents of my sedate Rover 75 were spread out on the long Customs table at Hegyeshalom, the border-post with Austria. Though their orders were to seal the frontier completely, there was nothing the Hungarian authorities could do about my entry visa. It had been properly stamped in a week before by their consulate in Vienna. I had applied on a hunch. After the turmoil in Poland which had culminated in the Poznan riots and the triumphant reinstatement of the popular Gomulka, might not the equally volatile Magyars take to the streets as well? Both countries were in my large journalistic parish as head of the *Daily Telegraph*'s Central and South-East European Bureau – a title which reflects the spacious yet specialised life of the foreign correspondent in the days before television news trampled across the scene.

Seven days later, in Budapest and most regional centres, the Hungarians had duly obliged by shattering the regime with a tidal wave of demonstrations. The tremors had not yet reached Hegyeshalom however, where the AVO (the Communist secret police) were still firmly established. Their lieutenant in charge, having grudgingly accepted he could not bar my entry, was determined I should bring in nothing which might be of use to those imperialist Fascist terrorists who were rocking the country.

I carried a tennis bag with me on any trip across the Iron Curtain, if only because it usually led on the courts to more off-the-record information than anything produced at their desks by press officers and the like. I had thrown it in while packing in Vienna that morning – partly on a *What the hell?* impulse but also to calm the nerves of a very anxious family. The lieutenant, unfamiliar with this item of luggage, zipped it eagerly open, hoping to see at least a rifle inside.

His chagrin at tipping out only two racquets, a box of balls and an orange found consolation when he turned to the handful of books I had also packed, in anticipation of a long stay. They included Boswell's *Journal of a Tour to the Hebrides with Samuel Johnson LLD* and this in turn included two large, pull-out maps made from a hand-drawn 1791 print. The dotted lines and crosses which marked the good doctor's progress around Mull, Coll and Skye in that autumn of 1773 might easily have been, to a suspicious mind without a word of English, the chart of some NATO invasion plan through the embattled Danube islands in this autumn of 1956. He ripped them away in triumph. '*Karte hier bleiben*' ('Map stops here') he barked in his pidgin German and – Stalinist honour satisfied – raised the frontier pole.

Mosonmagyaróvár, the first big town ten miles further (and one with which I was to become alarmingly familiar), already showed the scars of a world being violently torn apart: shattered windows and sprays of bullet-holes on some of the yellow-painted walls; a brown police car burned out and on its side. Yet that burst of fighting was over and an unreal peace reigned.

It was the same at Györ, the ancient county capital and seat of a bishopric: two Hungarian army tanks squatted on the Danube bridge but seemed to be on nobody's side in particular. Their crews were leaning out of open hatches, cigarettes in their mouths. It might have been a break in peace-time manœuvres.

For the next sixty miles the road was controlled by the patriot insurgents, by now almost synonymous with the people. Their banner was the ubiquitous symbol of the uprising: the red-white-green flag in Hungary's national colours but with a hole in the middle where the emblems of Communism – the wheatsheaf, hammer and sickle – had been torn out. To my surprise it was still very much in evidence at Almásfüzitö which I reached by mid-afternoon. This was an archetypal proletarian town whose massive aluminium plant was the pride of the People's Republic. The factory was still belching dark silver smoke from its chimneys and spreading a pall of grey powder over the town and across a five-mile radius of the surrounding fields. But it was evident that the pall of Marxist-Leninism no longer enveloped everything inside. Scores of the plant's workers had joined the cheering throng outside. Where, one began to wonder, would the cheering end? The answer came as we approached Budapest itself on the final, forty-mile stretch of the Vienna highway. For the first time the Red Army appeared in strength. So far, in the countryside, it had kept largely out of sight. Around the capital it had thrown a thick armoured ring.

This took some penetrating. Just north of the suburbs the road was completely blocked with Soviet light tanks and lorries. The officer in charge motioned us back, perhaps put out by the paper Union Jack that I had stuck on the inside of the windscreen. 'Journalist,' I shouted as he thumbed my passport, adding '*Izvestia*' as a somewhat outlandish inducement. The only reaction was a scowl. When I tried 'Diplomat' the scowl grew even deeper and he swung his machine-pistol through the window. On an inspiration I then cried '*Delagatie, Delagatie*'. As an old Iron Curtain hand I remembered that the workers' paradise fairly shimmered with delegates from someone to somewhere. It was a respectable Communist word. The scowl faded, the machine-pistol swung back, my passport was grudgingly returned and I was waved on. An hour later I reached the Lánchíd chain bridge (built by British engineers nearly a century before) where the Danube divides the hilly Vár district of the capital from the flat expanses of Pest.

There had been the occasional chatter of small-arms fire high up behind me, but no louder than a cricket chirping. A trolley-bus lay on its side near the bridge, the overhead wires coiled on the pavement like a Medusa's head of steel. But everything seemed frozen in time, giving a sense of stalemate heightened by proceedings at the Lánchíd crossing itself. Two heavy Soviet tanks guarded the left-hand approach. Opposite them stood a knot of civilians wearing their resistance armbands. These were the only ones to ask for my papers. They simply called '*Angol*' to the Russian who waved me on. Ten minutes later I was checking in at my regular Budapest watering-hole, the Duna. On all previous visits, to this or any other Communist-bloc hotel, the reception would retain the visitor's passport so it could be passed to the security police. But now mine was handed straight back with my room key. This was a novelty of some significance.

The timing of my arrival turned out to be another stroke of luck. A few hours before I checked in, Erne Gerö, the detested Stalinist stooge, had been replaced as prime minister by Imre Nagy, who was now busy implementing a state of emergency. Nagy was the darling of the insurgents, a moderate Communist with strong nationalistic leanings. The fact that he was somewhat of a cuddly Fatty Arbuckle in appearance did his popularity no harm. He actually looked human, in contrast to those colourless *apparatchiks* who stood against him.

His appointment – decided in an all-night session of the party's Central Committee with Soviet 'advisors' in the wings – was intended to calm things down. In fact it touched off fresh violence. Those 'workers of goodwill and honest Hungarian youth', whom Nagy first praised for their part in starting the disturbances, now went for the kill against the Soviet occupation army, ignoring his appeal to lay down their arms. What had started as student demonstrations had ended in popular revolt.

There was no fixed pattern to the street-fighting in the capital. It was as though the lava of revolution had burst through the crust, leaving the eruption to take its own course. This was shapeless and unpredictable and we were always darting from one part of the city to another as the rumour of some new skirmish or demonstration spread.

My first foray had to be to Stalin Square to see what remained of the memorial to the dead dictator. The crowd had wrenched the huge metal statue from its socket and dragged it, howling with joy, down the street like a sacrificial animal. All that was left of Stalin now – and, as it seemed, of Stalinism – were two jagged bronze feet, each the size of a man, on a stone pedestal.

As we were gazing at this piece of wholesome desecration, word of another blow at Moscow reached the square: 'They are burning the Russian books!' Back along the Rákoczy Út to the Soviet Information Centre in the Váci Utca. There, sure enough, was the bonfire – a pile of books six feet high and twelve feet across – blazing on the pavement. Whenever it threatened to die down, fresh faggots of Marx and Lenin were brought out from the looted store and tossed on the heap. And this 'information centre', until two days before, had been the cathedral of the Communist faith in Hungary.

It was on this drive that I had the worst of many similarly painful moments: yet another appeal for Western arms. A white-haired man who looked old enough to have fought against Genghis Khan, let alone Stalin, thrust his cavalry sword through the car window: 'These are our only weapons. When are you going to help us?'

The next day I saw for myself how the very young of the nation, as well as the very old (and seemingly every age-group in between), had been caught up in the ferment. A Hungarian friend had pulled me from the hotel dining-room promising that 'something special' was happening across in Buda: a group of youths, some of them children, were taking on a squad of heavy Red Army tanks with nothing more than stones and a few home-made petrol bombs. The battle-ground turned out to be the twin squares, the Moszkva Tér and the Széna Tér, just below the fortress hill. Normally a giant double loop for the capital's tramcar system, they now presented an extraordinary sight. Five or six Soviet tanks were lined up on a steep side-road, gun barrels tilted down to command the whole space below. The main attack was coming from behind an upturned tram fifty yards away, with much lobbing of missiles. Only one looked danger-ous. Something ominously like a heavy trench mortar was pushed into sight. The Russian lieutenant commanding decided to take no chances. He fired two rounds into it at point-blank range from his secondary cannon. The box disintegrated – to reveal a kitchen stove-pipe inside.

Without knowing it, the Russians were also being set upon from behind. A small boy, perhaps seven or eight years old, had clambered up the back of a battened-down tank and emptied a small can of petrol on its tracks. Unhappily he appeared to have forgotten the matches and, after a moment of vexed hesitation, he skipped away. When, half an hour later the lieutenant (who like all Red Army officers had been told he was putting down a Fascist insurrection backed by American troops) pulled out in embarrassment, we tried to find the boy who had played the mortar prank.

'Oh, he had to run off home,' we were told. 'He said there would be trouble if he was late for supper.' It was reassuring that a schoolchild who could defy six Soviet tanks was still afraid of a clipped ear from his mother.

That same day, Monday 29 October, the Hungarian Revolution suffered its first heavy blow. It was delivered not by the Russians but by two of its main anti-Communist sympathizers in the West. News of the Anglo-French Suez campaign reached Budapest. The implications were obvious. This new and even greater flare-up from the Iron Curtain might encourage the Kremlin to strike out more boldly to shore up its own quaking empire.

The irony was that this long-range threat to the revolution appeared just when its victory seemed assured. The night before, we had heard Imre Nagy announce that the Soviet commander-in-chief had agreed to withdraw his troops immediately from Budapest and that talks would start in Moscow for the evacuation of Soviet forces from the whole country.

Then, on the last day of October, the cry rang through Budapest like a carillon: 'The Cardinal is free'. Not merely free but already reinstated in his old town palace in the Uri Utca on the Vár, where the yellow-white papal flag now floated alongside the national colours of Hungary. The cardinal's eight years in Communist captivity had ended the night before when a patriot task force had burst at supper-time into the house north of Budapest where he was guarded by twenty-one AVO men. They surrendered their eminent prisoner without a struggle. When I arrived, questions were already raining down on his head from a flock of journalists in the courtyard, while a serpentine black chain of priests shuffled tearfully forward on their knees to kiss his ring.

Whether or not this was 'the only man who could save the country' (as Radio Budapest had declared) was never put to the test. But the next day, Thursday 1 November, a small group of us finally made contact with the man who had been leading the insurgents' salvation process thus far.

Istvan Dudas was a veteran of the War-time Communist resistance who had swung over later to the right-wing Smallholders Party, a conversion which brought him eight years' imprisonment without trial. He still looked like a defiant peasant: burly, thick-set and wearing leggings. But whatever his achievements on the barricades, I found his attitude now somewhat tawdry. It was all political intrigue and empire-building. As we were leaving I turned to one of his aides, a sallow young student who would have looked more at home fingering a laboratory microscope than his machine-pistol. What did he think?

'Plans! Plans! What's the point of them?' he fairly burst out. 'The Russians will never let us carry them out. We are deluding ourselves – in true Hungarian style! This revolution was not fought for the present, it was fought for the future, mark my words.'

They were words one could not help marking and already there were some ominous portents to underline them. The patriots had counted 304 Red Army tanks moving in from Záhony, the Soviet-Hungarian border village in the north-east. Another three hundred had come in from Romania. Moreover, since dawn that day, Russian troops had again ringed the capital's main air terminal at Ferihegy.

Yet Budapest itself was completely rid of Red Army soldiers and had the trance-like air of a normal Western capital. This feeling of normality increased the next day when, at the Ministry of Foreign Affairs (now of course in patriot hands), I was handed the ultimate symbol of freedom for any foreign correspondent: an unlimited and unrestricted visa for the 'Republic of Hungary'.

I decided to put it to good and speedy use by making a weekend trip back to Vienna, to collect some clothes and catch up with my wife who had been busy in emergency refugee camps along Hungary's open border with Austria. Moreover, I needed some reliable guidance about the

238

galloping Suez crisis. So that Saturday, 3 November, I drove away from Budapest heading west, but keeping my hotel room and leaving part of my luggage in it, expecting to be back on the Monday. Things turned out very differently.

The first uncomfortable sight came at the Danube crossing of Györ. Near the bridge my car had to pick its way through a chain of twenty-eight Soviet tanks, all with unfamiliar division-lettering on them. A handful of patriot tanks was also on hand, just watching. However, the atmosphere still seemed cheerful. One Red Army soldier was even delighting spectators by riding zigzag across the bridge on a borrowed bicycle.

It was at Mosonmagyarovár that real trouble loomed. A long line of Western cars with assorted number-plates was drawn up on the main road, their passengers pacing up and down and talking with local patriot leaders.

'The Red Army cut the border a few hours ago,' one of the American drivers told me after flagging me to pull in. 'We've tried to cross twice but their armoured cars pushed us firmly back. So we're all bedding down here for the night until we know what the hell is going on.'

Our emergency quarters turned out to be very comfortable – the dormitories of the Kossuth Lajos Gymnasium, once a hunting-lodge of the Austrian Archduke Frederick's and now a mixed senior school. Bowls of Hungarian bean soup with sweet-smelling black bread settled our appetites. We could even call Vienna via the town's switchboard. And so, fairly at ease, to bed.

I was awakened about five a.m. by an American woman with a very loud voice giving a very loud scream three rooms away. We wrenched open our dormitory door to find ourselves looking down the barrel of a Red Army machine-pistol. It seemed to sprout in direct horizontal level from a fur hat with ear-flaps and a pair of distinctly unfriendly, green Mongolian eyes. Similar unsavoury harbingers of dawn were guarding every room.

At the end of half an hour's pandemonium, punctuated by more feminine screams and strange barking noises coming from elderly male Swedes in pyjamas, it was clear that protest would get us nowhere. The game was up in Monsonmagyarovár and, as it soon emerged, in the whole of patriot Hungary. At that same hour a thousand Soviet tanks had moved into Budapest in a renewed and ultimately unstoppable bid to crush the revolution.

It would be idle to pretend that being held prisoner by the Red Army was not an adventure, even for someone who had four and a half years of war and various post-war excitements as a foreign correspondent behind him. It would, however, also be idle to claim that one ever felt unduly alarmed. Our American contingent, escorted by a member of their Budapest Legation, could scarcely be called combatant. It consisted mainly of children and pregnant wives. Moreover, there were several luminaries of the International Red Cross among our party.

I doubt therefore whether the Soviet general in command at Györ needed our protests (or the more formidable diplomatic ones being made on our behalf in Moscow that Sunday) to make up his mind. He was a harassed man who could recognise a very dispensable nuisance when he saw one. Soon after breakfast on Monday 5 November, he gave the order that we should be freed and escorted to safety across the Austrian frontier.

The order was not obeyed quite to the letter. True, the Soviet armoured car which had guarded our courtyard now joined the excitedly re-assembled convoy. But the crew were careful to ask one of the Red Cross ambulances in our party to lead the procession out of the silent, sullen town. And when we came in sight of the border, they turned tail and left us altogether. The reason was the frontier-post itself: the Customs building flew the patriots' flag and was held by a force of some forty insurgents, armed to the teeth.

We had nothing to declare except our sympathy and – in my case at least – embarrassment at leaving them to their fate. I asked one of them what they intended to do.

'Do?' he echoed. 'Why, just give the Russians hell when they do turn up and perhaps save a round or two for ourselves.'

And this, we learned later, was more or less what happened, despite the fact that, for those forty men and women, the Austrian border, and freedom, was a twelve-hundred-yard, unhampered stroll down the road.

I happen to have kept all the passports from my sixty-odd years of travels around the globe. In the one covering 1956 I now notice that there is no Hungarian exit stamp from November of that year. So technically, I never left that cauldron. I find the fantasy pleasing.

GORDON BROOK-SHEPHERD

A Patriot for Hungary

Budapest. Autumn 1963. The First Secretary's office in the British Legation. Dr István Gál, our valued Hungarian cultural adviser, put his head round the door and said: 'Have you a moment to see an unusual applicant for a visa? He is Count' (he used the title although the Communist regime had years before abolished the use of such distinctions) 'Zsigmond Széchenyi'.

I remembered that Count István Széchenyi had been the great modernizing reformer of mid-nineteenth-century Hungary and the man who had had the Chain Bridge built over the Danube to link Buda with Pest. Perhaps Zsigmond was one of his descendants?

A moment later Gál brought in a tall, powerfully built man in his sixties with strong features and a lined face. He had called to apply for a visa to visit Kenya, then still a British colony. The Budapest Natural History Museum, which had been all but destroyed during the War, needed some animal heads to display in its new building. The Hungarian government had therefore given permission for Széchenyi and his wife to go on safari to East Africa to shoot the animals and return with the trophies. The government would also arrange for an 'administrator' (i.e. a member of the secret police) to accompany them. Even so, this would be an exceptional experience for anyone to enjoy at a time when travel outside the Soviet bloc was still restricted to those on official business. Thus began my acquaintance with a remarkable Hungarian.

Over the next couple of years I was to learn more of his story. Born in 1898, Széchenyi had been the eldest of seven children brought up on a large country estate. There he had developed a passion for field sports and gradually become a fine naturalist as well as an outstanding marksman with both shotgun and rifle. He began to bag some record heads both at home and abroad. He was soon in demand at the best shoots. During the 1930s he continued his pursuit of red deer and roebuck in Hungary, ibex and chamois in the Alps, grizzly and bighorn in Alaska, panther and tiger in India, and the 'big five' in Africa. He once showed me his leather-bound big-game book, with pages of a different colour for each continent.

241

Hungary had in 1941 joined Germany in the 'crusade against Communism in the east'. When this ran into the sands of Russian resistance and subsequent retribution, many of the country's landowning class fled westwards to Austria, Germany and beyond. But Széchenyi, who had no interest in politics, made a momentous decision: he was Hungarian and, come what may, he would stay in Hungary. And, despite various opportunities to leave, there he remained.

In 1945, not long after the Russians had driven the German Sixth SS Panzer Army out of Hungary and occupied the whole country, Széchenyi was arrested. He had little idea why. One evening after he had been some weeks in prison, he was taken out, a sandbag was slipped over his head and he was pushed into a car. The car was then driven round the streets for a time, apparently to confuse him. Finally it stopped. He was pulled out, guided up a flight of steps, through a door and down a corridor at the end of which he was halted. There someone removed the sandbag.

He found himself standing on the threshold of a magnificent library – book-lined walls, a table with decanters and a bright fire at the far end. In front of the fire stood a Russian colonel.

'Come in, my dear Count,' he called. 'What would you prefer, cognac or whisky?' Thus began a strange interrogation. Its object was to discover where Széchenyi had hidden his famous collection of sporting guns. Eventually he was forced to lead the colonel to the orchard in his grandmother's garden where they were buried.

Under the subsequent Communist regime Széchenyi fared even worse. He was classified as a 'member of the former ruling classes' and, as such, came bottom of the ladder when it came to employment, housing and children's education. Even when I knew him in 1963 he was living with his wife and daughter in a tiny house cobbled together with bricks and rubble, the debris left over by the violence of war and the revolution of 1956. He had managed to salvage few possessions. But among them were his game books and his copy of Rowland Ward's *Records of Big Game*, the 1935 volume in which several of Széchenyi's record-breaking heads were documented.

As the Soviet Union installed a Stalinist regime in Hungary, Széchenyi was to endure misery. Although not purged, conceivably because of the famous name he bore, he was denied employment. So he began to write books about his pre-War adventures as a leading shot. Being non-political, their publication was allowed; and because they opened a window on what for Hungarians, who were then immured behind the Iron Curtain, must have seemed like a magical world – rajahs and elephants in India for example – they became best-sellers.

In early 1964 Zsigmond Széchenyi did manage to leave for his safari in Kenya, accompanied by his wife and an 'administrator'. He duly shot the buffalo, lion and other game on the Natural History Museum's list, had them skinned and the trophies dispatched to Hungary. A week or so later he returned to Budapest. At the airport he was accosted by an aggressive young Communist journalist.

'Well, Mr Széchenyi. As a member of the former ruling classes, how is it that when you were abroad you never did what all your family and friends have done and decided to abscond from Hungary?'

Széchenyi looked down on him and said: 'Young man, I must admit that Zsigmond occasionally toyed with the idea, but Széchenyi – never'.

HUGH CARLESS

The Search for the Leopard

For the first few moments after I climbed back into the Land Rover with Joshua and started winding through the streets of Arusha I wondered if this wasn't sheer madness. But as we hit the dusty red roads and moved out into the plains I knew I was right. Even if it seemed stupid and irresponsible, it was worth making the effort, whether or not it actually paid off.

It was dusty, hot, uncomfortable. We could stop halfway and find some kind of lodging somewhere or try to get all the way to Seronera in one go. Joshua was keen to press on. He knew the success of our crazy venture depended on him, and the Land Rover had a rough journey. It is a Serengeti Park rule that you cannot enter after sunset, so I understood something of his hurried driving. We had tried, unsuccessfully, to talk our way into the Ngorongoro Wildlife Lodge en route, and so had to get at

243

least to the park gate before six o'clock. We made it, but only just, and then wound across the plains, through the dramatic rock outcroppings, past the giant Simba kopje, which towered a hundred feet above us, and eventually reached Seronera as darkness was falling.

Joshua seemed to know exactly what he was doing. We drove through the forks of the Seronera River to a very secluded site under an acacia-tree. In almost complete silence we pitched the two small tents by the light of a bulb wired to the Land Rover's battery. After dinner Joshua told me that camping here was actually illegal: it was not a recognized site. He also told me he had camped here once before – with three nurses. They had all slept in one tent on the first night but one of them preferred to be alone on the second. She spent a fairly hectic night while an inquisitive male lion settled noisily next to her tent. The grunts and coughs terrified the poor woman; she got no sleep. It was, said Joshua, the last time she tried sleeping alone.

A freak thunder-storm hit Seronera that night, a dramatic downpour with sheet lightning that started just before midnight and lasted for the best part of an hour. Then about two hours later there was another downpour. It stopped quite suddenly and was followed by the noise of lions roaring all round the camp. We kept quiet and I lay awake listening as the deep, guttural sounds came closer. This nerve-racking experience continued for an hour. Then, just near Joshua's tent a few feet away, I heard a single, ear-splitting roar and a scraping and flapping against his tent. Joshua screamed. I thought that the lion had attacked him but in fact he was trying to scare the beast away. A few seconds later I heard the same scraping sound – but this time against my own tent, a few inches from my head. The lion bumped against the tent-pole and rubbed itself against the canvas, slinking around it. I didn't have the faintest idea what to do, but Joshua shouted to me to keep very quiet!

Before we went to bed, he had moved the Land Rover from under the acacia, where our supplies were, to the door of his tent. It was a lucky move that may have saved us. He leaped into the vehicle, started the motor and turned the lights on. A lioness and her five cubs stood there: she was looking for food. As Joshua rammed the Land Rover towards them, the lioness made a stealthy get-away, holding a plastic water-container in her jaws.

At first light we saw what had happened. It was clear from the paw prints around Joshua's tent that the lioness had tried to attack him. Her teeth had torn right through the wall of his tent. My tent too was surrounded by her large pugs, while the cubs' were scattered in the soft mud around. Joshua said that in future he would sleep in the vehicle in case something similar happened again. I didn't think it was possible for both lightning and lions to strike twice in exactly the same place.

Shaken but undeterred, we headed straight for the Magadi Road, which runs close to the Seronera River, and spent the remainder of the morning cruising slowly up the valley looking for tracks and searching the trees. In the recently created pools by the river the usually sinister marabous looked like solemn deacons in prayer.

In this great open brown country, the landscape is broken by shallow, dried-up river valleys and by the yellow-barked fever-trees, the flat-topped thorn-acacias and the sausage-trees. Yellow fever-trees prefer areas near water, and early explorers frequently camped under them because of the certainty of water and shade. Naturally, areas of water are also favoured camping grounds for the malarial mosquito. It was not known then that mosquitoes carry the malaria parasite, but people soon concluded that anyone who camped beneath the fever-tree was likely to contract malaria. An association was made between some mysterious power of the tree and the fever, hence its name.

It is in these trees that leopards usually spend most of the daylight hours. They lie in the low branches about twelve or fourteen feet above ground and are extremely difficult to see. When they move, they do so under cover in long grass or dense thicket. The rougher the terrain the better, and the leopard's spotted skin provides perfect camouflage. Only in the afternoon can leopards be seen more easily, but it is still like looking for a needle in a haystack. There are tails and limbs hanging down from the sausage- and acacia-trees all over Africa. However, most of these are imaginary; a real leopard's usually disappear as soon as it sees you.

We drove slowly along the valleys fruitlessly for nearly four hours then had a makeshift lunch, standing dejectedly beside the Land Rover. After lunch we headed for the Seronera Wildlife Lodge where Joshua managed to get a small single room for me to dump my bags. It seemed a better bet than camping in the lion range again.

Joshua left to try and get hold of someone he knew in the village. I waited for a good hour, wondering what he was up to. He returned with a smiling, thick-set man in a green shirt. Martin Darabe, an Irangu tribesman, was a National Parks guide who had been at Seronera for a number of years. Quiet and good-humoured, he spoke little English but he knew the lie of the land. Joshua had explained everything to him. Martin said our best bet would be in the early evening, when leopards begin to get ready for the evening's hunting. But he thought it was worth going out now, even though it was the hottest part of the day. We had only a few hours – the rest of this afternoon and perhaps part of the next morning – so we set out and tirelessly combed the fever-trees up and down the winding valley.

Two hours later we were still looking. I had almost given up hope when Martin said something quietly to Joshua in Swahili and Joshua said: 'I think der de lopard'. I peered at some acacias and saw nothing. The leopard wasn't in the first or the second group of trees but in a third, and very far away. How Martin saw it I have no idea. Just a tiny speck of a thing hanging down from a branch.

Joshua drove, for once carefully, keeping near cover in the rough terrain between us and the tree. I looked through my field-glasses and a chill of excitement went down my spine. It was indeed a leopard. A female, about five years old, Martin estimated, sprawled along a branch with all four legs and tail dangling down like extra branches, and her head in a fork of the tree facing us.

She seemed lazy, and was evidently quite content to spend the greater part of the day in the shade. From the shelter of a neighbouring tree, at a distance of about thirty yards, I was able to take photograph after photograph of her. Then, when I had taken every picture I possibly could, I said: 'OK Joshua. Now just go past her very slowly . . . Now turn left towards her . . . Just go under the branch'. Very disturbed, he said: 'I can't turn left'. He was afraid the leopard would jump into the open vehicle. Martin too was uneasy because we were breaking rules by driving off the track.

Joshua inched closer. Martin warned him worriedly not to, looking around uneasily to make sure there was no one to see us. Breaking the law because of a crazy guy who wants to get closer and closer. They wanted to leave. I wanted to get closer.

I had to capture that moment, and I was willing to take any risk to do so. I was frightened, not of the leopard but that she would leave. I kept taking shots, then I was really close. I got out the 300mm lens and very nearly shot her in the face. I could almost feel her breath on me. My eyes looked directly into hers in an uncanny moment of communication. Then I took the photograph I had been looking for. Everything came together – the light was right, the focus was right, the film was right.

Then, almost immediately, I knew I was outstaying my welcome. It was dangerous. I'd had one of the great thrills of my life, but it was time to go. We returned to Seronera in triumph.

CHRISTOPHER ONDAATJE

Placebos in the Mountains of the Moon

For our week's trek through Uganda's Ruwenzori Mountains my half-dozen companions and I indented for a team of Bakonjo porters. The Bakonjo live on the mountains' lower slopes but are familiar with the whole range. Over the years they had earned a reputation for physical stamina and cheerful reliability – qualities reminiscent of Sherpas in the Himalayas. Indeed, just as one seldom hears the slightest word in disparagement of a Sherpa, the same applies to the Bakonjo. No one who has dealt with them will forget their sterling virtues.

Situated on the Equator, the Ruwenzoris are a spectacular cluster of peaks between fifteen and seventeen thousand feet high that demarcate for some fifty miles the frontier between Uganda and the Congo. For days on end the peaks are often cloaked in impenetrable cloud, and invisible from below. But when they emerge the spectacle is unforgettable. Even so hard-bitten a traveller as Henry Morton Stanley, who witnessed it in 1889, was moved to pay it emotional tribute in his classic book *In Darkest Africa*.

'During the whole day our eyes had rested on a long line of dark and solemn spurs, their summits buried in leaden mist. But soon after 5 p.m.

the upper extremities of these spurs loomed up one after another, and a great line of mountain shoulders stood out. Then peak after peak struggled from behind night-black clouds into sight; until at last the snowy range, immense and beautiful, a perfect picture of majestic desolation, drew all eyes and riveted attention, while every face seemed awed.'

The Ruwenzoris had awed the Ancients also, though their *Montes Lunæ* – the Mountains of the Moon – remained for almost two millennia the subject of hearsay and conjecture. They had even been described as the source of the Nile by Ptolemy, the second-century Greek geographer, astronomer and mathematician who, living in Alexandria, probably met – and certainly heard of – travellers who had ventured far up river.

Apart from their visual splendour and their association with the mysterious source of the Nile, another inducement the mountains offered was the many plants grotesquely enlarged and strangely distorted by 'gigantism'. This was manifested, as on Mount Kenya, most commonly but not exclusively in the lobelia and groundsel/*senecio* growing at over eleven thousand feet. I had no knowledge of botany but had read Patrick Synge's *Mountains of the Moon*, the record of a botanical expedition in the 1930s.

'Our own familiar common herbs seemed to have gone mad. We saw groundsels, swollen and distorted with woody trunks twenty feet in height, lobelias like gigantic blue and green obelisks, heathers mighty as great trees. Most alpine plants are reduced to extreme dwarfness, but these have rushed to the opposite extreme and exhibit an exaggerated gigantism.'

Eager to see all this, we first consulted the District Commissioner at Fort Portal. He was an indispensable ally: he not only kept tabs on all intending climbers and co-ordinated any search and rescue actions needed, he also held the keys of the mountain huts. We drove to the roadhead at six thousand feet and left our cars in the safe-keeping of the chief. Here eight stalwart and sober Bakonjo clocked in punctually and set about sorting our baggage (food, bedding, clothing, cameras, ice-axes, a primus stove, even the fly of a tent) into manageable loads of similar bulk and weight. They were a tough breed who, with back-pack, head-strap and stick, would carry a fifty-pound burden all day, up and down exhaustingly steep and muddy gradients.

The DC had advised us to establish from the outset (more subtly than by over-paying them – which he deprecated) a close and cheerful working relationship. One element in this, he suggested, might relate to first-aid or amateur medical help – for which we had in fact already made provision with a stock of aspirin, sticking-plaster, bandages, antiseptic ointment, iodine, Gentian Violet and cheap brandy. Another element might be the porters' financial problems, which were apt to be chronic; but this was a dubious area to enter since they knew that their pay was pegged, that strike action was discouraged – besides being out of character – and that it was a buyers' market, with plenty of other Bakonjo ready to accept the going rate if they rejected it.

Language might have been a problem, since none of us spoke their vernacular Lukonjo. Although several of us spoke Swahili, the *lingua franca* of East Africa, we knew that in the far west of Uganda it could not be relied on as a medium for sophisticated communication. Matthew, our head porter, had however quite good Swahili and I found it easy to converse with him.

Amongst the personal items which we preferred to carry ourselves was a handsome biscuit tin I had acquired years before. Its lid featured a glamorous lady in period attire. Matthew found that she repaid close scrutiny, and was also much taken by my explanation of the 'By Appointment' emblazoned on the lid. It certified that Messrs Huntley & Palmer had been granted the privilege of making biscuits for King George VI. The tin, long emptied of biscuits, was handy for the stock of sweets which I fished out during halts on the march. I knew from experience that when sweatily engaged in tropical exertions one benefitted almost as much from sustaining one's sugar intake as from topping up on salt. Sugar, either in the elegant guise of Kendal Mint Cake (aristocrat of mountaineering provender, from the English Lakes to the Himalayas) or as stickily demotic boiled sweets, could refresh the palate and renew flagging energy.

Among the sweets in my tin was a large container of Smarties – which did not rank among the familiar comestibles of rural Uganda. They were, as always, in various strong colours, and these now caught Matthew's attention. He asked if they were pills.

'Yes, medicines,' I replied, using the word *dawa* which can be used ironically to mean almost anything which is good for you.

'But what do they cure?'

'They can treat various conditions, depending on their colour,' I said, and I remember straining my Swahili to express idiomatically what we now call colour-coding.

Matthew became confiding. 'I suffer from piles,' he said. I remembered the DC's advice.

'Then swallow this green one now,' I told him, 'and this red one tonight, with water, and tell me tomorrow if you notice any improvement.'

'Are you a doctor?' he asked.

'No,' said I. 'But medicines such as these are widely esteemed as palliatives if not as cures.'

An idea struck him. 'Is that why King George used to buy them?' I saw that – as they had both been accommodated in the same tin – Matthew was conflating the 'By Appointment' of the biscuits with the unprivileged status of my Smarties.

'I cannot say,' I replied. 'But you can be sure that the king would have chosen the best medicine available, and so does his daughter, our present Queen.'

By this stage I was flannelling, and the topic was turning surreal. Matthew also realised that our dialogue was attracting the notice of his porters, who were standing around in attentive silence. He quickly called them to order, finalized the distribution of the loads, made a point of leaving the biscuit tin in my charge, and at the same time made a little speech in Lukonjo. The gist was clearly that our expedition had royal patronage, and that I could provide 'sovereign remedies' which the Queen was known to favour. This was well received by the porters, who looked at me with a new deference and girded their loins with a flourish. We set off at a cracking pace.

The first day of our itinerary was not to have been too exacting: upward some three thousand feet, and forward a few miles, to a camping site called Nyinibitaba, 'Mother of Mud'. However, we were threading our way along a treacherous path in dense forest when we came to a deep and rock-strewn torrent plunging in a gully across our route. The only means of getting over was the trunk of a fallen tree lying athwart the gap, with the prospect of a broken leg or worse if we fell. Here the porters, unprompted, picked up our rucksacks in addition to their own loads, strode across the slippery tree-trunk in a trice and were kind enough to hide their feelings while we, looking as nervous and clumsy as we felt, crawled abjectly over on all fours.

On the second day, which took us up above the tree-line, we struggled with their help to cross a nasty swamp, at about eleven thousand feet, by jumping from one relatively firm tussock to another. The ground underfoot was as soft as porridge, and littered with the decayed remains of long-dead trees.

Our route had led us up through clear and surprisingly sudden changes of vegetation: from grass and bracken, through tree-fern, bamboo and arborescent heather, and at last to the weird guardians of the upper reaches, the giant lobelia and groundsel. Above that, at about fifteen thousand feet, we were into bare rock and ice. We even had to don crampons and cut a few steps with our ice-axes to reach the slippery summit of Mount Baker on our third day. On snow and ice, it was clearly understood, our porters did not accompany us; they lacked the equipment and experience. Their rôle was to support and supply us as far as the top hut in the Bujuku Valley, at about thirteen thousand feet, and this they did very well.

Less hypochondriacal people than our porters it would be hard to imagine, yet they all participated in a daily charade of reporting sick and asking me for medicine. This ritual was stage-managed by Matthew in his dual persona as head porter and cured patient. For he had spread the word that his hæmorrhoids had responded favourably and promptly to my prescription.

Every evening they would form up with a cheerfully frank account of the varied health problems that, contrary to appearances, afflicted them. Each would say he was suffering from serious headache, backache, stomach-ache, toothache or some other invisible affliction. I would ask a question or two before prescribing Smarties of whatever colour seemed apposite. I was careful to keep a mental note of what colours the different ailments were being treated with, so as to be consistent in my prescriptions, and to warn my patients that the *dawa* was exceedingly bitter and must be swallowed whole, without chewing. I was not sure that any such precautions were necessary for they were wholly uncritical and equally satisfied with any colour.

Although they knew that I also had some familiar first-aid items such as iodine and sticking-plaster, and that once or twice I had occasion to dispense these, I was left in no doubt that the *cachet* of the sovereign remedies was incomparably more attractive, and that I should try to ensure that these did not run out before the end of our trek. In fact, despite my attempts to husband this valuable resource, demand was so strong that it did run out, just a day before our return to base. So I improvised with dubbin. My patient had complained of backache so I told him to get his back massaged vigorously with this 'Prince Philip's Liniment'.

When we came down on the sixth day to rendezvous with the chief, our porters were all in good shape and good heart. In good voice too. They marched in singing a Bakonjo song which, with its repetitious style and ironic tone, sounded like a Swahili song popular in World War I:

> '*We are the porters who carry the food*
> *For the porters who carry the porters' food.*'

News of our return had preceded us and we were warmly greeted. Then, while a fire was kindled, pay sorted out and a valedictory brew of tea prepared, I began to wonder what the chief would make of my 'therapy by placebo'. Would he regard it as tastelessly condescending? To judge by his quizzical glances in my direction, he was just then being told about it by Matthew. So, over tea, I broached the subject.

'I hope you don't mind,' I said, 'but I invented a story about my medicines. You may think I took advantage of Matthew, and . . .'

'Not at all,' the chief cut in. 'I was going to congratulate you on that. As for what you told your porters, of course they didn't believe a word of it. But they liked your style.'

GEORGE WEBB

Don't Feed the Snake

It was a beautiful Californian afternoon in late August. Bright sunshine lit the trees in patches of translucent yellow and dark green, casting pools of mottled shadow on the sidewalk. I sped along with only a slight squeak, squeak, squeak trespassing on the tranquillity.

A perfect day, and now I had a bicycle to explore the areas that had hitherto been just that little bit too far to consider by foot. This consideration owed more of course to a certain attitude towards exertion than to the actual distances involved, but with a fine, if unoiled, set of wheels at my disposal the matter was resolved. After lunch that day I had set off from my base on Piedmont Avenue in the direction of the sea. It was rumoured that the university owned several boats at the marina and since I had little else to do that day I decided to see for myself.

Along Durant, over Shattuck, a right at Martin Luther King Jr., a left onto University Avenue and then follow my nose until I reached the sea. Easy. There was just one flaw in my plan. Almost within sight of the sea, what had started as a fairly busy street suddenly turned into a feeder road for the motorway that ran along the shore, and the only way to cross it was to join the motorway-bound traffic. I stopped and judged the situation from as close as I dared get. A solitary bicycle weaving its way through the traffic to the marina would be comparable to a rowing-boat navigating between fast-moving supertankers. I decided to turn back.

Rather than admit defeat I turned down the nearest street with the intention of at least seeing some new sights. A few yards down a pretty mundane road I noticed a wooded fence, not very wide but taller than a man. There was a door at which a young couple appeared, clutching a box. Looking very pleased with themselves, they crossed the street and drove away. Above the door was a sign 'Berkeley Vivarium'. This could also be construed as 'Open Invitation to Satisfy Mark's Curiosity'. So I locked my bike to the nearest lamp-post and made my way through the door.

Inside was a small yard and, at the far end, a flimsy-looking glazed door and next to it a large, wood-framed cage with chicken-wire sides. I strolled up to the cage and looked in. A chameleon with a large crest swivelled its eye to get a better look at me. With an air of jaundiced dismissal it then swivelled its eye away again and remained motionless.

A hidden world waited behind the glazed door. This uninspiring entrance gave onto a large room with rows of tanks piled on top of each other. A reptile supermarket. The stock ranged from the tiniest reptiles to huge lizards in glass pens lit by banks of lights.

I wandered along the aisles. The first tank contained a small lizard, only about six inches long and dark, with gimlet eyes. I stared at it in wonder. The lizard stared back. Suddenly it threw itself at my face, banging against the glass with a hiss. 'Don't make eye contact with them,' someone said, walking past. 'It's taken as a challenge.' Sheepishly I wandered on.

As I reached the end of the aisle I heard a crash and a shout behind me. I turned round to find a fearsome lizard, four feet long and built like a bull-terrier, shooting towards me. A young assistant on his hands and knees was scrabbling around behind it. Deftly I side-stepped the fast-moving beast, hoping that my legs were not what it wanted. The assistant made a valiant dive, caught the lizard by the tail and dragged it back into his arms, chastising it gently for such an audacious bid for freedom. 'Feeding time, they always get frisky at feeding time,' he explained, catching my look of astonishment as he carried the lizard back to its pen.

I turned back to my reptile-browsing, with one ear cocked for escaped lizards. To the right were two sizeable, grey plastic bins labelled 'Do Not Open'. Strange, I thought, but was distracted by an enclosure the size of a small garden-shed. I moved closer to see what wonder dwelt within. It was the big brother of the escapee, a big, stocky lizard sedately dozing under an electric sun. Next to this was another large cage with a slightly smaller lizard. A sign on the glass declared how rare this reptile was, justifying an enormous price-tag.

Behind me there was a loud thump. I spun round to see a different assistant with what must have been a twenty-foot python coiled tightly round his whole arm. He was gamely trying to fight it back into one of the grey plastic bins. Needless to say, the python was viciously intent on not going back, its huge coils working away to migrate closer to the man's throat. There was something so comical about the assistant battling the serpent back into the bin and slamming down the lid that it was easy to overlook how close he had come to having his neck broken.

'If that's the way you're gonna be, you can feed later!' said the young man with emotion as he stamped off. What amazed me was the speed of the attack. The snake must have practically leaped out of the bin. I noticed that the lids on neither of the bins were secured in any way, and edged away gingerly to what I hoped was the safer ground of the small cages and glass-fronted tanks.

These smaller tanks held various reptiles, with a large selection of aquatic beasts. I spotted a tiny, brightly coloured toad swimming in one tank. It was perhaps half an inch long and looked quite manageable. Something for my room, I thought; I could cope with a small toad in a tank. This was much more my style. I asked why it was in such a large tank on its own. 'Because it grows to over a foot long,' was the reply. I moved on swiftly.

I was quite taken by a tank of tiny lizards that really did grow no larger. They were livelier than the rest, but the thought of having to keep the crickets that they feed on ended that passing fancy. And then I spotted her! A very attractive young lady with jet-black hair and a Gothic look to her clothes. I moseyed in her direction, only to be stopped in my tracks by a black tarantula that leaped from her hands to my feet and scooted around at high speed. My face must have registered acute horror because she said: 'Don't worry, it's meant to do that, it's a jumping spider'. As if that was supposed to help! She scooped the furry black shape from the ground and demonstrated it jumping from hand to hand. I stayed to watch for a while, repelled but unable to draw myself away. An attendant came over to enjoy a jump or two with the spider, discussing its uniqueness and merits with the Gothic lady. He turned and offered me the bundle of black joy. I expressed my appreciation by jumping back six feet.

'Oh, arachnophobia?'

A polite, diplomatic understatement. 'A certain amount,' I replied, 'but I have it under control.' In fact, I was going to control my arachnophobia out of this place as fast as my legs would carry me before junior jumped onto my chest or, worse, shot up my trouser leg looking for a cool spot. I nodded goodbye and ducked away towards the door. The chameleon had still not moved, but did me the courtesy of a farewell swivel of its eye.

MARK BRETT-WARBURTON

Vietcong Come Home

The tragic absurdity of the Vietnam War came fully home to me when I found myself throwing leaflets out of a Second World War Dakota calling on Vietcong warriors to come home, have a bath, see mother and enjoy a more peaceful pursuit.

Only a few moments before, we had to stooge around for a bit while the best part of the American army's divisional artillery pasted the jungle below. Then we were given the word and out fluttered a million leaflets printed the day before by the Psychological Operations section of the Saigon command, the outfit known as Psyops.

It was early in 1968, just after the Tet Offensive had suddenly made the Americans worry that their use of the body count as a measure of success might not be a winning move. The Vietcong had penetrated Saigon as far as the US embassy, even fighting their way inside and holding out in a suicide mission.

Of course I had heard all about this on the BBC World Service, but it was a long way away and I never believed I would get caught up in the mess. At the time I was the BBC's Central Europe correspondent, based in Vienna, so it was a considerable surprise when the call came from London to get to Saigon fast. The man on the Foreign Desk at Broadcasting House said: 'Saigon is falling and we want you to get there soonest'.

At first I thought it was a leg-pull. After all the first three letters of Vienna and Vietnam are the same. But London insisted they were serious. 'Why me,' I asked foolishly.

'You happen to be the nearest man we have.' I suggested they get a bigger map.

There was no way of avoiding the assignment. Appeals about the inevitability of a vicious Soviet reaction against the then contemplated reforms in the Socialist camp went unheeded. So I set off on a Quantas flight for Bangkok where the Desk said I could get a visa. That took four days because the local South Vietnamese consul had instructions never to issue a visa to anyone with a Communist stamp in their passport. I was quite hopeful of being refused. Then I could take off for Singapore, 'lose' my passport and get another from the British High Commission there.

That was not to be. The consul in Bangkok had new instructions and I found myself on the next 'plane to Saigon. The first thing I noticed on arrival was a huge hole in the roof of Tan Son Nhut air base, one of the hang-overs from the Chinese New Year offensive the week before.

Ours seemed to be the only civilian aircraft among all the drably paint-ed C130s, Huey Choppers and DC3 Dakotas. I even spotted the very dis-tinctive shape of a U-2 spyplane. The last time I had seen anything like it was in Gorki Park in Moscow, when the Russians showed off the wreck-age of the machine Francis Gary Powers was flying when shot down over Sverdlovsk on Mayday 1960.

A bus deposited me at the city-centre Continental Palace Hotel, where the BBC man I was relieving had booked me a room. This was the place made famous by Graham Greene in *The Quiet American*, his book about previous US attempts to help the Vietnamese.

Almost the first person I saw there was an old friend, Carl Mydans, the late and famous news-photographer from *Life*. He and other former American colleagues from Moscow often drank together 'on the shelf', as everyone called the main bar of the Continental Palace. There too I met Sean Flynn. He had much of the charm and dash of his film-star father but never seemed to flaunt it. He struck me as a rather serious young man set on a career as a news-photographer. He disappeared in Cambodia a year or so after my time in Saigon.

It was Mydans, an old hand at wars, who told us youngsters as we wait-ed for what we thought might be yet another Vietcong attack: 'If you sur-vive the first few minutes you'll be OK'. A comforting thought.

There was a swift round to be done, first to the British embassy to get an attestation that I really was who I said I was, then to the South Vietnamese press headquarters where the censor presided. He never both-ered me but it was essential to get accreditation from him before pro-ceeding to the real power in the land, the redoubtable JUSPAO, the Joint US Public Affairs Office.

I quickly learned that the Americans were not conducting a war in Vietnam but simply offering assistance to the South Vietnamese. So my accreditation made it clear that I was attached to the Military Assistance

Command, Vietnam. It was here at MacV, in a former cinema in the centre of Saigon, that all reporters got their briefings. It was also where the military laid on transport for anyone wishing to go pretty well anywhere in the South. The best reporters made full use of this largesse, flying long distances up and down the country looking for a story. Some gloried in it, getting themselves up like John Wayne in various bits of army camouflage, and careering around in jeeps. I felt that the safer thing was to look as little like a military person as possible.

One of the odder features of Saigon was the attraction it seemed to have for female photographers of a certain age. They seemed to be everywhere, going about in pairs and obviously enjoying the glances they got from the GIs. A couple of them appeared once when I was out with a patrol. The lieutenant in charge shrugged and asked what could be done about them. 'I get my men out in the jungle away from the fleshpots and just when their minds are properly concentrated on the job and off sex, in they come.'

Some reporters never left the JUSPAO or MacV. One American who seemed to pick up the 'phone to New York or San Francisco practically every minute to report for a US radio network was reputed to have been here for ten years and earned several million dollars.

Against the backdrop of the surreal Saigon scene and the bizarre contrast between American good intentions and their deadly earnest business in the killing grounds around, the information war was being run by experts. The trouble was there was a world of difference between the picture they painted and the one the military had to deal with on the ground. It was clear from the start that the Pentagon was calling the shots. And that they were closely monitored by President Johnson himself.

I used to get private briefings from a State Department man whom I knew from Eastern Europe. We often lunched at the *Cercle Sportif Français* and I would follow that up with a chat with JUSPAO, so as to make better sense of what we were told at the 'Four o'clock Follies'. This, the main daily briefing, had had to be brought forward from five p.m. because the Tet Offensive had forced the South Vietnamese to install a nightly curfew starting at six.

There were plenty of bangs and crashes to tell us the war was close. Every evening the place to be was the roof of the Caravelle Hotel across from the Continental Palace. Here was a whiff of another and more civilized existence. White-coated waiters would ask in English what we would like to drink. They would bring it while we surveyed the scene from our high vantage point. The sun would go down and the battles commence. Flares being dropped; bombs falling; the gunship called Puff the Magic Dragon hosing down the jungle with awesome fire-power. When we had had enough, it was time to go down for a quite decent dinner.

Walking back to the Continental Palace after all this was a bit of an ordeal. The South Vietnamese were on patrol to make sure the curfew was solid. It was prudent to walk slowly, chatting as loudly as possible in order to avoid an unfortunate incident as the young recruits made a show of easing the springs of their weapons.

Having survived the Tet Offensive (probably South Vietnam's finest hour in that the Vietcong had been cleared out and the state had not collapsed), the military decided the time had come to take the war to the enemy. Every night we heard the B-52s outside Saigon in their remote flight from Guam to Cambodia and back. This milk run was naturally never acknowledged.

The military also demanded action on the ground, and devised an offensive called Operation Complete Victory. When this was presented to us, I put my hand up to ask whether, once the operation ended, complete victory would have been achieved. Our long-suffering civilian briefers merely commented that they didn't choose the names.

The scheme that took me up in the Dakota was Operation Chieu Hoi. It was carefully explained to us that this meant 'Rally to the Homeland'. The South Vietnamese government believed that the expulsion of the Tet attackers had given them their best chance to persuade the Vietcong to give up and come home.

Millions of leaflets were printed offering the bearer safe passage home and resettlement if needed. They were designed to be scattered far and wide over the jungle in a co-ordinated action using radio as well, a task given to Psyops. They were a welcoming lot and keen to be noticed. By the time I went round to enlist their help in making a film about Chieu Hoi, their signboard announced that they had printed several billion pamphlets of various kinds; the steadily mounting number was there on display to prove it.

One of the surprises for someone like me visiting Saigon for the first time was the fact that life continued with some semblance of normality in spite of the curfew and the explosions. The ordinary people of Saigon bustled about their business. Diplomatic life went on.

I attended the Easter service in the Anglican Church, conducted by the Bishop of Singapore. Nobody appeared to be affected by the explosions not far away as we knelt to pray for peace.

While the Americans always had Marines guarding their embassies, for the British in the Far East that rôle was undertaken by the Gurkhas. Chatting to the British military attaché after the service, I asked what had happened while the Vietcong were attacking the US embassy opposite. They had even established a machine-gun post in the embassy grounds. The attaché replied that at the height of the battle his Gurkhas had asked, fingering their kukris, 'When do we go, Sahib?'

'I had to lock them in the cellar and give them lots of rum to keep them quiet.'

It would have been consistent with the surreal nature of the Vietnam War had a footnote been added to its history reporting the mystery of the headless Vietcong corpses discovered in the British embassy grounds.

The office recalled me to my European duties just as the monsoon broke. When I left, the air base still sported its hole in the roof. I never heard how many Vietcong, if any, had 'rallied to the homeland'.

ROBERT ELPHICK

Cuba Libre

My first wife Marika and I spent our honeymoon on my brother Patrick's estate in Jamaica. His palatial Great House, Good Hope, lay between the Cockpit Country and the sea, where he owned a large stretch of beach. He had eighty horses and two hundred miles of marked rides, where one could canter safely past ruined sugar factories. Covered in creepers and trees, they looked like Caribbean Angkor Wats. The turquoise-blue Martha Brae River ran in a big curve through the estate, overhung with giant bamboos and full of crayfish. At that time Patrick ran the place as a private hotel so we lived in considerable luxury.

Our fellow-guests were an eclectic mix: old gents from the American deep south seeking gracious living, elegant equestrian widows, and émi-grés, none more exotic than the Baron Joseph de Biskei Dobronyi *alias* Sepy. He told us he had been a pilot in the Hungarian air force during World War II. In the chaos at the end of the War, he had flown his Spitfire to Sweden, abandoning his ancestral castle and estates to the Russians. In Sweden he had learned to be a jeweller and he had eventually made his way to Cuba. There, we gathered, as his stories became taller and taller through the night, he had become hugely successful, gathering the raw material of gold, silver and jewels for his business from the many wrecks around the coast. To these he regularly dived to collect treasure.

'You must come,' he told us, refusing to accept any denial. 'Cuba is a wonderful island and you will have an exciting time with me.'

We were persuaded, and arranged flights which would allow us a week there on our way home. The 'plane in which we flew to Havana was empty and we were surprised, in those easy-going days, how strict security was at the airport. But Sepy was waiting for us outside in his white Cadillac con-vertible, hood down, and he swept us into town.

'I'm afraid there's been a spot of bother this week – well a revolution actually – but that's normal in these parts and I promise it won't affect the fun we're going to have. In fact, I have a great friend also staying at the Hilton, where I'm putting you up, and you will enjoy meeting him.'

It turned out that Sepy's friend, with his girlfriend, were the only other guests in the hotel. It was the end of January 1959 and Fidel Castro had that week come down from the hills with his guerillas and driven Batista and his government out. The Hilton was occupied by young fighters of both sexes in green fatigues, draped with weapons. They had long hair and charming manners; they held open the lift-doors for us and, according to the bemused staff, didn't sleep in the beds but used the floor and left everything immaculate.

After changing, we went to have a drink in Sepy's friend's suite. An extremely attractive, suave, older man, he immediately started making a big play for Marika, while I talked to his beautiful and much younger girl-friend. My wife clearly had no idea who he was, although I had recognised him immediately from the movies. It was Errol Flynn. Apparently he had been the sole prominent Westerner to have identified himself with Castro's revolution and actively supported it. He even claimed to have fought with him in the hills and he threatened to show us his wound. As a result, he was an unassailable hero to the new masters of Havana and, as his friends, we too could do no wrong. It was an unusual feeling.

Life was carrying on as normal, although all the tourists had left; there was not much in the way of government yet and the entire police force had either run away or been shot. Fortunately, traffic lights had just been installed and so such traffic as there was ran smoothly. With Sepy we saw the sights: Hemingway's house and the bar he patronized. The great man was still alive, but not there. We visited and drank with many of Sepy's Cuban friends. Delighted to be rid of the much-hated Batista, but uncertain what the future held, they were soon to find out.

Meanwhile, Errol was observing the downside of revolution at close quarters. As an international figure he was useful to the regime, lending some legitimacy to the nastier things they felt had to be done to secure their hold on the country. Quick trials and kangaroo courts followed by executions took place every evening. Errol was expected to attend.

He appointed us guardians and playmates of Woodsie, his new and much-loved girlfriend, with whom he was trying at every spare moment, between trials, to make a baby. Having been one of the first people to have a vasectomy (following a series of scandals, which had resulted in paternity suits), he had recently become one of the first to have the operation reversed.

Woodsie's preferred entertainment was the legendary Tropicana nightclub, still functioning with all its gorgeous chorus girls and singers playing to an empty house – except for us. Sepy and I would dance with the girls until Errol arrived in the small hours. Grey with the strain and horror of what he had seen, he would soon in his inimitable way be ready for a party. He claimed he was down to two bottles of vodka a day.

One dawn, as we staggered out into the street where daylight was just breaking, we saw a sight which stopped the film star in his tracks. A cart with two huge wooden barrels filled with milk was trundling past. Between the shafts were six white mules. 'This is my scene!' he shouted, waving an imaginary sword and leaping onto the cart beside the startled driver. A wad of dollars soon dispatched the latter and, as we all climbed aboard, our swashbuckling hero cracked the whip over the astonished mules. Reluctantly they broke into a gallop and we careered through the streets of sleeping Havana, milk slopping out of the barrels onto the pavements. As soon as anyone saw us, the revolutionaries and the public, anyone around at that hour, they knew exactly who we were and what we were doing: '*El Flynn y sus amigos*' were doing their thing and reliving a hundred of his film rôles.

He was forty-four years old and died six months later of cirrhosis of the liver. Woodsie, whose real name was Beverly Aadland, did become pregnant but she lost the baby and got nothing from his estate.

Robin Hanbury-Tenison

In the Shade of the Traveller's Palm

Nonsuch is a place to which I have regularly travelled over many years. It is on a loop hill-road with precipitous bends, and is near to places called Cambridge, Windsor and Sherwood Forest. The land is rocky, with soil not dissimilar to that of the Cotswolds' oolite limestone, and exceedingly fruitful. Everything in nature is speedy at Nonsuch. The moon rises before your eyes as if in a hurry to get high in the sky. Immemorial-looking trees called 'figs' and 'cedars', but not like the figs and cedars of Europe, grow huge within decades. Throw out an orange pip and up leaps a sprig of a tree. The fence-posts sprout leaves and blossom.

The house at Nonsuch stands on top of a hummocky hill that is precipitous in places but covered thickly with trees on its slopes – cedar, fig, lime, papaya, poinciana, tropical almond, palm, nutmeg, sour apple, sweetwood, trumpet-trees and tulip-trees and so on. The only places where you can make out the trees from the wood are on the grassy slopes nearer to the house, which are planted with a variety of palms: coconut, fig, thatch and of course the Traveller's Palm.

I go to this place as a visitor and observer, for the house and the property were created many years ago by my wife. I don't wish to appear possessive or 'move in' on her ground. It is beautiful ground, a place in the foot-hills of Jamaica's Blue Mountains, which are the backdrop to the view toward the south-west. To the north, over lower hills, there is a great stretch of sea. A freighter, tanker or cruise-ship will glide along the horizon from time to time.

Despite the frantic rate at which everything grows, Nonsuch is a tranquil world. Tranquil except when screeching flocks of olive-throated parakeets whizz through the skies in a communal effort to drive off some predatory crow. A malicious marauder is the chestnut-bellied cuckoo, which Jamaicans call 'the old-man bird' because it is clumsy and falls about in trees making a snarling, guttural cry. Another oddity is the common potoo, a large, grey bird with a long tail that lays a single egg on top of a stub or fence-post and incubates in an upright posture with its eyes shut and beak in the air, the very picture of supercilious disdain.

It is difficult for a stranger to reach the Nonsuch property without interception and cross-examination. The lane that winds up to it is guarded at its junction with the road by a rum-shop kept by Mr Clarence King. He is also a coffin-maker and he has but one leg. In days gone by he would go about on a mule; now he is very deaf and nearly blind. But he has a number of sons who keep watch from the shop when they are not making coffins on the edge of the lane. Over that edge, in the valley below, is the graveyard, dotted with all the tombs of Nonsuch.

Aside from the Kings there are numerous Bishops in the neighbourhood, these last sired by a Rastafarian preacher of that name. Both families boast sons with fine names like Jason, Valentine and Canute. Clarence King is a neighbour on one side; on the other is Mr Coles. Mr Coles is dilatory in bushing his steep land, preferring that his six goats should keep down the ferns. He has eighty acres, but the goats seem magnetized by the proximity of delectables that grow on Binns land.

The neighbourhood plumber, one McClashlan, is obliged to make regular visits because plumbing in rural Jamaica is more imaginative than functional. His son Andrew bushes the land together with Ricardo, the son of Carpenter McKenzie. Andrew is theatrical in style, wears a Turkish cap and swings a cape from one shoulder.

In the mornings a villainous-looking man with a warm heart, called Johnny Walker, brings a sack of oranges up to the house. One of these nearly fills a half-pint glass when squeezed. There are twenty-one big oranges, for which Johnny gets one hundred Jamaican dollars, or £1·75. Apart from growing oranges, he keeps hens and is 'by profession' a house-painter. He wears a Rastafarian knitted beret and has a forked and plaited beard. He has with him a young man named Lue who, it transpires, has no intention of being 'enumerated' on the voters' registration list. I ask why and am scornfully reminded that enumeration involves finger-printing, and giving one's finger-prints to Authority is not a thing a freedom-loving man ever does. 'We no want nutt'n fi do with politricks!'

Then there is Devon, a handsome older man seemingly carved out of polished dark mahogany. He is an expert gardener, quietly authoritative, who knows all the Latin names for plants. He prunes and plants and puts down fertilizer. His method is to scratch a ring round a plant, more or less in its own shade, with a cutlass. He will then ease in the fertilizer (one mug for each tree) with the point of the blade. The fertilizer is twelve per cent nitrogen, four per cent phosphate and twenty-eight per cent potash. The remaining fifty-six per cent is a mystery.

Devon usually comes on a Sunday but that depends on his cow, which has a habit of running away up the mountain so that it has to be chased and retrieved. Devon's only tool, his cutlass, can be put to any use horti-culture requires. Now he trims the lower, browning fronds from the edges of a Traveller's Palm.

The Traveller's Palm is not, strictly speaking, a palm at all but is relat-ed to the banana family, as is the heliconia. The tree that Devon has tidied is a handsome example, nearly thirty feet in height, its long, narrow leaves ragged at the edges and spread out into a perfect but enormous fan. Where the arms of the fan join the trunk, each one holds in its armpit half a litre of pure water. This is most welcome to a thirsty traveller and, some say, gives the tree its name. Not all agree. The great fan invariably lines up along a north-south axis so that the spread of its flag-like leaves faces east-west. This on an overcast or stormy day indicates one's direc-tion, and may equally well explain the name of the Traveller's Palm – *alias* the 'Traveller's Tree' which makes the main title of Patrick Leigh Fermor's *A Journey through the Caribbean Islands.*

GRAHAM BINNS

Coming Home

Last week a man with a flat-bed trailer came to take away my tractor, so he could fit it with a backhoe.

This sentence, which I found myself writing the other day in an email home to my aged parents in England, is not one I could have ever imagined myself writing, or even thinking of writing, as little as a year ago. Back then I lived something of a dashing existence, either wandering across the remoter parts of the planet or, when settled, inhabiting a world of gritty and costly apartments in capital cities, of business-class travel and fancy cafés and edgy urban chatter. I wouldn't have known then what a flat-bed trailer was, I certainly had no idea of the functions of a backhoe – glory be! – and to my certain knowledge tractors were merely burbling little beasts that chugged around in farmers' fields in that curious beyond one saw from train windows and which was known as 'the country'. The notion that I'd ever own or want to own one, or live and take my ease among those to whom they were a customary form of transport, was well beyond what I prided myself in considering my fairly acute powers of imagination.

Well – that was then and this is now. Now I own a tractor. I own two tractors, in fact. And last week a man with a flat-bed trailer came to take one of them away, to fix it up with a backhoe – something which weighs half a ton, needs greasing every week and costs a great deal more than I'd expected. And all of this (which includes learning how to wield a mysterious device that I now know to be a grease gun) has happened because, after fifty-seven fairly exciting, exacting, sophisticated and mainly metropolitan years, I have become – voluntarily and, so far as I can tell, forever and for good – a hayseed. It is a rôle that I find I have slipped into as easily as a deerskin work glove, and I find also that by doing so I have become as happy as something that I was wont to eat at New York's Nobu, but which has proved as rare as hen's teeth here: and that is, to wit, *a clam*.

The notion of settling anywhere was to me once utterly alien. I was sixteen when I began to travel seriously; I hitch-hiked the entire circumference of populated North America one summer, and it was then that I developed a taste for the risks and rewards of solitary wandering. Over the following years, thanks to the indulgence of a number of newspaper editors, I lived in (or perhaps more appropriately, I was *based* in) Africa, India, Ireland, China and the United States. I believe I travelled to every country on the planet – except for a scattering of those Central Asian entities that are now called the 'stans' – and I was able for a long while to say with the pride of an inverse snob that I had never been either to Peru or to the Hamptons. (Both I have been to lately and am happy to say that for each, once is quite enough.)

I have had more homes than I can remember, more telephone numbers, more email addresses; and friends who are kind enough to keep me in their little black books grumble at the 'W' page, dominated as it is by so many rubbings-out and fillings-in. *Can't you ever settle down?* they ask in kindly-weary exasperation. *Of course*, they add, *we envy you mightily.*

And for a while I used to think they did, especially if their lives depended on the catching of morning commuter trains and the sitting in soft-sided office cubes and the looking forward to games of golf on summer weekends. My life, *sans* both commuter trains and weekends, did seem at first blush quite appealing, I am sure. Except that they saw their daughters' bliss on wedding days, and they curled up at firesides on winter nights; and I suspect if they remembered me at all then, they saw my life a little differently – that my unsettlement and unshacklement were not quite everything, that the solitary and the empty and the rootless can also be co-equal with the joyless, and that the life of the fancy-free was often much more fancy than, in many ways, it was truly free.

And as my years began to tick on I confess that slightly, and only intermittently, I began to ponder such matters too, and to wonder at the supposed benefits of endless wanderings. This feeling gradually strengthened until, in a sudden moment of hopeful whim last year, I bought a rambling old house and a few acres of weary farmland in the Berkshire Hills of western Massachusetts. And in doing so I wondered at that very moment if I too – a little late, perhaps even too late – might for the first time take a shot at settling down at last. It might work, I thought. It might not. And if it didn't – well, then at least it would be another adventure out of which I could make another anecdote, to tell in some distant watering-hole once the travelling had started once again.

That was nine months ago. Since then, aside from two journeys to Java and a mere handful to Europe, I have not budged. Eight months ago – four weeks into the experiment, in other words – came an epiphany. And this epiphany involved, just as is demanded by the symmetry of classic story-telling (and in this case, by the truth), a tractor.

I mentioned that I now own two tractors. One of them came with the property. It is not as old as the house (which was constructed a little after what to me, an Englishman, were those melancholy events of 1776), but it sports a fair half-century of yeoman service. It is a faded blue Ford (model 8N, I mention for the aficionados out there, who I gather exist in healthy numbers). It is a little rusty. It needs to be cranked into life with much care and gentle words.

But once so eased into what passes for mechanical vivacity it runs really quite merrily, chugging and pulsing steadily like a heartbeat. It has a little exhaust-pipe that emits what I am sure is the kind of blue smoke that could kill, but which in fact, when borne on country air, seems to have a rare sweetness about it. I wouldn't exactly bend down and attach my mouth to the pipe, unless I was feeling exceptionally gloomy, but when the tractor has passed by and I get the faint scent of its exhaust on the breeze, it is, I must say, an aroma most pleasing. When I mentioned this rather dull observation to the farmer who helped me, he looked at me straight in the eye and he did something farmers rarely do: he cracked a smile.

Anyway, attached to the rear of my burbling little Ford 8N, held up by what is known in hayseed-speak as a 'three-point hitch', and powered by a shaft that emerges dangerously from a connection to what is known similarly as a 'PTO' (a power take-off), is a spinning blade, covered by a large, yellow iron shield, which is known as a 'brush-hog'. This is what people who live in the Berkshires like to use, I was told, to mow their fields. Not to make their lawns satin-smooth, mind you, but merely to get the thistles and crab-grass and timothy down to a height in which passing children and small animals don't get totally lost.

One warm early evening, as the sun was going down over the locust-trees (one of which housed a big, fat porcupine contentedly munching twigs), I decided to have a go. I sat on the machine, lit my pipe, gently coaxed and fired up the engine, backed the brush-hog off the two baulks of timber on which it had been resting for the past many months, and set off unsteadily down the meadow.

No sweeter smell have I ever known in any place I have ever been. In the background – I am sure the scent-makers of Grasse have a name for such a thing – were the commingled aromas of tractor exhaust and my Balkan Sobranie Mixture, with its accents of sweet Latakia leaf. But in the foreground was something nicer still: the smell of new-mown grass, new-mown *hay* in fact, for what I was cutting in a wide swathe behind me was tall grass and blue alfalfa, which smells more unimaginably lovely than anything, except what came next. And that came when, as I directed the puttering little Ford over to a patch of richer, wilder green than the rest of the field, there wafted through the air the overwhelming aroma of fresh mint.

In that moment I was utterly hooked, totally transformed. Tractor smoke, fine Syrian tobacco, blue alfalfa and wild mint made a cocktail of, well, probably pheromones, someone will one day write and tell me, that produced for me a true olfactory epiphany. It was as though – and if this sounds sentimentally unreal, I make no apology for it – in that one instant the earth sang out: *Stay here*, it said. *Dig holes here. Put down roots.* Nurture and gentle them with sun and rain and seasons, until, like that old Ford, they burble into life as well, and show that something that grows has more point to it than anything else borne from a ceaseless wandering.

Well, to come down from the magic of the moment, to reattach to a more sober reality, you have to understand a little of farming. To dig holes in which to plant roots either real or metaphorical, one needs a far, far bigger tractor than my dear little 1952 blue monster, which serious farmers refer to only as a toy. So now in consequence, and since the epiphany lasted, and since its effects last still, I possess a great big orange monster of a new tractor, with forty-six wild horses under its hood, a big orange bucket and thick black forks at its front end, and ever since its brief, flat-bed-assisted absence of last week, a backhoe attached wherever it is that backhoes hoe.

And with this machine so far, in just the last ten days, I have accomplished much. I have shifted the branches of fifty newly pruned apple-trees. I have moved a ton of clay onto the floors of four stalls in a barn built for two Norwegian fjord-horses. I have moved vast piles of firewood for the coming winter. I have dug out a section of the garden in which the lady who kindly partners me in this delightful madness wishes to plant rhubarb. I have helped a neighbour pull out an aged tree stump, and I have worked with another to reshape an old stone wall.

Soon, when the forty tons of topsoil arrives, I will rake and smooth it around the old Vermont carriage barn that I have turned into my library, and I will plant box-trees there and hope the Massachusetts winter won't make me rue the expense – for that, too, is a smell that works wonders on a flagging spirit, and might just be right for when a book is going less so.

I have plans for a thousand-and-one other tasks, as my girlfriend and I try to turn this weary old farm back into a productive little organic clutch of acres. We have plans to send out apple-finished lamb to the local restaurants (many of whom now have a policy of buying only home-made produce from local farms); of sending to our friends blossom and clover honey (for the bees arrive any day, just in time to catch the apple flowers, and we have plans for painting their hives tonight) and to make home-smoked bacon from the pigs that soon will be snorting and snuffling their way in the pens we are building (with the help of the tractor, naturally).

Yes, we have plans all right. And I have plans, at last, to stay. I never imagined that there might one day be a place in Massachusetts for a wandering Englishman like me. And I confess I still find it difficult to believe that the wandering will ever stop – for, mistakenly and foolishly I now realise, there was a long time in my life when such persona as I had was perhaps defined by the fact of travel. I was only useful to people when I wasn't around – amusing to them when I came back and told the tales, but someone to be prodded back to the airport or the dockside, and made to go away again.

Well, that is no more (or more or less no more: I am off to London tomorrow, and Hong Kong in July, and briefly back to Java after that). No, it was that evening of aromas that convinced me, and the simple fact that I was at that moment performing a task that is ageless and eternal and should, were we all so lucky, be done at some moment by us all. *I was making hay while the sun shines* – as good a way to run a life, I know at last, as any I can suppose.

SIMON WINCHESTER

The Authors

We asked each contributor to write his own biography for us. M.A. & F.H.

ALLEN, MICHAEL (*b*.1932) Read Russian at Cambridge and English at Oxford. Joined EMI 1956; spent over 30 years in international management of classical records. General manager Angel Records USA (Los Angeles 1974-76); otherwise based in London, travelling frequently in Europe, USA and Far East. Retired 1989 as commercial director of EMI Classics. Interests: early music movement and classic American musicals. *See pages 28, 137, 172 and 195*

ARMITAGE, ST JOHN CBE (1924-2004) Specialist in Middle East affairs. Served with Arab armies in Transjordan, Saudi Arabia and Oman, searched for locusts in Kenya and the Aden Protectorate and for oil in Libya and, as a member of HM Diplomatic Service, spent 16 years in Iraq, Lebanon, Saudi Arabia and the United Arab Emirates. *See pages 13 and 38*

BAND, GEORGE (*b*.1929) Mountaineer and oilman. Member of first successful expeditions to climb Everest in 1953 and Kangchenjunga in 1955, where he was the first to summit with Joe Brown. Spent 36 years in the international oil industry, mostly with the Shell Group in 7 different countries, and then as director general of the UK Offshore Operators' Association. Continues to enjoy escorting adventurous treks in Central Asia for 'Far Frontiers'. *See page 27*

BARRATT, ALICK (*b*.1930) Read History at New College, Oxford. Solicitor in London for 23 years and then a Chancery Master in the High Court for 17 years. Holidays spent in most European and Arab countries and sometimes farther afield. Travellers Club member for 45 years. *See page 213*

BARRY O'BRIEN, RICHARD (*b*.1930) Journalist: 37 years as reporter on *The Daily Telegraph, The Sunday Telegraph* and *Daily Mail* covering home and foreign news ranging from Profumo affair in 1963 to Middle East wars and African famine in 1970s and 1980s. Travelled widely in Middle East and Africa reporting from Israel, Lebanon, Jordan, Egypt, Turkey, Cyprus, Iraq, Sudan, Ethiopia, South Africa and other countries. *See pages 223 and 228*

BINNS, GRAHAM (1925-2003) Served in World War II in both Royal Navy and Indian Army. Fulbright Scholar USA. Five years in Arts Council followed by 30 years in broadcasting and communications. Managed radio and TV stations overseas. Deputy chairman Capital Radio 1974-82; director Duke of York's Theatre 1980-84. Hellenophile with contrasting interest in Wild West Indies. *See pages 10 and 263*

BONINGTON, SIR CHRIS CBE (*b.*1934) Educated University College School, Hampstead & Sandhurst. Commissioned in Royal Tank Regiment 1956. First British ascent south-west pillar of the Drus 1956 and north wall of the Eiger 1962. Since then free-lance career as writer, lecturer, photographer and mountaineer with many famous climbs to his credit. Author of *Quest for Adventure* and 20 books in all. Frequent television work. Chancellor Lancaster University 2005. *See page 24*

BRAMALL, FIELD MARSHAL THE LORD KG GCB OBE MC (*b.*1923) Professional soldier. Enlisted 1942; commissioned 1943; War service in N.W. Europe June 1944-May 1945. Served in British Commonwealth Occupation Force in Japan 1947; in UK, Middle East and Berlin 1948-62; on staff of Earl Mountbatten 1962-64; CO 2nd Battalion Royal Greenjackets during confrontation with Indonesia 1965-67; commanded 5th Airborne Brigade 1967-69; 1st Armoured Division 1970-72; British Forces Hong Kong 1973-76. C-in-C UK Land Forces 1976-78. Chief of General Staff 1979-82 (during Falklands). Chief of Defence Staff 1982-85. HM Lord Lieutenant of Greater London 1986-98. President of MCC 1988-89. Chairman of Trustees Imperial War Museum 1989-98. Chairman of Travellers Club 1999-2003. Joint author of *The Chiefs: an anecdotal History of the Chiefs of Staff.* Interests: international affairs on defence, cricket, painting and travel. *See pages 145 and 193*

BRETT-WARBURTON, MARK (*b*.1966) Studied architecture at University College London & Royal College of Art, followed by MA in Design at University of California, Berkeley. Has worked at various times as interior designer, graphic designer, CAD specialist and CD-ROM producer. Currently runs own architectural practice. Interests: The Worshipful Company of Masons, photography, making the occasional short film. *See pages 122 and 253*

BROOK-SHEPHERD, GORDON CBE (1918-2003) Double First History, Cambridge 1938. Lieutenant-colonel Intelligence Corps in World War II (mentioned in despatches). Foreign correspondent, diplomatic correspondent and associate editor *Daily* and *Sunday Telegraph* 1948-86, travelling worldwide. Chairman SOS Children's Villages UK 1989-2003. Author of 19 works on modern European history specializing in Central Europe. Interests: shooting, fly-fishing, tennis, travel, music and good food. *See page 232*

BROWNING, JULIAN, THE REV. (*b*.1951) Assists in the Parish of Little Venice, London; is also an antiquarian bookseller with a particular interest in manuscripts and autograph letters of all periods. *See page 107*

BROWNRIGG, HENRY (*b*.1943) Educated Winchester & New College, Oxford (Secretary Oxford Union). Worked for international mining group Charter Consolidated, latterly as divisional manager. Sloan Fellow of London Business School. Collects and deals in Asiatic & Islamic art. Author of *Betel Cutters in the Samuel Eilenberg Collection* (1992). Interests: Asian culture and politics. *See page 114*

CAMERON, PETER DUNCANSON (*b*.1952) Professor of Law at University of Dundee & European University Institute in Florence. Has worked extensively in former Soviet Union, Africa, Latin America and China as legal adviser on energy and natural resource issues for governments, companies and international organisations; lived in the Netherlands 1986-97. Most recent publication is *Competition in Energy: Law and Regulation in the European Union* (2002). *See page 162*

CARLESS, HUGH CMG (*b*.1925) Studied Persian at SOAS 1942-43. After 4 years in army and 3 years at Cambridge, joined Foreign Service 1950. Served in Foreign Office, Afghanistan, Iran, Europe and Latin America, lastly as ambassador to Venezuela. Married to painter Rosa Maria Frontini. Travelled with Eric Newby to the Hindu Kush 1956. *See page 241*

CARSWELL, PROFESSOR JOHN (*b*.1931) Artist, writer and historian. Archæological draughtsman at Jericho 1951. Taught Fine Art at American University of Beirut 1956-76. Museum director at University of Chicago 1978-87. Director Islamic Department, Sotheby's 1987-96. Archæological research in Middle East, Maldives, Indian sub-continent, Central Asia and Gobi Desert. Author of *Coptic Tattoo Designs* (1958), *New Julfa* (1968), *Kütahya Tiles* (1972), *Blue-and-White* (1984), *Arab Seafaring* (new edn. 1996), *Iznik Pottery* (1998). One-man exhibitions in London 1966, New York 1968 and retrospective in Stockholm 1998. Interests: travel and research. *See pages 210 and 215*

CAWKWELL, SIMON (*b*.1946) Qualified as chartered accountant 1969 and so practised on own account 1975-2003. Specialized in short-selling on the world's stock exchanges and author of the UK's only published guide to that subject. Inveterate gambler. *See page 96*

CRAIG, SIR JAMES GCMG (*b*.1924) Read Classics and Oriental Languages at Oxford. Academic for 10 years, then HM Diplomatic Service, ending as ambassador to Syria and to Saudi Arabia. After retirement various academic, business and benevolent activities. *See page 41*

CREWDSON, RICHARD (*b*.1932) Solicitor; senior partner Field Fisher Waterhouse; retired 1992. Founder and first chairman of Cultural Property Law Committee of International Bar Association. Retained by UNESCO to assist in drafting heritage legislation for Namibia, Eritrea and South Africa 1993-97. Interests: music, art and history. *See page 190*

DALBY, STEWART (*b*.1944) Educated Sussex University. Journalist since 1967: news editor, foreign correspondent and travel writer for the *Financial Times*; war correspondent for *The Observer* and various

American publications, notably in Vietnam where he stayed on after the American pull-out in 1975; has written about Ireland for the *New Statesman*, *The Spectator* and *The Economist* and about collecting and alternative investments for *The Guardian*. Since 2003 has been part-owner of an internet and conference business and editorial director and publisher of a group of e-newspapers specializing in natural resources. First novel *The Friends of Rathlin Ireland* published 2005. *See page 226*

DAVIES, ROGER (*b*.1940) Read Law and Theology at King's College London. Called to the Bar; Gray's Inn 1965. Practised at Bar until 1985 when appointed metropolitan stipendiary magistrate (now district judge) and sat in Westminster (Senior at Horseferry Road Court) until retired 2004. Recorder of Crown Court (1990-). Currently (2005) chairman House Committee, Travellers Club. Interests: history, music, travel and conversation. *See page 95*

ELPHICK, ROBERT (*b*.1930) Spent most of his life in journalism, ending his career as spokesman for European Commission in Brussels and London. Reuters correspondent in Moscow 1958-62 and Algiers 1963-64. Joined BBC as assistant diplomatic correspondent 1964, covering Eastern and Central Europe from Vienna. Transferred to Bonn as BBC-TV's first Europe correspondent 1972. Other lengthy assignments in India, Vietnam, Amman and Beirut. Joined the EC 1977. *See page 256*

ELY, ROBERT (*b*.1930) After National Service in the Suffolks and Modern Languages at Trinity Hall, Cambridge, joined BAT 1953. Worked in Europe, East and West Africa, Trinidad and Chile. Retired as head of Public Affairs worldwide 1990. Now works voluntarily for several charities. Interests: languages, travel and meeting people. *See page 222*

FABER, SIR RICHARD KCVO CMG (*b*.1924) Educated Westminster & Christ Church, Oxford (President of the Union). War-time service in Royal Navy. Entered Foreign Service 1950; served in Baghdad, Paris, Abidjan, Washington, Rhodesia, The Hague and Cairo. Ambassador to Algeria 1977-81. Author of various books on historical topics and *A Chain of Cities: Diplomacy at the end of Empire. See page 149*

FIELDING, SIR LESLIE KCMG FRSA FRGS HON.LLD (*b.*1932) Joined Foreign Service 1956; served in Tehran (Oriental Secretary), Singapore, Phnom Penh (chargé d'affaires 1964-66), Paris and on West European desk and Policy Planning Staff, London. Transferred to European Commission in Brussels as director 1973; EC ambassador in Tokyo 1978-82; Director General for External Relations, Brussels 1982-87. Vice-Chancellor University of Sussex 1987-92. Industrial consultant 1992-97. Anglican lay reader since 1981 (licensed successively in dioceses of Exeter, Europe, Japan, Chichester and Hereford). Interests: teleology in the natural sciences and in comparative religion. *See page 36*

FIENNES, SIR RANULPH OBE (*b.*1954) Expedition leader and writer. Has led over 30 expeditions in both hot and cold climes, established several world expedition records, was awarded the OBE for 'human endeavour and charitable services' and has published 16 titles to date. Currently pursuing his love of adventure racing, and training for an attempt at the Eiger. *See page 61*

GALL, SANDY CBE (*b.*1927) Writer and broadcaster. Learned French, German and Spanish at Glenalmond & Aberdeen University, climbed in the Cairngorms and caught the travel bug. Foreign correspondent for Reuters 1953-63, then joined ITN, covering Middle East, USA, Vietnam, Africa (where jailed by Idi Amin) and Afghanistan. Co-presented *News at Ten* 1970-90. First to report Coalition liberation of Kuwait 1991 and fall of Kabul 1992. Chairman Sandy Gall's Afghanistan Appeal. Author of 10 books. Interests: golf, swimming in the Mediterranean and wine. *See page 177*

GLAZEBROOK, PHILIP (*b.*1937) Educated Eton & Trinity College, Cambridge. Honorary Attaché at British Embassy in Rome 1959-63. Author of novels and 3 books of travel. Lived in Dorset 1970-2001 and helped bring up 4 children there. *See page 21*

GORE-BOOTH, SIR DAVID KCMG KCVO (1943-2004) Educated Eton & Christ Church, Oxford. Joined Foreign Service 1964; Middle East Centre for Arab Studies (MECAS) in Shemlan and various postings in Arab world thereafter, culminating as ambassador to Saudi Arabia in 1993 and (like his father before him) High Commissioner to India. A witty and erudite public speaker and outspoken diplomat who throughout his career supported the Palestinian cause, urging a just solution to the Arab-Israeli conflict based on UN resolutions for a viable state of Palestine within its 1967 borders. *See page 39*

HANBURY-TENISON, ROBIN OBE DL (*b*.1936) Educated Eton & Magdalen College, Oxford. Explorer of rain forests and deserts (Royal Geographical Society Patron's Gold Medal), campaigner for indigenous peoples (president of Survival International) and author of some 20 books. Chief executive of Countryside Alliance 1995-98. Farms on Bodmin Moor, Cornwall. *See pages 99, 136 and 260*

HAWKSLEY, HUMPHREY (*b*.1954) Educated at St Lawrence College, Ramsgate, then by working as deck-hand on 100,000-ton bulk carrier *Chelsea Bridge*, which launched his career in travel. Author and BBC foreign correspondent with postings in Colombo, Delhi, Manila, Hong Kong and Beijing, where he opened BBC's first television bureau. Currently living in London; recent work has taken him to Greenland, Mali and the notorious Triple Border about which he writes here. His books include the international military and political trilogy *Dragon Strike*, *Dragon Fire* and *The Third World War*. *See page 92*

HERRMANN, FRANK FSA (*b*.1927) Book publisher 1947-76 (Faber, Methuen, Ward Lock etc). Director Overseas Operations, Sotheby's (1978-81). Antiquarian book auctioneer (founder-director Bloomsbury Book Auctions). Now retired. Author of *The English as Collectors* (1972 & 1999), *Sotheby's: Portrait of an Auction House* (1981), the *Giant Alexander* series (children's books 1964-72) and *Low Profile: a Life in the World of Books* (2002). Regency porcelain enthusiast. Conceived the idea of *Travellers' Tales*. *See page 34*

HOPKINS, PETER GWYNVAY (*b*.1946) Member of an old Welsh family that has strong links with both sea and land, is a classical sociologist by training and has spent his life in scholarly publishing. Travels widely and constantly and is co-founder of the *Rough Guides*, co-author with John Guest of *The Ancient Road: From Aleppo to Baghdad in the Days of the Ottoman Empire* and editor of *The Kenana Handbook of Sudan*. Currently completing a biography of the late ruler of Bahrain, Shaikh 'Isa; lives in London and Wales with his wife, young daughter and two Bengal cats. *See page 101*

KEALY, ROBIN CMG (*b.*1944) Spent 37 years in the Diplomatic Service until retirement as ambassador to Tunisia 2004. Also served in Libya, Kuwait and Iraq 1967-90 and as consul-general in Jerusalem (effectively Britain's representative to the Palestinian Authority) during the Camp David and Taba talks 1997-2001. Now lives in Hampshire, a consultant on the Arab world and trustee of two Palestinian-linked NGOs. *See page 83*

LEIGH FERMOR, SIR PATRICK MICHAEL DSO OBE (MIL.) DLITT (KENT & WARWICK) CLITT Travelled in Europe and Balkans 1933-35. Enlisted Irish Guards 1939; 'I' Corps 1940; SOE 1941; campaigns of Albania, Greece, Crete, Middle East and Western Europe. Author of a number of books: one novel, translations from French and Greek, occasional verse. Now lives in southern Greece. Interests: literature, history, travel, painting, religions etc. *See page 1*

MACKENZIE-YOUNG, PETER LDS RCS (*b.*1915) Qualified as dental surgeon; appointed house surgeon London Hospital 1940-41. Served in Royal Navy as dental surgeon; demobilised 1946 as Surgeon Lt Commander. Opened dental practice in London 1946; appointed registrar then onto teaching staff of dental schools at London Hospital and Royal Dental Hospital. Retired from private practice 1989. Interests: music, family and cooking. *See page 139*

MIDDLETON, ROBERT MORRICE (*b.*1931) Born in Nova Scotia, raised in British Columbia, graduated from University of British Columbia and entered Canadian Foreign Service 1955. Served in Indonesia, Brazil and Washington and as High Commissioner or ambassador to Ghana, South Africa and Cuba. On home postings much of his work involved the UN in one capacity or another. *See page 218*

MORGAN, SIR JOHN KCMG (*b*.1929) HM Foreign Service; served in Moscow (twice), Peking and Rio de Janeiro. Ambassador to Korea, Poland and Mexico. Now retired. *See pages 57 and 168*

NEWBY, ERIC CBE MC (*b*.1919) Educated St Paul's School; worked in advertising, then made voyage to Australia and back around the Horn, described in *The Last Grain Race*. War-time service in SBS; captured in 1942; later married girl who helped him escape from prison camp, described in *Love and War in the Apennines*. Subsequently worked in the family and other fashion businesses (*Something Wholesale: My Life and Times in the Rag Trade*). Journeyed through Nuristan with Hugh Carless, described in *A Short Walk in the Hindu Kush*. Travel editor *The Observer* 1964-73. Other books include *Slowly down the Ganges*, *The Big Train Ride*, *A Traveller's Life* and *On the Shores of the Mediterranean*. *See pages 14 and 201*

ONDAATJE, SIR CHRISTOPHER CBE OC FRGS (*b*.1933) Born in Ceylon, educated in England and emigrated to Canada 1956. Worked at several magazines and newspapers; founded Pagurian Press 1967, which eventually became the enormously successful Pagurian Corporation. Sold all his business interests and returned to the literary world 1988. Author of 7 books including the Burton biographies *Sindh Revisited* and *Journey to the Source of the Nile*. Member of Canada's Olympic bobsled team 1964 and Trustee of the National Portrait Gallery. Lives in London. *See page 243*

ORR, NEIL (*b*.1939) Educated Loretto School; medical training at Cambridge & St Thomas's Hospital. Oxford University Expedition to Socotra 1956, collecting blood groups from the mountain cave-dwellers. Medical officer in the Antarctic 1958-61, where his main interests were the food requirements of men and dogs in Antarctica (Polar Medal). Subsequently consultant general surgeon in Colchester. Interests: sailing, gardening, water-colour painting and travel. *See pages 68 and 198*

QUINTON, RICHARD FRCP (*b*.1963) Consultant endocrinologist at Royal Victoria Infirmary, Newcastle-upon-Tyne and Senior Lecturer in Medicine at University of Newcastle. Attended Corpus Christi College, Cambridge, graduating in Anthropology 1986 and Medicine 1988. Subsequently trained in London at St Bartholomew's, University College, the Royal Free and Middlesex hospitals and at Erasmus University Hospital, Rotterdam. *See page 114*

TALLBOYS, RICHARD CMG OBE FCA LLB (*b*.1931) Eight years at sea 1947-55, 7 years in accounting. Australian Government trade commissioner 1962-68 (Africa, Singapore, Indonesia). HM Diplomatic Service 1968-88; served in Brasilia, Phnom Penh, Seoul, Houston (as consul-general) and Hanoi (as ambassador). Chief executive World Coal Institute 1988-93. Since 1993 occasional consultant and lecturer on Asia. Co-author of *Fifty Years of Business in Indonesia* (1996). *See page 170*

TANTUM, GEOFFREY CMG OBE (*b*.1940) Served in the army before reading Oriental Studies at St John's College, Oxford. Spent 26 years in the Foreign Service, working mostly in or on the Arab world. Since retirement in 1995 has combined running a consultancy on Middle East affairs with sailing and leisurely country living in Devon. *See page 59*

THESIGER, SIR WILFRED KBE DSO (1910-2003) Educated Eton & Oxford. As early as 1934 showed his aptitude as an intrepid traveller, successfully completing a hazardous exploration of the Aussa Sultanate in Abyssinia. Joined Sudan Political Service 1935 and soon found an opportunity off-duty for serious Saharan travel. During the War served with distinction under Wingate in liberation of Abyssinia; and with SOE in Syria and SAS in Libya. Spent 5 years with the nomadic Bedu in southern Arabia and several more among the marsh dwellers of Iraq; these experiences he described in 2 classic books which, with his fine photographs, made his reputation – *Arabian Sands* (1959) and *The Marsh Arabs* (1964). Continued for years to travel adventurously in Africa and Asia and to publish a series of remarkable books: *Desert, Marsh and Mountain* (1979), *Visions of a Nomad* (1987), *The Life of My Choice* (1987), *My Kenya Days* (1994), *The Danakil Diary* (1996) and *Among the Mountains* (1998). Joined the Travellers Club 1929, died in England 2003. *See page 75*

Composed for Wilfred Thesiger by George Webb

THORNTON, TIMOTHY (1938-2004) Educated Clifton College & Brasenose College, Oxford. Spent his working life as a teacher, culminating as Principal of the Croft Preparatory School, Stratford-upon-Avon. Served on management committee of Eritrean Relief Association. *See page 85*

TOMKINSON, MICHAEL FIL FRGS (*b*.1940) Author and publisher 1970-. Read Modern Languages at Oxford and Arabic at the École des Langues Orientales, Paris, before returning to the Foreign Office to relearn Arabic at MECAS. Served in Kuwait, Doha, Baghdad and Jedda before resigning in 1968 to write, photograph and publish independently. His Cotswold-based company functioning better in his absence, his *Kenya, Norway, The Gambia, Tunisia* and *The United Arab Emirates* have largely been written, and translations of them edited in 15 languages, in Tunisia (1970-1990), Kenya (1990-1994) and by laptop, mobile and email on sundry African beaches since. *See pages 47, 127 and 182*

TULLY, SIR MARK OBE (*b*.1935) Was BBC correspondent in Delhi for over 20 years and still lives there. Author of several books on India and now a free-lance writer and broadcaster. *See page 174*

WAITE, TERRY CBE (*b*.1939) Served as personal assistant to the Archbishop of Canterbury on most of his foreign travels and has written a humorous book about his experiences, *Travels with a Primate*. Has also travelled extensively and written the autobiographical *Taken on Trust: Recollections from Captivity* (1993). *See page 111*

WEBB, GEORGE HANNAM CMG OBE (*b*.1929) Colonial Service Kenya 1954-63; Diplomatic Service 1963-85 in Thailand, Ghana, Iran and USA. Staff of City University, London 1985-93, Senior Fellow; chairman of Travellers Club 1987-91. Author of *The Bigger Bang – a financial revolution* (1987) and *Kipling's Japan* (with Sir Hugh Cortazzi, 1988). Interests: literary (editor since 1980 of quarterly *Kipling Journal*). *See page 247*

WINCHESTER, SIMON (*b*.1944) Until 1994 foreign correspondent for *The Guardian* and *The Sunday Times* based in Ireland, America, India and China, covering most of the non-European world. Currently a free-lance writer living in Massachusetts. *See pages 155 and 266*

WITTS, FRANCIS (*b*.1941) Merchant banker with Morgan Grenfell, spending much time in the Middle East 1965-91. Adviser for Middle East affairs to the Archbishop of Canterbury 1991-92. Launched Lords of the Manor Hotel, Upper Slaughter 1972. Has more recently been trustee of various charities, including St Andrew's Trust. Interests: hill walking, cricket and old family papers. *See page 72*

WOODCOCK, THOMAS LVO FSA (*b*.1951) Since 1997 Norroy and Ulster King of Arms. Read Law at Durham & Cambridge. Called to the Bar, Inner Temple 1975; research assistant to Sir Anthony Wagner, Garter King of Arms 1975-78, Rouge Croix Pursuivant 1978-82; Somerset Herald 1982-97. Author with J.M. Robinson of *Oxford Guide to Heraldry* (1982) and *Heraldry in National Trust Houses* (2000). Editor of *Dictionary of British Arms – Mediæval Ordinary, Vol. I* (1992), *Vol II* (1996), *Vols III & IV* (in progress). *See page 40*

WRIGHT, SIR DENIS GCMG (*b*.1911) HM Ambassador to Iran 1963-71 and Ethiopia 1959-63; also served in Romania, Turkey, Yugoslavia and USA. Hon Fellow of St Edmund Hall and St Antony's College, Oxford. Author (with James Morris and Roger Wood) of *Persia* (1969) and of *The English amongst the Persians* (1977), *The Persians amongst the English* (1986) and *Britain and Iran 1790-1980: Collected Essays* (2003). *See page 88*

ORDNANCE SURVEY
OF
ENGLAND & WALES